Literature and Lite
Young Children

The 8th edition of this bestselling text provides a framework and instructional strategies for identifying, selecting, and teaching high-quality children's literature for ages 0–8. This new edition's emphasis on diverse literature will assist in positively impacting the lives of all young people. Effective instructional approaches for using literature as a teaching tool are coupled with developmentally appropriate methods for sharing literature with young children. This book is a foundational text for graduate and undergraduate students in early childhood education, early literacy, literacy methods, children's literature, and literature instruction.

Cyndi Giorgis is a Professor of Literacy Education and Children's Literature at Arizona State University, where she teaches courses in children's literature, multimodal literature, reading, writing, and action research. She is the recipient of the International Reading Association's Arbuthnot Award for Outstanding Professor of Children's and Young Adult Literature. Cyndi has served on many children's book award committees including the Caldecott Medal, Newbery Medal, Theodor Seuss Geisel Award, Pura Belpré Award, and the Orbis Pictus Award for Outstanding Nonfiction.

Literature and Literacy for Young Children

Envisioning Possibilities in Early Childhood Education for Ages 0–8

8th Edition

Cyndi Giorgis

NEW YORK AND LONDON

Designed cover image: © Eric Rohmann

Eighth edition published 2024
by Routledge
605 Third Avenue, New York, NY 10158

and by Routledge
4 Park Square, Milton Park, Abingdon, Oxon, OX14 4RN

Routledge is an imprint of the Taylor & Francis Group, an informa business

First edition published by Pearson Education, Inc. 1981
Seventh edition published by Pearson Education, Inc. 2009

ISBN: 978-1-032-43503-9 (hbk)
ISBN: 978-1-032-43282-3 (pbk)
ISBN: 978-1-003-36763-5 (ebk)

DOI: 10.4324/9781003367635

Typeset in Palatino
by codeMantra

Literature and Literacy for Young Children: Envisioning Possibilities in Early Childhood Education for Ages 0–8 is dedicated to early childhood educators, childcare providers, and parents who make a difference in the lives of young children every day by sharing the power and pleasure of literature

and

Megan Sullivan Sloan, who is not only an incredibly imaginative, innovative, and extraordinary educator, but is also a colleague, mentor, and friend. Thank you for sharing your expertise with me over the years and for allowing your students' responses to literature to be featured in this book. I am constantly in awe of you!

Contents

Preface

Literature and Literacy for Young Children: Envisioning Possibilities in Early Childhood Education for Ages 0–8 is written for early childhood teachers and childcare providers to help them learn to recognize high-quality children's literature and to share it effectively to support emerging literacy development in infants (ages 0–12 months), toddlers (ages 12–24 months), preschoolers (ages 2–4), and primary-age children (ages 5–8). The text presents the literary merits of literature intended for young children, explains how to share children's literature as a teaching tool, and offers myriad developmentally appropriate strategies for partnering with literature in the early childhood setting.

The 8th edition provides:

- an evaluation of various genres and criteria for selecting and using high-quality literature with young children;
- discussions of classic and contemporary literature appropriate for infants, toddlers, preschoolers, and primary-age children;
- explanations and strategies to demonstrate how literature supports the development of children's language, cognitive skills, personality, social and moral development, and aesthetic and creative development;
- suggestions for integrating a variety of literature into the early childhood curriculum;
- educational theory and research pertinent to the topic of each chapter;
- strategies to extend learning beyond the chapter's focus;
- developmental goals, teaching suggestions, and recommended literature presented in a boxed format.

New to the 8th edition:

- reorganization of chapters to create a strong foundation for supporting children as emergent readers;
- extensive examples of literature, both classic and contemporary, aligned to chapter concepts;

- inclusion of instructional strategies to support all learners through reading aloud, selecting appropriate literature, generating a literature-rich curriculum, and enhancing reading comprehension;
- updated lists and suggestions of literature that promote literary quality;
- children's written and visual responses to literature;
- websites related to authors, illustrations, organizations, teaching ideas, and digital media;
- detailed explanation of how to generate curriculum through a thematic unit, author-illustrator study, and cornerstone text.

Organization of the Text

The first two chapters of this text define the formats and genres of children's literature and provide criteria by which to evaluate them. The next two chapters offer possibilities for creating a literate environment while Chapter 4 highlights how literature can be a teaching partner, collaborator, and mentor. Chapters 5–9 present how literature can support children's language, intellectual, personality, social-emotional, moral, aesthetic, and creative development. Chapter 10 provides a detailed step-by-step look at how a specific book with toddlers and preschoolers, and two with primary-age children can support the developmental goals described in the previous chapters.

Acknowledgments

I have always believed that early childhood is a magical time for learning and exploration. Part of that magic comes from the books that children are introduced to as infants, toddlers, preschoolers, and primary-grade students. This book stems from that belief as well as my love for children's literature. Since no book is created without a team of individuals and supporters behind it, I would like to acknowledge the following:

Karen Adler, my initial editor at Routledge, who understood the importance and need for this book to continue to support those individuals entering or currently teaching in early childhood education. And Megha Patel who stepped in as my new editor and offered continued support throughout the submission and production process.

Eric Rohmann who created the original artwork gracing the cover of this 8th edition. It expresses the delight and wonder that comes from reading books—no matter who you are.

Sarah Lechner, Marie LeJeune, Nicole Noline, Daria Nalborczyk, April Robert, Paige Robison, and Megan Sloan who each provided a glimpse into classrooms where literature and literacy serve a critical role in young children's development.

Librarians at the Paseo Verde Library in Henderson, Nevada for responding to my endless requests for books in such a timely manner.

The anonymous reviewers for this text.

My husband, Jim Kruger, who is an excellent proofreader and dog walker. Thank you for your ongoing love and support.

Instructional Strategy from the Field Contributors

Sarah Lechner who served as Charlie's nanny while living in Phoenix, Arizona (Chapter 3). She is currently in California working as a nanny for a new family! "I love working one-on-one with the little ones to help them grow and develop into tiny humans."

Marie LeJeune is a Professor at Western Oregon University where she serves as the Associate Dean of Teacher Education. She is a former reading and language arts teacher. Marie has conducted extensive research in elementary and secondary classrooms focused on adolescent literacy and on readers' response to literature. She has published numerous scholarly and practitioner-based articles and presented her research at regional, national, and international conferences.

Daria Nalborczyk is a kindergarten teacher at Oakbrook Elementary School in Wood Dale, Illinois which is a small suburban district outside of Chicago, Illinois. She has been teaching for four years and has her English as a Second Language endorsement and her Special Education Seal of Approval. Daria grew up speaking Polish and was born in the United States to immigrant parents from Poland. Daria's classroom has 16 students with diverse backgrounds and needs. "Four of my 16 students have an IEP for Autism and Developmental Delay. I have nine students who have been identified as English Language Learners that are participating in the Transitional Bilingual Program. I support students who speak Polish, Russian, Ukrainian, Spanish, and Urdu."

Nicole Noline is a first-grade teacher in Window Rock, Arizona, which is located on the Navajo Nation. In her community, "the students are not exposed to as many experiences as people in modern America. Running water, air conditioning, and individual housing are a luxury. Students do not travel to nearby cities which in part results in a smaller vocabulary and a need for learning a lot of background knowledge through literature."

April Robert owns a nature-based Microschool, Little Leaders Academy, in St. Louis, Missouri. "I am building a program for homeschool moms/ educators on operating a Microschool that educates through a mind-body approach. I am also a whole-child content creator and photographer." April is a graduate of Arizona State University with a bachelor's degree in elementary education and an endorsement in ESL. https://aprilmaura.com/about-april-maura/microschool-coaching/

Paige Robison teaches first grade at High Tech Elementary North County in San Marcos, California. She taught kindergarten and second grade previously. "Writing at this school is usually centered around our project-based learning, so students are engaged and motivated to create meaningful work for an authentic audience."

Megan Sullivan Sloan currently teaches second grade at Cathcart Elementary School in the Snohomish School District in Snohomish, Washington. She has been teaching over 30 years. Megan is a frequent presenter at national conferences and serves as an educational consultant. Megan is the author of numerous books about writing including *Into Writing: The Primary Teacher's Guide to Writing Workshop* (Heinemann, 2009), *Teaching Young Writers to Elaborate: Mini-Lessons and Strategies that Help Students Find Their Topics and Learn to Tell More* (Scholastic, 2008), *and Trait-Based Mini-Lessons for Teaching Writing in Grades 2–4* (Teaching Resources, 2005).

1

Defining Literature for Young Children

> A childhood without books – that would be no childhood. That would be like being shut out from the enchanted place where you can go and find the rarest kind of joy.
>
> (Astrid Lindgren, author)

Quality literature has the ability to impact children's thinking, enhance their lives, and provide them with joy. Whether it's reading for pleasure or information, each phrase, passage, or page has the potential to touch hearts, impart humor, or build knowledge. As author Astrid Lindgren pointed out, books take readers to enchanted places. In settings, both real and imagined, children meet unique, clever, kindhearted, or heroic characters. They might even encounter a red-haired, freckled character who is totally unpredictable but endlessly entertaining such as Lindgren's Pippi Longstocking (1945). Children who discover the importance of literature and value what it offers will attain a lifelong source of emotional and intellectual enrichment. Teachers of young children in preschool through grade three, childcare providers, librarians, and parents are in an ideal position to instill a positive outlook about literature and literacy.

This book presents the many ways literature can and does support the goals of early childhood education. It illustrates how books can be shared to assist children in developing and maintaining a positive attitude toward literary experiences. Before appreciating how literature contributes to the achievement of developmental goals, you must be aware of the wide range

DOI: 10.4324/9781003367635-1

of stories, poems, and informational books currently available for young children. This first chapter defines the different types and formats of books for young children ages 0–8. The ensuing chapters describe the attributes of high-quality literature for children, children's preferences for literature, and suggestions and strategies for envisioning the possibilities of sharing this literature with young children.

Importance of Literature in the Lives of Children

Before embarking on the types and formats of books available for young children, it is imperative we recognize the critical role literature plays in literacy development. The National Children's Book and Literacy Alliance compiled a lengthy list for "Why Do Kids Need Books?" Here are the top ten:

- *Books create warm emotional bonds between adults and children when they read together* because of the interaction that reading provides.
- *Books help to develop basic language skills and profoundly expand children's vocabularies,* particularly when these books contain unique words generally not heard in everyday conversation.
- *Books support critical thinking skills* as children respond to stories that reflect their own experiences, share perspectives of others, and increase knowledge of the world around them.
- *Books foster and nourish children's imaginations and expand their world* by stimulating their sensory awareness as they see, hear, taste, feel, and smell on an imagined level.
- *Books entertain and offer an escape* when children laugh at characters' antics and sometimes cry at their misfortune.
- *Books offer various perspectives of the world* through the opportunity to experience something through the pages of a book before it possibly happens to them in real life.
- *Books assist children in charting their own moral and ethical course,* in reflecting upon right and wrong, good and evil. Books can provide guidance as children develop their own set of values.
- *Books answer and generate questions* through engaging text and eye-catching illustrations in fiction, nonfiction, and poetry.
- *Books serve as great companions* and offer a hopeful and comforting message to children that they are not alone.
- *Books provide children with the tools to achieve their dreams* because they offer possibilities while expanding the children's universe and inspiring creativity.

Early childhood is a significant and magical time for learning and exploration. The influence and impact of literature on a child's life cannot be underestimated. At an early age, children recognize the pages of a book contain something wonderful and enjoyable. As the adult in a child's life, you can encourage and support this enjoyment of stories and learning by providing opportunities that result in joyous encounters with books.

Categories of Literature

There is a wide range of books that authors and illustrators create with an intended audience of young children in mind. Several categorization systems are used to describe and classify books but they are frequently grouped by their format or their genre.

Format

The format of a book is its general makeup. This includes the size, shape, arrangement of illustrations, end pages, cover, paper quality, typography, and spacing. For example, the description of the Caldecott Honor book *Color Zoo* (1989) by Lois Ehlert, which introduces initial concepts of colors, shapes, and animals, might include its measurements of 9 by 9 inches. It has a hardcover but no book jacket. When opened, bright green end pages greet the reader. The pages are sturdy and durable while featuring perfectly die-cut shapes ingeniously designed that line up to unfold nine distinctly recognizable and abstractly formed animal heads. Ehlert uses bold primary and secondary colors throughout the book. Limited text is placed on the corner of each page that names the shape or animal featured. The book concludes with a listing of colors in the book and the animals created from the shapes.

Color Zoo (1997) is also available in a board-book format that measures 7 by 7 inches. However, the end pages are not included nor are the three pages that begin and end the book. Board books are generally ideal for infants and toddlers. *Color Zoo* is better suited in the hardcover format for sharing with preschoolers who are learning shapes and colors alongside an adult who will assist them in identifying abstract animal faces.

When publishing hardcover picture books in a board book or electronic format, some aspects of the book might not be included, similar to the missing pages described above for *Color Zoo*. The hardcover version of the popular *Goodnight, Goodnight, Construction Site* (2011) by Sherri Duskey Rinker and illustrated by Tom Lichtenheld as well as the Spanish-language version,

Buenas noches, construcción. Buenas noches, diversión, measures 10 inches high and 20 inches wide. The size of the board-book version is 5¾ by 6 inches. There is also an e-book format that will adhere to the size of smartphone or tablet screens, which generally measure smaller than a hardcover picture book. The e-book and board-book versions of *Goodnight, Goodnight, Construction Site* both eliminate the depiction of the sun rising behind the construction site on the opening end pages (which is how the story and day begin) and the sun setting on the closing end pages showing that all the trucks have gone to sleep.

Many children's books are also published in paperback editions. Paperbacks are less expensive and enable quality literature to be available within the economic reach of more families and classrooms. However, paperbacks are generally not as long-lasting as hardcover books which might be a consideration depending on the age of the child(ren) and the need for durability. Also, a paperback of a picture book may differ in size from the original. For example, Robert McCloskey's classic *Make Way for Ducklings* (1941) paperback edition is approximately one-third the size of the original Caldecott Medal winner. This reduced size significantly affects the ability of a group of children to view McCloskey's expressive illustrations, which might also impact their enjoyment and response to the story.

Unusual Formats

Some books stand out because of their unique format. *When's My Birthday?* (Fogliano, 2017) echoes a question asked by young children: "when's my birthday?/where's my birthday?/how many days until my birthday?" Written in lowercase letters, the text has a frenetic pace that begs to be read aloud. The distinctive vertical design feature is the book's tall, thin shape. When the book is open, the two pages form a square rather than a rectangle, as with most picture books. Lolly Robinson, a reviewer for *Horn Book Magazine*, considered the odd shape of this book and finally decided, "If a wide book reveals a story that covers a long time period, then the opposite makes sense about the frustrations of waiting for something to happen." The narrator in *When's My Birthday?* is anxiously awaiting her birthday, and the tall design calls for rapid page turns and the hurried passage of time. The book also resembles a birthday card.

Format should be used to make storytelling engaging and effective. Eric Carle's *The Very Busy Spider* (1984) uses expansive white space to draw the eye to the spider and its web. On each page, strands of the spider's web are raised offering a tactile experience and illustrating how a spider web develops from the outer edge and spokes to the full pattern of concentric circles. In the Caldecott Medal-winning wordless picture book *My Friend Rabbit* (2002), illustrator Eric Rohmann uses frames to create a comic effect while allowing huge animals such as an elephant and hippo to make sudden entrances from the side or top of the page. This technique artfully captures the expressions on the animals' faces. The book format changes at a dramatic point in the story, requiring readers to tilt the book vertically to view the climactic spread showing a stack of very annoyed animals sitting on each other's backs. Always consider how a picture book's format enhances, rather than detracts from, the presentation of the story.

The graphic style of storytelling is gaining popularity with young children. You'll find this comic-style format in the TOON Books for emergent readers and the *Babymouse* series for children ready for a little more text. Jeff Smith's *Little Mouse Gets Ready* (2009) is one that children will relate to as Little Mouse puts on numerous articles of clothing, including underpants, socks, shoes, pants, and a shirt so that he can go to the barn with his mama and siblings. The comic-book format has limited text and one or two panels per page.

Jennifer L. Holm and Matthew Holm's clever and adventurous heroine Babymouse has become a hit with readers attracted to the book's comic-strip-style format containing black-and-white illustrations splashed with pink. The final book in the series, *Babymouse #20: Babymouse Goes for the Gold* (2016), will delight readers with the antics of the sassy, wise-cracking rodent, who has big dreams and wet whiskers, as she joins the swim team in hopes of winning a gold medal. The graphic format of these books and others is particularly attractive to visual learners, emergent and reluctant readers, and multilingual learners because of the reliance on illustration rather than text to tell a story.

While there are unusual formats, classifications related to format generally identify types of books, the most common being board books, toy and novelty books, wordless picture books, and picture books. Other classifications are beginning-to-read books, early chapter books (which are often series), and chapter books.

Board Books

Board books are printed on heavy cardboard with rounded corners. They are designed considerably smaller than picture books, making them perfect for the small hands of babies and toddlers just learning how to handle books. Because of the stiffness of the pages, board books can be grasped and turned more easily than lighter-weight pages and are less likely to tear. The pages are generally laminated, making them easy to wipe off if the enjoyment of the reading experience includes chewing on the book.

Board books are generally designed to provide stories with simple direct plots or basic concepts. They also create a bonding moment when the sharing of the book has the infant sitting on a parent's lap. Board books contain uncluttered and brightly colored illustrations of familiar objects, activities, food, or animals. Reading them might prompt a parent or caregiver to make the sounds of a cow, a pig, or a cat to engage the child in the experience. Even the action of turning the pages can elicit sheer delight from an infant or toddler. In addition, board books can nurture a love of books and reading, provide sensory stimulation in support of brain development, encourage language, and build knowledge about the world and how it works.

Originating during the 1930s, board books were made of thick cardboard that could be bitten or thrown with little to no damage. Tiny fingers with limited fine motor skills had difficulty turning the pages of a picture book, and paper cuts were common. Board books provided a safe alternative while allowing a young child to learn how a book "works" in orientation and directionality (Campbell, 2017).

The publication of board books has increased tremendously in recent years. In 2023, two board books received the inaugural Margaret Wise Brown Board Book Award for excellence in children's literature: *Give Me a Snickle!* (2022) by Alisha Sevigny won in the 0–18 months range, and *Me and the Family Tree* (2022) by Carole Boston Weatherford and illustrated by Ashleigh Corrin, won in the 18–36 months category.

Due to their small size, durability, and issues of cleanliness, board books are often not available in public libraries. This has prompted parents to seek them out in bookstores and through online vendors. Some of the most enjoyable and effective board books are those that are created specifically for the audience of infants and toddlers. Helen Oxenbury's classic board books *I Can* (1995a), *I Hear* (1995b), *I See* (1995c), and *I Touch* (1995d) provide an excellent introduction to the senses for babies and invite interaction through language and movement. Emily Bolam's board books contain bold colors and a tactile experience for toddlers as they explore eye-catching stripes and dazzling polka dots in *Patterns* (2018b) or cuddly bears and changing chameleons in *Animals* (2018a). Toddlers will enjoy interacting with Karen Katz's lift-the-flap books, *Baby Loves Summer!* (2012), *Where is Baby's Puppy?* (2011), or *Zoom, Zoom, Baby!* (2014). These theme-based board books contain bright, attractive art along with sturdy, easy-to-lift flaps that will engage even the most active two-year-old. Sandra Boynton's board books are probably the most familiar and include *Pajama Time!* (2022), *Belly Button Book* (2023), and *Peekaboo Rex!* (2023).

Many board books have been adapted from books originally published as picture books. Take into consideration that these smaller versions may eliminate portions of the books, condense illustrations, or rewrite and simplify the text. Picture books usually contain 32 pages whereas board books are 12 pages—text or illustrations are altered to fit a condensed format. Some make the transition well like Hervé Tullet's *Press Here* (2019), a highly interactive book that instructs readers and listeners to push the button, shake or tilt the book, and clap their hands to make the dots multiply and increase in size. As mentioned previously, the board-book version of *Goodnight, Goodnight, Construction Site* (Rinker, 2017) is missing the pages from the picture book version. A better choice with the same construction theme would be *Bulldozer's Shapes: Goodnight, Goodnight, Construction Site* (Rinker, 2019a) and *Excavator's 123: Goodnight, Goodnight Construction Site* (Rinker, 2019b). These board books are specifically designed for the toddler audience and offer basic concepts focused on characters from the original picture book. Generally speaking, it is better to wait until a child can appreciate a particular story than to reduce it in size for a younger audience. When assessing a board book, look at it as a new publication and judge it for its own merit.

Toy and Novelty Books

Toy books include a special feature that enables them to be played with as well as to be read. Often toy books contain materials like fabric that children can touch and feel. *Where's the Astronaut?* (Arrhenius, 2019) celebrates the 50th anniversary of the moon landing by inviting young children to lift the felt flaps to discover four hidden space-themed characters. The last page asks, "And where are you?" with a mirror under the final moon flap. Nosy Crow publications have a variety of "Where's the . . .?" books highlighting animals including a dog, duck, penguin, and bear. They also publish Camilla Reid's board books containing a slide mechanism just right for small fingers. These titles include *Peekaboo Apple* (2020a), *Peekaboo Farm* (2020b), and *Peekaboo Moon* (2021). Rilla Alexander's *Animals* (2019a) and *Food* (2019b) present a tactile experience as well as an opportunity to increase vocabulary. In *Animals*, a raised image of a familiar animal such as a cat, dog, frog, or cow appears on the right side of the book with the name of the animal in raised letters along with words describing the animal on the left side. For example, the words for a cat include ears, whiskers, claws, frisky, purring, and playing. Sharing *Animals* will engage toddlers in touching the images; preschoolers will have the opportunity to learn new vocabulary associated with the different animals. This same format is used in *Food*.

Lift-the-flap books, such as those by Karen Katz mentioned previously, are considered toy books because they include interactive features. "Who needs to be tucked in?" is the question posed in the charming, *Tuck Me In!* (Hacohen, 2010). Seven baby animals, from peacocks to pigs, are asked the same question and provide the identical response, "I do!" Readers then turn the page and lift the oversized flaps that serve as blankets covering each little creature. The vibrant colors and the adorable baby animals will engage children as much as the novelty of the flaps. In another lift-the-flap book, Bee, Dog, Elephant, Ladybug, and Penguin each have something inside their backpack in *My Backpack!* (Swanson, 2013). By lifting the flaps, the object is revealed. Additionally, the series of Sophie the Giraffe board books, which originated in France and are based on the popular toy, might be those to touch and feel as with *Sophie la girafe: Good Night Sophie* (2017) while others contain tabs and flaps including *Sophie la girafe: Hide and Seek* (2016). This chunky, beautifully illustrated board book features six easy-to-grab tabs and flaps that keep young children entertained as they play hide-and-seek with Sophie and her friends.

A recent study by Jeanne Shinskey (2016) explored toddlers' interaction with lift-the-flap books to determine if two-year-olds learned the story vocabulary. The findings suggest that toddlers found the feature of the flaps distracting rather than enhancing their learning of new words. Shinskey's recommendation, based on the study, was to consider this format as another type of physical toy rather than a tool for learning. As with any book, the enjoyment and learning that results is the interaction that is enhanced due to the participating parent, caregiver, or teacher.

Novelty books are usually highly interactive and go beyond lifting flaps to include pop-ups, jigsaw puzzle pieces, stickers, or other devices to engage children. While many of these books might not be as durable as board books, or even picture books, they do attract children's attention and keep them entertained for repeated readings.

Janet and Allan Ahlberg encourage participation through pages constructed as envelopes in the classic *The Jolly Postman or Other People's Letters* (1986/2006). This unique book has been in print for three decades but has never lost its appeal. The jolly postman rides around on his bicycle, delivering letters addressed to storybook characters. His mail deliveries include Baby Bear's invitation to Goldilocks' party and a letter to the wolf from the attorneys representing Little Red Riding Hood. *Give and Take* (Félix, 2016) is a book of opposites containing shapes that can be removed and inserted on the next page. Young children, with the assistance of an adult, can practice early motor skills, shape recognition, sorting, and opposites.

Nothing captures the attention of a child more than a pop-up book. Toddlers can identify colors, numbers, shapes, and letters. In *The Color Monster: A Pop-Up Book of Feelings* (Llenas, 2015), they can also explore and discuss common emotions such as happiness, sadness, anger, and fear. David E. Carter's "bug" pop-up books are great for little ones including *Bugs that Go!: A*

Bustling Pop-Up Book (2011) with bugs using all forms of transportation or *Builder Bugs: A Busy Pop-Up Book* (2012) which is construction themed where bugs are building, digging, hammering, and moving. Pop-up books are more fragile than other books and often more expensive, but the visual display they provide will enchant children and adults.

Picture Books

The text and illustrations in picture books work in concert to create meaning. Picture books are a format (form/design) and not a genre (content), although sometimes the term genre is used to describe picture books as a whole. Generally, picture books are 32 pages, but may range from 24 to 48 pages. The illustrations integrate with the narrative to bring the story to a conclusion. The overall design serves to build a relationship between text and illustrations; this includes front matter, back matter, book jacket, casing, and end pages.

Contemporary picture books represent some of the finest storytelling and eye-catching art being created today. *A Parade of Elephants* (2018) by Kevin Henkes is an excellent example of a picture book for young children. The pastel purple cover shows three lines of elephants that are placed above and below the book title and Henkes's name. Inside, the front end pages depict a sun and butterflies. Following the title page, there is a countdown of one to five elephants who are going marching, marching, marching. Concepts such as numbers, shapes, adjectives, and adverbs become part of the story. Bright pastel illustrations, large, readable font, and simple text will engage young children. The book concludes with end pages showing the moon and stars as the elephants' day has come to an end.

Stories for young children are often filled with emotion that can be exhibited by people, animals, and even inanimate objects. In *Bulldozer's Big Day* (Fleming, 2015), children will understand how the Bulldozer is feeling by looking at its changing expressions as the story progresses. The little Bulldozer is hopeful the other machinery remembers what day it is, but for them, it's business as usual in scooping, sifting, filling, and lifting. Sheer happiness is exuded by the Bulldozer at the conclusion of the story as everyone gathers to celebrate his birthday. Different emotions are on display in *Bulldozer Helps Out* (Fleming, 2017) as Bulldozer attempts to show how he can handle a rough and tough job. *Bulldozer's Christmas Dig* (Fleming, 2021) is holiday themed as the little bulldozer digs up a most unexpected gift. These books by Henkes and Fleming prompt connections and comments from children as they can relate to emotions they may have felt as well.

Over the years, text and illustrations in picture books have become more sophisticated. A good example is Jon Klassen's "hat trilogy." *I Want My Hat Back* (2011) tells of a bear who has lost his hat and politely asks a series of animals if they have seen it. All deny having knowledge of the whereabouts of this missing head covering but observant readers will notice a rabbit wearing a red hat. At the conclusion of the story, the bear is shown with a red hat on his head and the rabbit is nowhere to be seen. Did he eat the offending bunny? This book provides a perfect example for allowing children to come to their own conclusion as to the rabbit's fate. In *This Is Not My Hat* (2012) the hat-wearing thief openly admits to stealing the blue bowler on his head. He rationalizes that the hat didn't even fit the big sleeping fish so there was no harm in taking it. This second "hat" book received the Caldecott Medal. The third book, *We Found a Hat* (2016), focuses on two turtles who have found a 10-gallon hat. The hat looks good on both of them, but there are two turtles and one hat, so what should they do? All three books by Klassen evoke hilarity and empathy while highlighting visual comedy and deceptive simplicity. The open-endings of the stories make these books appropriate for a range of ages.

Because picture book denotes a format, it is important to remember these books do not indicate the interest level or reading ability of young children. Children of all ages and grade levels enjoy listening to and reading picture books. The topics presented vary in complexity so parents, caregivers, teachers, and librarians should pre-read them before sharing the books to determine if the content is appropriate for the intended audience.

Wordless Picture Books

Wordless picture books are exactly what the name implies. They are books containing no text and showcase the art of visual storytelling (Salisbury & Styles, 2012). Wordless picture books can be used to develop language and thinking skills in young children. They assist very young children in becoming accustomed to the left-to-right pattern of reading. More importantly, these books enhance emergent readers' ability to detect sequence, identify details, note cause-and-effect relationships, generate judgments, determine main ideas, and make inferences. Wordless picture books are well suited for multilingual learners because they allow them to engage with complex content as they discuss meaning and gain oral language proficiency (Louie & Sierschynski, 2015). Without written text, children are invited to serve as co-authors in constructing narrative and meaning from the images.

A wordless picture book that encourages children to engage in these types of skills is Molly Idle's *Flora and the Flamingo* (2013). Flora and her graceful friend, Flamingo, move from synchronized dance to a performance executed in perfect harmony. Children will enjoy telling the story and trying out some of Flora and Flamingo's movements. Jerry Pinkney's *The Lion & the Mouse* (2009) is an adaptation of an Aesop fable where a lion spares a meek mouse he planned to eat only to have the mouse return the favor in a big way. This Caldecott Medal-winning book features vivid images of the African Serengeti and expressively drawn characters. Other illustrators such as Jeannie Baker, Matthew Cordell, Regis Faller, Barbara Lehman, and David Wiesner create wordless picture books with visual stories that enhance language development and imagination.

Wordless picture books can be used to differentiate language instruction by labeling actions and objects in the illustrations, telling the story using sentence stems, and retelling stories using story maps or structural frames. Another strategy is to create text for wordless picture books using sticky notes that might include dialogue or narrative. The sticky notes can then be placed on the page where appropriate. This strategy enables children to read the text they have created whether they are multilingual learners or emergent readers.

Box 1.1 Wordless Picture Books

Field Trip to the Ocean Deep (John Hare, 2020)
Fly (Mark Teague, 2019)
The Great Zapfino (Mac Barnett; ill. Marla Frazee, 2022)
Hike (Pete Oswald, 2020)
Inside Cat (Brendan Wenzel, 2021)

Concept Books

A specialized type of picture book is the concept book—a book that explicates a general idea or concept by presenting specific examples of it. As young children encounter sights, sounds, smells, tastes, and textures around them, they need help in grasping the basic concepts people use to put the world in order (Roach, 2015). These concepts include colors, shapes, letters, numbers, counting, and size. As children acquire language, they are often able to speak words before they completely understand their meanings. Concept books assist young children in gaining this understanding.

The name of colors is a simple concept that children begin learning when they are around 18 months. Books intended to teach colors such as red, blue, yellow, green, and so on are appropriate for toddlers and preschoolers. A book for toddlers will generally show an object paired with the color word such as in Keith Baker's *Little Green Peas* (2014). Playful green peas experience the colorful world around them from blue boats, to red kites, to yellow buses.

The large letters and bold colors reinforce the color concept. Once children learn the primary colors of red, yellow, and blue, introduce books showing secondary colors such as Hervé Tullet's *Mix It Up!* (2014) that combine colors in a fun and imaginative way through an interactive format.

Alphabet and counting books are two of the most popular types of concept books. As with other picture books, these are written at many levels of sophistication. You cannot assume the subject matter automatically makes them appropriate for children who are beginning to recognize letters or learning to count. Always consider a child's level of development and the purpose of using the book.

If you want children to explore the sounds letters make, pay particular attention to the objects that are illustrated representing the sounds of the letters. Also, consider whether the picture could be known by another name such as a rabbit for the letter r which might be called a bunny by a young child. Suse MacDonald's *A Was Once an Apple Pie* (2005) adapts Edward Lear's whimsical alphabet rhyme with bright bold illustrations. A Bear sniffs an apple pie, a Cat and Dog are friends, an Eel and Fish share an ocean, and so on. A favorite alphabet book is *Chicka Chicka Boom Boom* (Martin & Archambault, 1989) because of its lively rhyme and naming of the letters. This is also one of the few alphabet books that include both uppercase and lowercase letters.

It's often difficult to locate books that contain a sound–symbol relationship between words and letters. Many alphabet books are simply a way of organizing content. Others use the alphabet as a vehicle for telling a story rather than teaching the letters. Patrick McDonnell's *The Little Red Cat Who Ran Away and Learned His ABCs (the Hard Way)* (2017) begins with an alligator and a bear chasing a cat. When a dragon, a chicken, and an egg join in the pursuit, a wild and wacky chase takes the characters through snow and ice, to jungles, and over mountaintops. While the letters are clearly visible, many of the words, such as dragon, are blends rather than pure sounds of the letter. *Z is for Moose* (Bingham, 2012) presents the alphabet through a particularly clever and inventive story. Zebra is organizing the play's cast members Apple, Ball, Cat, Duck, and Elephant, and asks for an orderly progression onto the stage. Unfortunately, Moose just cannot wait and foils the entrance of the other letters to be featured. While this book won't necessarily provide an orderly ABC exploration, it will have children laughing as they attempt to determine what letters have been smashed, stomped on, and mangled in Moose's quest to be part of Zebra's play. *Not an Alphabet Book: The Case of the Missing Cake* (McLaughlin, 2020) was supposed to be a simple alphabet book but that was before a most horrible, terrible crime had been committed—the most completely "delicious, tongue-jinglingly chocolaty cake" has been stolen. Bear goes in hot pursuit of the thief who might be closer than he wants you to believe. Each letter of the alphabet becomes part of the search while other animals, and a few familiar book characters, are all suspects.

These alphabet books present well-crafted illustrations that may stimulate discussion between you and a child about the objects, letters, and scenes presented. Very young children may look at a single illustration and name it. Seven-year-olds may look at a page filled with action, hidden letters, or objects and test their letter knowledge and observation skills.

Counting books often follow the same format as alphabet books. They show a numeral, a word, and a picture illustrating the number. Books for babies and toddlers concentrate on number recognition and matching a numeral or number word to the objects on a page. Clarity of illustrations is essential because children are checking their skill at counting and their understanding of its concept. Sometimes the best counting books for babies and toddlers are ones you create yourself with photos of common objects or food, coupled with the numeral.

Adorable black, brown, tan, or white puppies bounce and pounce, nibble on kibble, and exhibit peppy puppy grins in *One Pup's Up* (Chall, 2010). Preschoolers will need to look closely to count the pups as they enter and exit pages where only noses, paws, or tails are evidence of them still engaging in the romp. *One Is a Piñata: A Book of Numbers* (Thong, 2019) incorporates Spanish words as children discover a fiesta of numbers from one to ten. Emily Gravett's *10 Cats* (2023) depicts 10 lively kittens who are white, black, or have patches and stripes. While their mother sleeps, the cats explore cans of paint which quickly turn the kittens into colorful works of art. Color words and counting are both incorporated into this delightful book for young children.

Lois Ehlert's *Fish Eyes: A Book You Can Count On* (1990) adds several elements to basic counting. Using the premise that if the author were a fish, she would swim far into the ocean and see, first, one green fish, then two jumping fish, and so on through the number 10. Each page states the number of fish seen, "plus me," makes ____, and the next number is stated, thus introducing both the concept and the language of addition. The "me" is a tiny black fish on each double-page spread. The other fish are pictured in patterned neon colors shown on a deep blue background with eyes cut out so colors from the previous and the next page are showing. In *Fish Eyes,* the end pages, title page, and introductory and concluding pages have numerous fish, allowing for counting to higher numbers and counting by categories—such as a black fish or fish with blue eyes. Individual pages throughout the book can also be used for categorization and counting, using the number of dots or stripes on a fish or the number of fins.

When you select counting books, keep in mind what you expect them to accomplish and the child's level of comprehension. Toddlers enjoy interacting with books and pointing to different things they can name. Although these concept books may appear simple, they often become favorites because of their bold colors and photographs or paintings of familiar, everyday objects. Preschool-age children are gaining proficiency in counting, so books selected for three- and four-year-olds should allow them to focus on learning this skill. For primary-grade students, the objective is often to reinforce the ability to count as well as mathematical operations.

Other concept books include learning about shapes and opposites. *Go, Shapes, Go!* (2014) by Denise Fleming introduces clearly labeled shapes of circles, rectangles, ovals, arcs, and more. The shapes eventually form a monkey until something goes wrong and a new animal is formed. Mike Twohy's *Stop, Go, Yes, No!: A Story of Opposites* (2018) features an enthusiastic dog and a please-go-away cat who engage in a silly chase. Repeated readings will have children giggling as they name the opposite pairs.

Box 1.2 Counting to 100

100 Things That Make Me Happy (Amy Schwartz, 2014)
Centipede's One Hundred Shoes (Tony Ross, 2003)
Counting Our Way to the 100th Day (Betsy Franco; ill. Steve Salerno, 2004)
Miss Bindergarten Celebrates the 100th Day of Kindergarten (Joseph Slate, 1998)
Miss Mingo and the 100th Day of School (Jaime Harper, 2020)
My Very First 100 Words (Rosemary Wells, 2022)

Predictable Books

Predictable books have a structure that allows children to predict, with some accuracy, what will happen next. Sometimes that structure is in the repetition of a similar refrain. Many children are familiar with *Brown Bear Brown Bear, What Do You See?* (Martin, 1967). This predictable story is written using an appealing cadence as it introduces a sequence of animals such as a red bird, blue horse, and green frog. Eric Carle's signature collage illustrations capture the true sense of the animal while effectively using white space and color.

Predictable books are valuable for a variety of reasons. First, they encourage children's participation as they listen. Bob Shea's *Dinosaur vs. Bedtime* (2008) will have children roaring as Little Dinosaur encounters a pile of leaves, a slide, a bowl of spaghetti, and talking grown-ups. Little Dinosaur wins every time until he faces his biggest challenge. Not only is the word "roar" repeated frequently but it is also shown in colorful large font. Predictable books can stimulate children to begin learning to read naturally as they recognize new words, such as roar, and then match the words they hear with the written text on the page. In this way, children gain quick control over a story and the words used to tell it, giving them confidence in their ability to learn to read.

Many of the current books published in large format and labeled Big Books are predictable stories. This oversized format allows the teacher to share the story with a group of children as they follow along with the print. In this way, children are encouraged to learn to read whole refrains, then sentences, and then individual words. Childcare providers and parents deliver the same stimulus for learning to read when they sit next to a child and share a book so the child can see the print as the adult reads. In fact, it was from parents reading to children in this natural way that educators came to realize the importance and potential of working with big books.

Predictable books are also extremely useful in helping children, for whom English is their second language, to learn the sounds, cadences, and meanings of words and sentences. The emphasis on meaning, the use of context, and the enjoyment produced by good literature combine to provide both incentives and the tools needed for second-language learning.

Cumulative tales such as *A Bear Sat on My Porch Today* (Yolen, 2018) are predictable because what has happened before is repeated with each new event. What would you do if a bear sat on your porch and just wouldn't leave? He is soon followed by a shaggy squirrel, a spraying skunk, a playful possum, and a host of other forest creatures who all want to stay. So, the protagonist exclaims, "Okay! Okay! You can stay." That is until the porch begins to sway with a disastrous effect. The narrative text is accompanied by the character's repetitive phrasing that will surely have children saying, "What should I do? Boo! Shoo!" *Me and Annie McPhee* (Dunrea, 2016) is a cumulative counting tale about two curious monkeys who appear to be on a deserted island. The tranquility is disturbed by an array of ridiculous animals who emerge from their hiding places in a desire to frolic. The repetitive rhyming text invites readers to chime in at the end of each phrase. Adjectives and verbs are peppered throughout this humorous story while the illustrations, which are chock-full of details, will help children navigate the increasingly cumulative story action.

Beginning-to-Read Books

Publishers use labels such as *I Can Read*, *Read Alone*, *Step into Reading*, and *Easy-to-Read* to denote books that have limited vocabulary and regulated sentence length. These factors contribute to the ease with which material can be read and are designed for beginning readers. Attention is given to the number of difficult words, but the writing is not done from a standardized word list, as are some stories in grade-leveled basal readers. Beginning-to-read books are excellent choices for children as they learn to read independently.

Reading aloud a book intended to support independent reading is a great way to introduce them to children. The *Elephant & Piggie* series by Mo Willems is one that begs to be read aloud but also attracts emergent readers because there is limited text on a page and the stories are always entertaining. Children will often join in when a book has repetitive phrasing such as in *Let's Go for a Drive!* (Willems, 2012). After Elephant and Piggie have gathered all of the items needed to go for a drive, they realize an important element is missing—a car. Children quickly become engaged as they repeat lines such as "Drive, drive, drivey, drivey, drive." The beginning-to-read format has become popular in recent years as numerous new series, like *Elephant & Piggie*, have been introduced that feature enjoyable storylines and comical characters. Preschoolers will enjoy *Hello, Hedgehog! Do You Like My Bike?* (Feuti, 2019) because it is about a familiar experience of learning how to ride a bike. The comic-book-style format and the brief dialogue shown in speech balloons will help children gain reading confidence.

In 2004, the Association for Library Service to Children established the Theodor Seuss Geisel Award to honor the most distinguished beginning reader book. Dr. Seuss's *The Cat in the Hat* (1957) has long been considered the first book using this format with a controlled vocabulary of only 50 different words. When it was published, the trim size of 6 inches wide and 9 inches high was smaller than a picture book but larger than most chapter books. The authors of some beginning readers have tried in the past to work within the constraints of vocabulary and sentence length to produce interesting and well-written stories. One of the best known is Arnold Lobel's *Frog and Toad Are Friends* (1970). In three clever and humorous stories, Lobel has captured the natural cadence of speech through brief sentences and easy vocabulary.

Young independent readers can begin to make friends with book characters such as Elephant and Piggie or Frog and Toad as they get to know them through several books that feature their adventures. Enjoying one book in a series often leads to requesting and reading another.

Early Chapter Book Series

Children's book publishers are beginning to recognize the need for high-quality books that will engage transitional readers and set them on the path toward independent reading. These series have relatable characters and are heavily illustrated to assist in making the transition to chapter books and novels.

Some early series chapter books contain short stories, generally three to five pages long such as in *Fox + Chick: The Party and Other Stories* (Ruzzier, 2018). Fox and Chick are the most unlikely of friends but the short stories about their antics coupled with ink-and-watercolor illustrations have great appeal for young children. Another book in the series, *Fox + Chick: Up and Down and Other Stories* (Ruzzier, 2022), shows Chick unable to climb down from a tree, the anticipation of sledding, and receiving a gift from Fox. Another engaging series is Kate Messner's *Fergus and Zeke* featuring two adorable mice. Fergus and Zeke are class pets in Miss Maxwell's room that enjoy doing everything the children do. In *Fergus and Zeke and the 100th Day of School* (2021), the loveable rodents are trying to contribute to the 100th-day celebration. Attempting to create their own field day contests that are mouse-sized gets hilarious results in *Fergus and Zeke and the Field Day Challenge* (2020).

As children progress in reading independently, *The Magic Treehouse* series of books by Mary Pope Osborne will definitely become favorites. Annie and Jack discover a treehouse that transports them back in time. An engaging narrative and short chapters will propel readers to the story's conclusion. The *Princess in Black* series by Shannon Hale and Dean Hale features heroine Princess Magnolia who can battle sea monsters or hungry bunnies at a moment's notice. This popular series is perfect for boys and girls.

When selecting early chapter book series, be sure the story is entertaining and the illustrations are engaging. The goal is to support children's ongoing literacy development while helping them to find success as transitional readers.

Chapter Books

Chapter books, as the name indicates, are books with chapters. The format has importance for kindergarten and primary-grade children because it provides a transition between picture books and novels. The reading level is similar to many picture books, but the stories are longer and the text predominates with minimal, if any, illustrations. Often the plot is episodic, with a character having a different adventure in each chapter.

For many children, their first introduction to chapter books is through the read-aloud. *Charlotte's Web* (White, 1952) continues to be a popular story for reading aloud as it has withstood the test of time. Charlotte's spider web shows her feelings through words for a little pig named Wilbur. The enduring tale of friendship and loyalty is one that has been loved by generations of children and has essentially become a part of our literary heritage. The *Poppy* (1995) series of chapter books by Avi are also ones that children have enjoyed over the years by hearing them read aloud. Like an evil dictator, a great horned owl keeps the growing deer mouse population in Dimwood Forest under his fierce control. When Poppy's boyfriend is killed by the owl, the little mouse dares to go where no other mouse has gone before—to the world beyond Dimwood.

Often, chapter books whose intended audience is children in grades first through third may also be series books. Readers delight in the antics of characters such as Sophia Martinez, Judy Moody, Juana and Lucas, Alvin Ho, Keena Ford, or the Infamous Ratsos. The key is to consider the storyline and the writing style to determine the suitability for primary-grade children.

Genre

Although *format* refers to the physical qualities of a book, *genre* refers to the content. The major genre classifications are prose and poetry. Prose is divided into fiction and nonfiction, with fiction being invented work and nonfiction presenting factual information. Each of these is further subdivided.

Fiction

Fiction includes all stories that are created from an author's imagination, even if based on real happenings. If the story could happen, it is called realism similar to *When's My Birthday?* (Fogliano, 2017). If the setting is present day, the genre is contemporary realism; if the setting is in the past, it is historical fiction similar to the story *Henry's Freedom Box* (Levine, 2007) which is based on the true story of Henry Brown, an enslaved man, who mails himself to freedom. A book is categorized as fantasy if the story includes any actions that could not happen in the world as we know it today, such as in *Charlotte's Web* (White, 1952).

Traditional literature, which began in the oral tradition of storytelling and includes folktales, fairy tales, epics, myths, and legends, is a rich source of stories for children. The tales were adapted by various storytellers to fit particular audiences. With their quick action and clear portrayal of good and evil, folktales have survived for generations in a number of versions. Some have been told in single picture-book editions while others appear in collections. The book's title page often indicates the tale is "retold by" or "adapted by" an author or illustrator because the original authors are unknown.

Nonfiction

Nonfiction includes informational books and biography. Informational books are designed to tell about a specific subject such as dinosaurs, trucks, or how to plant a garden. Sometimes the information is conveyed through the narrative with child characters sharing their knowledge about a subject or with the use of *you* and *we* to make it more personal. At other times, the information is presented directly, organized by topic. Concept books are related to informational books in that they too deal with facts as building blocks, but concept books tend to be simpler. If a book contains information about an animal but the creature is anthropomorphic, meaning it has taken on human qualities such as speaking or feeling, then the book is considered fiction, rather than nonfiction.

A biography is a story of a person's life or a segment of it. Authentic biographies use only statements the person is known to have made and base all incidents on documented happenings. The back matter in nonfiction, particularly biographies, should offer a listing of sources of where the information was obtained. For example, *Me, Jane* (2011) by Patrick McDonnell tells the story of a young Jane Goodall and her childhood toy chimpanzee named Jubilee. As a child, Jane observed the world around her and dreamed of a life living and helping all animals, which eventually occurred. This biography is accessible to young children and contains engaging illustrations and quotes taken directly from Goodall's autobiography.

Box 1.3 Nonfiction Science Picture Books

The Bug Girl: A True Story (Sophia Spencer; ill. Kerascoët, 2020)
Can An Aardvark Bark? (Melissa Stewart; ill. Steve Jenkins, 2017)
Giant Squid (Candace Fleming; ill. Eric Rohmann, 2016)
Mystery of the Monarchs: How Kids, Teachers, and Butterfly Fans Helped Fred and Norah Urquhart Track the Great Monarch Migration (Barb Rosenstock; ill. Erika Mez, 2022)
Our Planet: There's No Place Like Earth (Stacy McAnulty; ill. David Litchfield, 2022)
A Seed Grows (Antoinette Portis, 2022)
Seeds Move (Robin Page, 2019)
Water is Water: A Book About the Water Cycle (Miranda Paul; ill. Jason Chin, 2015)

Poetry

Poetry for young children often rhymes. Poetry has a depth of emotion and imaginative quality. The sound of poetry is pleasing and the meaning often comes from the sound as well as the words. A large part of young children's poetry experiences is Mother Goose rhymes. Picture books may contain a single illustrated poem or a collection of poems focused on a specific theme or topic. Rebecca Kai Dotlich, Douglas Florian, Lee Bennett Hopkins, J. Patrick Lewis, Pat Mora, Laura Purdie Salas, and Jane Yolen are a few well-known poets whose writing appeals to young children.

Diversity in Children's Literature

Leland and Lewison (2018) assert that multicultural literature and global literature provide stories that have the potential to "open up new spaces that break down boundaries" (p. 70). Multicultural literature has been defined in many ways but typically refers to major cultural groups in the United States: African American, Asian American, Hispanic, and Native American (Bishop, 1997). Short (2016) has offered the definition that multicultural literature encompasses "books that highlight the lives of people from marginalized and underrepresented groups in the United States" (p. 5). López-Robertson & Haney (2017) have expanded on these definitions by "including the stance that multicultural literature enhances the reader's sense of identity and self-empowerment" (p. 49). When children do not see themselves, their families or communities, their language, or their culture represented in books, they "encounter difficulties in validating their own identities" (Ada, 2016, p. x), which can negatively impact their schooling.

Multicultural literature, more commonly referred to as diverse, offers authentic stories about cultures. These stories are told through rich language and captivating illustrations and share the diversity of both local and global societies as well as validate the life experiences of readers (Mathis, 2011). Diverse books are found across genres and content areas and provide varied perspectives to young children. The website We Need Diverse Books (www.diversebooks.org) offers various booklists and resources.

Black Is a Rainbow Color (2020) by Angela Joy is a delightful overview of Black culture and history through the eyes of a child. The back matter of this picture book includes information on the numerous phrases and references within the text. In *Drawn Together* (2018) by Minh Lê, a young Thai-American boy and his grandfather do not speak the same language, eat the same food, or have similar tastes in television shows. What they discover they do share is a love of art that bridges their two worlds. Both books highlight the individuality of the characters by sharing what is unique within their cultures.

Global literature is defined by Freeman and Lehman (2001) as, "Books written and published first in countries other than the United States . . . books written by immigrants . . . about their home countries and published in the United States . . . and books written by American authors with settings in other countries" (p. 10). Linda Sue Park's *Nya's Long Walk: A Step at a Time* (2019) is set in South Sudan where girls must walk to fetch water for their families from a remote water hole that is hours away from their home. The story of *Lubna and Pebble* (Meddour, 2019) is set in a refugee camp and explores a young girl's generous act of kindness. Lubna's best friend is a pebble that listens to her stories and makes her feel safe. She cannot imagine parting with it until the day when a little boy arrives in the "World of Tents." This powerful story by Wendy Meddour shows that friendship can be found in places around the world. An excellent resource for global literature for children is Worlds of Words (www.wowlit.org) which offers book reviews, recommended booklists, and articles with the mission focused on "global literature so that children can reflect on their own cultural experiences and connect to the experiences of children across the globe."

There are a number of awards that recognize diverse and global literature. The American Library Association's (ALA) Coretta Scott King Book Award is given annually to African American authors and illustrators, while the Pura Belpré Award honors Latino writers and illustrators for outstanding portrayals of the Latino cultural experience. The ALA awards also include, among many others, the American Indian Youth Literature Award and the Asian/Pacific American Award for Literature.

There are awards established for global literature as well. The United States Board on Books for Young People selects an annual list of outstanding international literature to recognize children's literature from other countries. The American Library Association's Mildred L. Batchelder Award acknowledges the translation and publication of quality literature first published in other countries. The Hans Christian Andersen Award and the Astrid Lindgren Memorial Award recognize authors and illustrators of international literature. Finally, the Jane Addams Children's Book Award recognizes works that promote peace, social justice, equality, and world community.

Throughout *Literature and Literacy for Young Children: Envisioning Possibilities in Early Childhood Education for Ages 0–8,* recommended titles of diverse literature will be incorporated into each chapter. Lehman (2018) states, "Children gain agency if they understand an issue in society, believe they can make a difference, and take action to be part of the solution" (p. 17). Introducing young children to a range of literature in which they can see themselves and learn more about others can nurture all aspects of their ongoing development.

This book also shows the many ways in which literature supports the goals of early childhood education. At the center of any literature program for children is the literature itself and its contribution to the development of children's imaginations and the pleasure of reading. As the quote by Astrid Lindgren points out at the beginning of this chapter, books offer "the rarest kind of joy." Beyond this, reading regularly to children and engaging them in active response to literature supports their language, intellectual, personality, social, moral, aesthetic, and creative development.

Instructional Strategy from the Field: Responding to Literature through Words and Images

At the beginning of the school year, second-grade teacher Megan Sullivan Sloan read aloud the book *This Is a School* by John Schu (2022). This engaging and relatable story presents school as a place that offers the opportunity to discover, share, help, heal, and hope, while the community that is created emphasizes growth, celebrations, and transformations. School is featured as more than a building where teachers, librarians, coaches, staff, and particularly students all work and learn together. Coupled with Schu's upbeat text are Veronica Miller Jamison's watercolor, acrylic, and digital-collage illustrations that provide a sunny and cheerful palette.

Following the reading of *This Is a School,* Megan's students talked about the people and places that make their school a school. They brainstormed words that described their school and made squares with images depicting them. After each child shared their square it was added to a larger piece of paper to create a quilt.

joy
Cathcart!

Rayleigh
Welcoming
We lCome to Cathcart
Welcom

Box 1.4 Books About School Community

All Are Welcome (Penfold, 2018)
The Day You Begin (Woodson, 2018)
Principal Tate is Running Late (Cole, 2021)
School's First Day of School (Adam Rex, 2016)
School People (Lee Bennett Hopkins, 2018)

Professional References Cited

Ada, A. (2016). Foreword: Literature in the lives of Latino children. In E. R. Clark, B. B. Flores, H. L. Smith, & D. A. González (Eds.), *Multicultural literature for Latino bilingual children: Their words, their worlds* (pp. ix–xviii). Rowman & Littlefield.

Bishop, R. S. (1997). Selecting literature for a multicultural curriculum. In V. Harris (Ed.), *Using multicultural literature in the K-8 classroom* (pp. 1–20). Christopher-Gordon.

Campbell, O. (2017). The history of the bendable, durable, chewable board book. *Literary Hub*. https://lithub.com/the-history-of-the-bendable-durable-chewable-board-book/

Freeman, E. & Lehman, B. (2001). *Global perspectives in children's literature*. Allyn & Bacon.

Lehman, B. (2018). Reading multiculturally, globally, and critically. In D. A. Wooten, L. Aimonette Liang, & B. E. Cullinan (Eds.), *Children's literature in the reading program: Engaging young readers in the 21st century* (pp. 3–20). Guilford.

Leland, C. H. & Lewison, M. (2018). *Teaching children's literature: It's critical!* 2nd ed. Routledge.

Lindgren, A. https://ispiritpublishing.com/2021/04/quotes-about-childrens-books-writing-for-children/

López-Robertson, J. & Haney, M. J. (2017). Their eyes sparkled: Building classroom community through multicultural literature. *Journal of Children's Literature, 43*(1), 48–54.

Louie, B. & Sierschynski, J. (2015). Enhancing English learners' language development using wordless picture books. *The Reading Teacher, 69*(1), 103–111.

Mathis, J. (2011). Multicultural literature: Reading and responding within contemporary contexts. In A. Whatley Bedford & L. K. Albright (Eds.), *A master class in children's literature: Trends and issues in an evolving field* (pp. 93–108). National Council of Teachers of English.

National Children's and Book Literacy Alliance. "Why Do Kids Need Books?" https://thencbla.org/advocacy/why-do-kids-need-books/#:~:text=-Books%20create%20warm%20emotional%20bonds, they%20demand%20that%20kids%20think

Roach, J. (2015). C is for concept. *School Library Journal, 61*(7), 32–36.

Robinson, L. (2017). *Horn Book Magazine Blog: Calling Caldecott.* November 21, 2017. https://www.hbook.com/2017/11/blogs/calling-caldecott/whens-my-birthday/

Salisbury, M. & Styles, M. (2012). *Children's picturebooks: The art of visual storytelling*. Laurence King Publishing.

Schu, John. (2022). *This is a school.* Ill. Veronica Miller Jamison. Candlewick Press.

Shinskey, J. (2016) Lift-the-flap may stop toddlers from learning new words, say scientists. *The Telegraph*, September 14. https://www.telegraph.co.uk/science/2016/09/14/lift-the-flap-books-may-stop-toddlers-learning-new-words-say-sci/

Short, K. G. (2016). A curriculum that is intercultural. In K. G. Short, D. Day, & J. Schroeder (Eds.), *Teaching globally: Reading the world through literature* (pp. 3–24). Stenhouse.

Children's Literature Cited

Ahlberg, Janet & Ahlberg, Allan. (1986/2006). *The jolly postman or other people's letters*. Little, Brown and Company.

Alexander, Rilla. (2019a). *Animals*. Chronicle Books.

Alexander, Rilla. (2019b). *Food*. Chronicle Books.

Arrhenius, Ingela. (2019). *Where's the astronaut?* Nosy Crow.

Avi. (1995). *Poppy*. Ill. Brian Floca. Orchard.

Baker, Keith. (2014). *Little green peas*. Beach Lane.

Bingham, Kelly. (2012). *Z is for moose*. Ill. Paul Zelinsky. Greenwillow.

Bolam, Emily. (2018a). *Animals*. Silver Dolphin Books.

Bolam, Emily. (2018b). *Patterns*. Silver Dolphin Books.

Boynton, Sandra. (2022). *Pajama time!* Boynton Books.

Boynton, Sandra. (2023a). *Belly button book*. Boynton Books.

Boynton, Sandra. (2023b). *Peekaboo Rex!* Boynton Books.

Carle, Eric. (1984). *The very busy spider*. Philomel.

Carter, David E. (2011). *Bugs that go!: A bustling pop-up book*. Little Simon.

Carter, David E. (2012). *Builder bugs: A busy pop-up book*. Little Simon.

Chall, Marsha Wilson. (2010). *One pup's up*. Ill. Henry Cole. McElderry Books for Young Readers.

Dunrea, Olivier. (2016). *Me and Annie McPhee*. Ill. Will Hillenbrand. Philomel.
Ehlert, Lois. (1989). *Color zoo*. HarperCollins.
Ehlert, Lois. (1990). *Fish eyes: A book you can count on*. Houghton Mifflin.
Ehlert, Lois. (1997). *Color zoo*. HarperCollins. (board-book format)
Félix, Lucie. (2016). *Give and take*. Candlewick Studio.
Feuti, Norm. (2019). *Hello, Hedgehog! Do you like my bike?* Scholastic Press.
Fleming, Candace. (2015). *Bulldozer's big day*. Ill. Eric Rohmann. Atheneum.
Fleming, Candace. (2017). *Bulldozer helps out*. Ill. Eric Rohmann. Atheneum.
Fleming, Candace. (2021). *Bulldozer's Christmas dig*. Ill. Eric Rohmann. Atheneum.
Fleming, Denise. (2014). *Go, shapes, go!* Beach Lane.
Fogliano, Julie. (2017). *When's my birthday?* Ill. Christian Robinson. Roaring Brook Press.
Gravett, Emily. (2023). *10 cats*. Boxer Books.
Hacohen, Dean. (2010). *Tuck me in!* Ill. Sherry Scharschmidt. Candlewick Press.
Henkes, Kevin. (2018). *A parade of elephants*. Greenwillow.
Holm, Jennifer L. (2016). *Babymouse #20: Babymouse goes for the gold*. Ill. Matthew Holm. Random House.
Idle, Molly. (2013). *Flora and the flamingo*. Chronicle Books.
Joy, Angela. (2020). *Black is a rainbow color*. Ill. Ekua Holmes. Roaring Brook Press.
Katz, Karen. (2011). *Where is baby's puppy?* Little Simon.
Katz, Karen. (2012). *Baby loves summer*. Little Simon.
Katz, Karen. (2014). *Zoom, zoom, baby!* Little Simon.
Klassen, Jon. (2011). *I want my hat back*. Candlewick Press.
Klassen, Jon. (2012). *This is not my hat*. Candlewick Press.
Klassen, Jon. (2016). *We found a hat*. Candlewick Press.
Lê, Minh. (2018). *Drawn together*. Ill. Dan Santat. Disney Hyperion.
Levine, Ellen. (2007). *Henry's freedom box*. Ill. Kadir Nelson. Scholastic.
Lindgren, Astrid. (1945). *Pippi Longstocking*. Rabén & Sjögren
Llenas, Anna. (2015). *The color monster: A pop-up book of feelings*. Union Square Kids.
Lobel, Arnold. (1970). *Frog and Toad are friends*. HarperCollins.
MacDonald, Suse. (2005). *A was once an apple pie*. Orchard.
Martin, Bill Jr. (1967). *Brown bear brown bear, what do you see?* Ill. Eric Carle. Doubleday.
Martin, Bill Jr. & Archambault, John. (1989). *Chicka chicka boom boom*. Ill. Lois Ehlert. Simon & Schuster.
McCloskey, Robert. (1941). *Make way for ducklings*. Viking.
McDonnell, Patrick. (2011). *Me, Jane*. Little, Brown and Company

McDonnell, Patrick. (2017). *The little red cat who ran away and learned his ABCs (the hard way)*. Little, Brown and Company.
McLaughlin, Eoin. (2020). *Not an alphabet book: The case of the missing cake*. Candlewick Press.
Meddour, Wendy. (2019). *Lubna and Pebble*. Ill. Daniel Egneus. Dial.
Messner, Kate. (2020). *Fergus and Zeke and the field day challenge*. Candlewick Press.
Messner, Kate. (2021). *Fergus and Zeke and the 100th day of school*. Candlewick Press.
Oxenbury, Helen. (1995a). *I can*. Candlewick Press.
Oxenbury, Helen. (1995b). *I hear*. Candlewick Press.
Oxenbury, Helen. (1995c). *I see*. Candlewick Press.
Oxenbury, Helen. (1995d). *I touch*. Candlewick Press.
Park, Linda Sue. (2019). *Nya's long walk: A step at a time*. Ill. Brian Pinkney. Clarion.
Pinkney, Jerry. (2009). *The Lion & the Mouse*. Little, Brown and Company.
Reid, Camilla. (2020a). *Peekaboo apple*. Nosy Crow.
Reid, Camilla. (2020b). *Peekaboo farm*. Nosy Crow.
Reid, Camilla. (2021). *Peekaboo moon*. Nosy Crow.
Rinker, Sherri Duskey. (2011a). *Buenas noches, construcción. Buenas noches diversión*. Ill. Tom Lichtenheld. Chronicle Books.
Rinker, Sherri Duskey. (2011b). *Goodnight, goodnight, construction site*. Ill. Tom Lichtenheld. Chronicle Books.
Rinker, Sherri Duskey. (2017). *Goodnight, goodnight, construction site*. Ill. Tom Lichtenheld. Chronicle Books. (board-book format)
Rinker, Sherri Duskey. (2019a). *Bulldozer's shapes: Goodnight, goodnight, construction site*. Ill. Ethan Long. Chronicle Books.
Rinker, Sherri Duskey. (2019b). *Excavator's 123: Goodnight, goodnight, construction site*. Ill. Ethan Long. Chronicle Books.
Rohmann, Eric. (2002). *My friend rabbit*. Roaring Brook Press.
Ruzzier, Sergio. (2018). *Fox + Chick: The party and other stories*. Chronicle Books.
Ruzzier, Sergio. (2022). *Fox + Chick: Up and down and other stories*. Chronicle Books.
Seuss, Dr. (1957). *The cat in the hat*. Random House.
Sevigny, Alisha. (2022). *Give me a snickle!* Orca Book Publishers.
Shea, Bob. (2008). *Dinosaur vs. bedtime*. Disney Hyperion.
Smith, Jeff. (2009). *Little mouse gets ready*. TOON Book.
Sophie la girafe: Hide and Seek (2016). DK Children.
Sophie la girafe: Good Night Sophie (2017). DK Children.
Swanson, Weldon. (2013). *My backpack!* Scholastic Press.
Thong, Roseanne Greenfield. (2019). *One is a piñata: A book of numbers*. Ill. John Parra. Chronicle Books.

Tullet, Hervé. (2014). *Mix it up!* Chronicle Books.
Tullet, Hervé. (2019). *Press here*. Chronicle Books. (board-book format)
Twohy, Mike. (2018). *Stop, go, yes, no!: A story of opposites*. Balzer + Bray.
Weatherford, Carole Boston. (2022). *Me and the family tree: Celebrate family love and connection!* Ill. Ashleigh Corrin. Sourcebooks Jabberwocky.
White, E. B. (1952). *Charlotte's web*. Ill. Garth Williams. Harper.
Willems, Mo. (2012). *Let's go for a drive!: An Elephant and Piggie Book*. Disney Hyperion.
Yolen, Jane. (2018). *A bear sat on my porch today*. Ill. Rilla Alexander. Chronicle Books.

2

Evaluating Literature for Young Children

> A picture book isn't didactic but rather something that tick-tick-ticks in the back of your mind like a time-release capsule. It unfolds in your thought and moves you in some way. It makes you feel connected to your own humanity, and maybe makes you able to see your own behavior in a way that resonates for you. And maybe even changes you a tiny bit.
>
> (Antoinette Portis, author-illustrator, 2019)

Books written and illustrated for children should represent the best by literary and artistic standards. During an interview, author and illustrator Antoinette Portis shares that picture books should move you in some way and possibly even change you a tiny bit. This is the power of stories. As you begin applying criteria and developing your expertise in evaluating literature that is the "best," you might want to access book reviews. Several print and online journals, such as *The Horn Book Magazine* and *School Library Journal*, offer reviews of new books. In addition, various blogs, Pinterest boards, and online sources such as https://www.ReadBrightly.com, www.goodreads.com, and www.thechildrensbookreview.com offer summaries of books grouped by age, theme, and topic, along with author interviews. Reading book reviews on these sites suggests how critics and readers apply literary criteria.

Each year, the Association for Library Service to Children (ALSC) presents the Caldecott Medal to the illustrator of the most distinguished picture book published for children. The selection committee, comprising school and public librarians, children's literature educators, and book reviewers, determines

DOI: 10.4324/9781003367635-2

what they consider outstanding illustrations. The Theodor Seuss Geisel Award is presented by the ALSC and recognizes books for beginning readers. There are also numerous book awards given by national organizations such as the National Council of Teachers of English, the National Council of Social Studies, and the Children's Book Council. These awards are generally determined by adults while young readers choose recipients of state awards for children's literature. Awards such as the Texas Bluebonnet Award or the California Young Reader Medal can offer insight into the possible difference between books selected by adults versus those chosen by children.

As you begin to read children's literature and share these books with young children, you will develop your own criteria for book selection. You will also gain an understanding of the type of stories that engage children and prompt discussion and response.

Evaluating Fiction

One way to analyze fiction is to look at literary elements. You can identify strengths and weaknesses in plot, setting, characterization, theme, and writing style.

Plot

The plot of a story is what happens in it. In Ariel Bernstein's *We Love Fishing!* (2021), the story is told through a simple narrative that begins, "Bear, Porcupine, Otter, and Squirrel love fishing." Other statements explain things the foursome like that are associated with fishing, such as walking through the woods, sitting in the boat for hours, enjoying rain showers, and feeling excited about the big fish they have caught. However, dialogue between the animals coupled with exaggerated expressions, particularly by Squirrel, tells a very different story. When Squirrel accidentally bungles the net holding the fish, the slippery catch slides through his hands and back into the water. The other animals no longer love fishing quite so much. However, Squirrel has the perfect solution and solves the dinner dilemma by calling a taxi to whisk them away to a restaurant—possibly for a fish dinner.

A good plot should be interesting. It builds suspense, so the reader will want to know what will happen next. Remembering that text and illustrations work in concert to create meaning is essential. *We Love Fishing!* depicts a different attitude of the Squirrel about fishing than is stated in the narrative. While all the animals rave about the joys of fishing, comments by Squirrel include, "Fish smell too fishy" and "Rain makes my fur frizz." The cover illustration presents Bear, Porcupine, and Otter with smiling faces while

Squirrel sits in the background with his arms crossed and a scowl on his face. As the story evolves and the animals bask in the fishing experience, Squirrel expresses his displeasure and boredom. The story propels the reader forward because of the different character perspectives and the reader's desire to discover how this fishing expedition ends. The climax occurs with Squirrel's fish calamity, even though the fish seems happy to be off the hook and back in the water. The plot builds suspense so the reader will continue turning the pages to discover what happens next.

A good plot builds logically. Causal relationships connect the events which are plausible within the story's context. For example, even though some children may not have experienced a fishing trip, they will relate to doing something where they were bored or unhappy. Likewise, going fishing, or engaging in any experience with friends because they enjoy it, is also plausible.

Plots in picture books and chapter books vary in complexity. There may be only one problem or several to be solved. There may be two characters or 20. Occasionally, there will be parallel plots, two storylines weaving together by the conclusion. However simple or complex the plot, the events should be logically related.

Setting

The setting, where and when a story takes place, should be an integral part of the story, not just a backdrop that could be changed without affecting the plot. The setting for *We Love Fishing!* includes walking through the woods on the way to the fishing boat. Bear, Porcupine, and Otter enjoy the fresh air and the trek while Squirrel is complaining about the bugs, stepping on a pebble, and the steep terrain he has to climb. Illustrator Marc Rosenthal incorporates visual images on double-page spreads to offer the reader an understanding of the setting and also emotions such as when the animals are sitting on the boat or as the animals look dejectedly into the water as the fish swims away. The setting in *We Love Fishing!* is easily understood because of the simple yet bold art.

The descriptions should be accurate if the story has a specific setting, with the exact time and place identified. Other settings may be depicted more generally, such as in a town, in the country, or "long ago in a faraway land." Even when the location is not precisely spelled out, the reader should be given a taste of what life is like at that place and time.

Characterization

Characterization—how the author portrays each character—often makes a book memorable. Children know Madeline, The Princess in Black, Max and Ruby, Junie B. Jones, and Judy Moody's brother Stink, because these characters are clearly delineated. The reader knows what they like and dislike, how they will behave in a given situation, and what is special about them. They have more than one dimension so that the reader can respond to the many aspects of their personalities. There are some likable things they do or think and some not so likable. A good author lets the reader know about characters by showing what they do, think, or say, and sometimes by offering what others say or think about them or how they are treated.

The dialogue between Bear, Porcupine, Otter, and Squirrel reveals much about what they are thinking about going fishing. The illustrations add another layer and often contradict the text. The three storytelling devices—narrative storyline, dialogue, and illustrations—create a unified and enjoyable picture book.

In some stories, the characters change or develop due to what happens to them. It is difficult to have extensive character development in books for young children simply because the stories are fairly short in picture book and chapter book formats. There is little time to delineate a character fully, then have a believable change occur. It is doubtful Squirrel will grow to love fishing, but he will continue to enjoy being with his friends.

Theme

The theme of a book is its underlying idea. It may be a general theme, such as friendship or courage, or more specific and stated in sentence form, such as "Even though the characters seem alike, each one is unique" or "We should make our own decisions and not let others make them for us." A story may have no theme, one theme, or multiple themes. The themes underlying *We Love Fishing!* are friendship and acceptance of each other despite having different opinions and interests. The theme is not fishing but rather embeds the story within that context. If there is a theme, it should be an integral part of the story but not overpower it. There should be no need for closing comments by the author to make certain the theme is understood.

Style of Writing

The style of writing—which words are chosen and how they are arranged—helps create the mood and tone of the story. *We Love Fishing!* incorporates brief, "factual" statements that the entire foursome loves doing the same things. The dialogue, shown in speech balloons, offers a different perspective on the fishing outing and highlights actions and feelings.

The creative vocabulary includes phrases such as "skewer my fish for a shish kebab" and words like *escalator*, *peaceful*, *refreshing*, and *restaurant*. Some words and phrases have visual clues, while others might need context clues, such as "escalator."

There is humor in *We Love Fishing!* in both text and illustrations. On the cover and the title page, it is apparent how Squirrel is feeling as opposed to the beaming smiles of the Bear, Porcupine, and Otter. As the other animals extol their love of fishing, Squirrel states, "They love fishing," as he gazes lovingly at his supply of nuts. Once the fish is caught, Bear is ecstatic, Otter has hearts surrounding him as he licks his chops, and Squirrel is utterly clueless that something is happening because he has been drawing pictures of acorns. Even the fish's happy expression after he plops back into the water is quite humorous.

Other authors, especially in chapter books, may use descriptive passages that achieve the same end of advancing the plot but give a tale a slower pace. The style should be appropriate to the story being told. It should appear natural so that readers are not distracted by it and are scarcely aware of how it is functioning.

Plot, setting, characterization, theme, and style should be mutually compatible while complementing the others. In addition to these marks of good writing, books for children should be free of stereotypes and condescension in tone. Stereotypes generally indicate poor writing and are intellectually and socially offensive. Stereotypes present a person not as an individual but as a representative of a group whose members are deemed to possess the same characteristics. A condescending tone should be avoided because it disrespects children's ability to comprehend a story.

Coherence

Another way of evaluating fiction is to look at the story's overall coherence. There should be a sense of completeness when the book is finished, as the author has taken or created an incident, developed it, and structured it. The story will not have the lags, random happenings, or intrusions that characterize real life. Instead, it should flow meaningfully, with each part related to other parts and the whole. Storytelling is recognized as one of the ways in which we make sense of our lives and the lives of others.

Coherence depends on a carefully structured plot and compatibility between the individual elements of the plot, setting, characterization, theme, and style of writing. *We Love Fishing!* works because the plot revolves around the joy of Bear, Porcupine, and Otter and the annoyance and lack of interest of Squirrel. The dialogue and characters' actions and emotions reinforce elements of characterization and advance the plot. The style of writing and illustrations contribute to understanding the characters and the mood of the entire story. The book presents a coherent whole.

Evelyn Del Rey Is Moving Away by Meg Medina (2020) uses a different but equally effective structure. Evelyn Del Rey is Daniela's best friend, her *mejor amiga*. Unfortunately, it's moving day for Evelyn and her family. The two best friends take advantage of their remaining hours together by waving to Mr. Soo as he's feeding the pigeons, stopping at Señora Flores's door for a cookie, and playing with an empty box that is transformed into an imaginary bus. As the last boxes are loaded into the van, Daniela and Evelyn discuss how they will talk every day after school and visit each other in the summer. A final hug, a secret handshake, and a heartfelt wave one last time, and Evelyn Del Rey is gone. However, Daniela knows Evelyn will always be her "first mejor amiga and número uno best friend." A concluding illustration depicts Daniela years later with photos and letters that indicate the friendship with Evelyn is still present and precious. This diverse story celebrates friendship and acknowledges the inevitable changes that test that bond.

Literary elements reinforce one another. In *Evelyn Del Rey Is Moving Away*, the characters are believable, the setting is contemporary, and the story is universal. The story is also well developed and has completeness as the book concludes. After reading a book, ask yourself if you have a sense of satisfaction with the overall experience. Then go back and carefully look at the book to discern what has or has not given coherence to the work as a whole.

Integrity

Good children's literature contains freshness and honesty. It may touch children's emotions; it may stimulate their imaginations. It may make them think about new ideas or old ideas in new ways. The child's world expands through the inventiveness of the author and illustrator. *We Love Fishing!* uses a concise, humorous, and deftly told narrative with a brief storyline and dialogue that expresses the happiness of engaging in a pastime with friends and honoring the idea that not everyone enjoys the same activities. Daniela values her friendship in *Evelyn Del Rey Is Moving Away* to the extent the two best friends enjoy being together and having fun rather than commiserating about the impending move. Both stories bring a creative approach to their topics and an honest presentation of the story.

Evaluating Nonfiction

Standards for nonfiction and biography should be applied as rigorously as those for fiction. Like fiction, nonfiction should be well written, engaging, and accurate. Nonfiction appeals to young children because of the brief, concise text and colorful illustrations that pique their interest. In addition, nonfiction written in students' native language can support multilingual learners transitioning from their first language to their second (Young et al., 2007). This applies to nonfiction written as either narrative or expository text.

Organization

Good writing in nonfiction is clear and informative. The material presented should have a careful and logical organization. The table of contents, index, and back matter standard in nonfiction for older readers sometimes are omitted in books for young children. Text may also appear more like a story which is true for narrative nonfiction. However, information should follow a pattern that helps to make the content understandable to younger readers.

Nonfiction is presented in a variety of formats. For toddlers, board books such as *How It Works: Dinosaur* (Hepworth, 2022) can be informative and fun. The topic of dinosaurs is always fascinating for young children, and this interactive board book has layered die-cuts sprinkled throughout the pages. Labeled illustrations support vocabulary words such as teeth, skull, and tail. Also, fun facts about Tyrannosaurus rex make this an enjoyable book for young children. The board-book series Animal Families features animals from different settings. *Animal Families: Forest* (Ormes, 2020), published by Nosy Crow, shows a variety of forest animals with the correct terms for daddy, mommy, and baby. For example, a mommy rabbit is called a doe, a daddy rabbit is called a buck, and baby rabbits are called kits. You can reveal the baby animals by lifting the flaps.

Hey, Water! by Antoinette Portis (2019) is a nonfiction picture book that is just right for preschool and early grades. "Hey, water! I know you! You're all around" begins this exploration of how we use water and its various forms, such as tears, rain, steam, fog, and iceberg. A spunky little girl arrives at the realization that water is everywhere. As Portis pointed out in the cited interview, books such as *Hey, Water!* can assist children in realizing the interconnectedness of individuals with the world around them. In this brief picture book, there is a call to conserve water and for children to consider their own uses of this valuable resource. The text is also coupled with terms for places (river, ocean, rink) and forms of water, which will undoubtedly enhance vocabulary development. *Hey, Water!* is also available as a board book and e-book.

Another book focusing on water as well as land is Christy Hale's *Water Land: Land and Water Forms around the World* (2018). A lake turns into an island, a cozy bay into a secluded cape, and a gulf with sea turtles transforms into a peninsula surrounded by pirate ships. Strategic cutouts on each page switch between bodies of water and corresponding land masses. A large fold-out map at the book's conclusion explains land forms and water forms from around the world. Pairing *Hey, Water!* with *Water Land* provides information about water on a small and grand scale. The information in both books is organized to engage young children as they learn about something they use in their daily lives.

Another item that is used every day by children is crayons. *The Crayon Man: The True Story of the Invention of Crayola Crayons* (Biebow, 2019) is a picture-book biography of Edwin Binney, who is credited with inventing colored crayons. Crayons were first created in Europe from a mixture of charcoal and oil but broke easily. Also, some of them were toxic and made children sick if they might eat or chew them. Edwin's wife was a schoolteacher and encouraged her husband to invent cheaper crayons that were easier to hold and not poisonous. In a top-secret lab in Pennsylvania, Edwin assembled a team of workers who each day melted paraffin wax and ground up rocks and minerals as pigment for the crayons. After much experimentation, Edwin created green, orange, violet, pink, red, blue, and yellow crayons. They were also nontoxic. What to call them? His wife suggested mixing the French words *craie* and *ola*, which became Crayola. The crayons were a hit at home and around the world. Photographs at the book's conclusion show the crayon-making process, while the back matter provides additional information about Edwin Binney and a selected bibliography about him and crayons. This biography does not focus on Edwin's entire life but instead on his process of inventing the crayon. Picture-book biographies might tell about an individual's entire life, concentrate only on childhood, or present a slice of life based on a significant time or achievement such as in *The Crayon Man*.

Accurate Presentations of Facts

Factual accuracy is one of the most important criteria when choosing nonfiction books. Nonfiction for any age level should not contain misinformation or oversimplify a topic to the point of inaccuracy. Look at concept books for infants and toddlers with the same critical eye you use for all nonfiction. These beginning informational books should be accurate in the information they present and the examples they use to illustrate a concept. Nonfiction author and illustrator Gail Gibbons is known for her succinct text and colorful watercolor illustrations. *Volcanoes* (2022) details the types of volcanoes, their explosions, and their earth-altering abilities. Children learn about dormant and active volcanoes using direct sentences, maps, infographics, and visual images. Gibbons has an extensive offering of well-researched nonfiction books on various topics that contain accurate facts and information just right for young children.

Look for information that is excluded as well as what is included. Although not a direct misstatement of fact, leaving out essential information can be just as misleading. Authors writing about broad topics must make choices, of course, and it is impossible to include everything. Gail Gibbons has a knack for knowing just how much information to include in her nonfiction picture books. Natascha Biebow presented the biography of Edwin Binney through narrative text while infusing factual information in separate boxes throughout the book. In doing so, the flow of the narrative was not interrupted, but intriguing tidbits about crayons could be shared through other means.

Expository nonfiction explains, describes, or informs in a straightforward and accessible fashion (Stewart & Young, 2022). Written in this style are many nonfiction books for young children, including those by Gail Gibbons. Greg Pizzoli (2022) looks at a favorite food in *Pizza! A Slice of History*. Did you know that people in the United States eat 350 slices of pizza every second? But what is the origin of pizza, and how did it come to this country? Pizzoli explains that pizza possibly started in ancient Greece or maybe Persia. The type of pizza we are most familiar with was probably created in Naples, Italy, hundreds of years ago. Today, there are many variations of pizza not only in the U.S. but worldwide. This captivating nonfiction book will appeal to a wide range of readers and listeners.

Facts can be presented in a variety of ways in addition to expository and narrative texts. *Lift, Mix, Fling! Machines Can Do Anything* (Schaefer, 2022) uses lively, rhyming text to introduce young children to several machines. "Simple machines have one or two parts." Items such as a spoon, knives, or lids on jars are examples of these types of machines, while rockets, trucks, and vacuums are compound machines. James Yang's bold, colorful illustrations make this STEM topic easy to understand. The book concludes with additional definitions and suggests searching for simple and compound machines used daily.

Current Information and Resources

Nonfiction books that you use should present current information. Please pay attention to the copyright date and the data themselves. Some areas, such as science, are changing more quickly than others, so the topic may alert you. When a field is changing rapidly, it is imperative to select recently published books and alert children to the date of publication when you use older books.

During the pandemic in 2020, the Children's Book Council compiled various publisher websites that offer lesson plans and instructional guides for fiction and nonfiction picture books and chapter books. While it might take a bit of searching the numerous websites, there are dozens of ideas and resources for a range of books. The website is located at https://www.cbcbooks.org/readers/reader-resources/publisher-online-resources/

Evaluating Poetry

Poetry takes careful reading. There is a compactness of language—every word counts. The sound of the language as it is read aloud is vital. The rhythm should be strong and natural. Even free verse with no rhyme has a rhythm to it. If it is a rhyming poem, the rhyme should have a pattern or cadence. The rhythm in poetry should sing.

Poems use language for its sound as well as its meaning. However, the rhyme in poems should not take precedence over the meaning. Words should not be stated in an awkward order just so the last words will rhyme. Nor should lines be included that would not make sense if found in a prose selection just because they rhyme.

The language in poetry should be fresh. It may show a new way of looking at something or telling about it. Poetry often uses figurative language and makes comparisons. It relies heavily on imagery, describing how the senses perceive experiences. Read poems to see if the comparison and descriptions make sense and are vivid, such as *When Green Becomes Tomatoes: Poems for All Seasons* by Julie Fogliano (2016). The four seasons are celebrated through poems describing blooming crocuses, rainy spring days, and falling leaves. The poems convey the beauty of the four seasons and the human emotions that the changing seasons evoke. Don't underestimate children's ability to comprehend figurative language as you read poetry. The key is to allow them time to discuss their interpretations rather than being told what the poem means by an adult.

Collections of poetry should be evaluated the same as individual poems. *The Dream Train: Poems for Bedtime* (Taylor, 2023) contains original verses and rhymes for young children that explores the ritual of bedtime. Thirty poems written in a variety of styles, such as shape poems, free verse, and ballads, are divided into three sections titled "Night Arrives," "Shut-Your-Eyes-Time," and "Dream Wheels Turning." Collections and anthologies by children's poets Lee Bennett Hopkins, Rebecca Kai Dotlich, Douglas Florian, J. Patrick Lewis, and Mary Ann Hoberman are also recommended for young children.

The literary standards by which poetry for children is judged are no less demanding than those for adult poetry. A poem that is poor by adult standards is also poor for children. Nor is there any need to talk down to children or make poems cute or easy. To do so is to show a fundamental disrespect for the child reader or listener. Teachers have a responsibility to children to select poems that have literary merit.

Evaluating Illustrations

The previous sections focused on evaluating the text in literature for young children. Equally as important are the illustrations. A distinguishing feature of quality picture books is the "use of illustrations that tell part of the story (and sometimes a very significant part of the story)" (Villarreal et al., 2015,

p. 266). Color, line, texture, shape, and space, along with font, framing, perspective, and positionality, are all tools used by illustrators to craft the art in picture books. Chapter 9 in this textbook, Generating Children's Aesthetic and Creative Development, provides an in-depth look at these art and design elements.

When you select books to share with young children, look at the overall effectiveness of the total book. Then, as you look at various books more carefully, you will better analyze the art and the text.

Proximity to Text

Illustrations in a picture book should be located near the text they depict, either on the same or opposite page. Children look at illustrations as the story is being read, and if they read the book independently they may use the pictures as clues to meaning. If the story is unified, text and illustrations must then appear together. In books of poetry, the illustration should be tied to the poem by its placement on the page and its content. This is particularly true if several poems appear on a single page.

Developing the Text

Illustrations should match both the description and action in the text. When the text in *Evelyn Del Ray is Moving Away* says, "But the walls in Evelyn's room are sunny yellow, while mine are pink like cotton candy," they show Daniela in her pink room, and in the apartment where Evelyn lives the walls of her room are yellow. Then, of course, the illustrator can add any actions or details that might extend the story, develop the setting, or enhance the characterization.

The illustrator need not show everything mentioned in the text. The primary criterion is that there should be no conflict between text and illustration unless it is clearly part of the storytelling, such as in *We Love Fishing!* Sometimes illustrations can be confusing rather than helpful, even without direct conflict. For example, postmodern picture books may have illustrations combining realism with fantasy, such as surrealistic images, the inclusion of nontraditional formats, or the juxtaposition of unrelated images (Serafini, 2014). These storytelling devices may overwhelm a young child and complicate the story.

Capturing the Emotional Link

Caldecott Medal-winning illustrator, Jon Klassen whose "hat trilogy" books were discussed in Chapter 1, says that sometimes it is a struggle to draw people so the reader knows what the character is feeling and thinking. Drawing animals is easier for Klassen because there are many ways to depict symbols of emotion but not actual emotion. For example, when he is drawing a dog, children will look at the eyes—if the eyes are looking straight ahead, the dog might feel guilty or hungry, whereas if the eyes are looking downward, the dog might feel ashamed or sad. Klassen's "hat trilogy" provides excellent examples of how this award-winning illustrator effectively displays emotions, including guilt, that enable the reader to know precisely how the character feels.

As you examine the art in children's books, consider those aspects of art that develop an emotional link between the story and the reader. View the media, colors, perspectives, style of illustration, use of white space, and shape of the book that all assist in telling the story well.

When readers view Ian Falconer's illustrations of *Olivia* (2000), an irresistible pig with limitless energy, they will notice that she is constantly on the move while showcasing her talents and dreaming big dreams. Falconer's charcoal illustrations with dollops of bright red are highly amusing. When the text states, "She is *very* good at wearing people out," we see Olivia engaged in various activities through 13 black-and-white vignettes, with an occasional splash of red. Falconer illustrates Olivia's ongoing sense of movement until eventually, "She even wears herself out." The artist uses lines to convey Olivia's movement and emotions. These lines also enable the readers' eyes to move across the page. The use of white space effectively displays the vignettes and full scenes. The focus is always on Olivia, which is simply the story's theme.

The illustrations in *Olivia* are effective both as art and in combination with the spare text. The style and medium are highly unique and eye-catching. The spacious design of the book, clever illustrations, humorous storyline, and opportunity for readers to see a little of themselves in Olivia make this Caldecott Honor book one to revisit for repeated readings. Olivia makes an emotional link that Klassen describes and is true to the mood and content of the text, blending words and pictures effectively.

Appropriateness of Illustrations

The purpose for which the book was designed can help define criteria for evaluating the illustrations. In alphabet books, those used particularly with toddlers to name objects, the illustrations should be clear and uncluttered. Designing the alphabet book to emphasize the sound or sounds made by each letter means the illustrations must be accurate. That is, *s* should not be represented by an object such as a shoe because even though the word does begin with *s*, it is the sound of the *sh* blend that children hear. If the book is designed to help children learn to count and recognize numerals, then the illustrations must show the objects clearly. The child should know what is to be counted. There should be no confusing background and no questions about whether the bugs or the legs on the bugs should be counted. This means that diagrams must make a concept clearer, photographs must convey information and beauty, and drawings must help the reader understand. Illustrations in nonfiction can be categorized by the degree of representation. Photographs, for example, are usually highly representative, showing the object's features as they appear naturally. Diagrams combining pictures with labels are less representational and more abstract, and tables and charts are the least and most abstract.

Photographs should be of high technical quality. For example, April Pulley Sayre spent four hours a day for months photographing frogs for *Being Frog* (2020). The subject of each photograph is vividly clear as the book explores the question, "What is it like to be a frog?" Diagrams in children's books vary in complexity, from simply labeling objects or parts of objects to cutaway or cross-sectional drawings. These should clarify or extend the information in the text. Of particular interest in nonfiction is how scale is shown or whether it is shown at all. Often an artist will include in the illustrations something whose size is known—such as a hand holding a baby mouse or a car parked next to a redwood tree—or may label the size of the object. The illustrations help the reader visualize not only the subject itself but also the subject in context.

Captions, although not essential, can make photographs, diagrams, maps, tables, and other ways of presenting data much more straightforward. They may also help to capture the reader's interest. Captions are often found in nonfiction books that contain extension information. When evaluating the illustrations in a nonfiction book, you may want to think of how you plan to share the book with children. Consider whether the book can help children become careful observers and interpreters of visual data.

Illustrations are central to the success of all picture books. Carefully evaluate them because they are essential to a young child's literary and artistic education. Books shared with children should be the best available based on literary and artistic standards. Childcare providers and teachers must therefore be able to judge the quality of children's books. You can evaluate fiction by assessing the effectiveness of the literary elements of plot, setting, characterization, theme, and style of writing as well as how the elements are integrated to provide a unified whole. Judge nonfiction for factual accuracy, current information, and clear differentiation between fact and opinion. The organization and choice of material affect the quality of nonfiction. Finally, you can assess poetry for children on the freshness and compactness of language, use of rhythm and rhyme, and emotional content.

Evaluating Interactive Media and Children's Books

The number and range of media, including audiobooks, e-books, and book apps, is expanding rapidly. The National Association for the Education of Young Children (NAEYC) refers to interactive media as digital and analog materials that include apps, streaming media, some children's television programming, e-books, and other forms of content that are designed to facilitate active and creative use by young children.

As the ability to access technology has increased, there have been concerns raised as to whether young children should be using their parents' smartphones or tablets to view videos or play games. The American Academy of Pediatrics (2016) discourages any amount of screen time for children under the age of two and one hour or less per day of high-quality programming for children older than two. One issue is that when young children engage with technology, it is often a passive activity rather than one in which a parent or caregiver is interacting with the child.

NAEYC and the Fred Rogers Center (2012) have developed principles to guide the use of technology and digital media with young children. Some of these principles include selecting technology and media that is age appropriate. The developmental level, needs, interests, linguistic background, and abilities of each child should be considered. The tools that children use that help them explore, create, problem solve, think, and listen should apply to literature as well as digital media. When used appropriately, technology and media should enhance children's cognitive and social abilities. Overall, technology and media have the capability to enhance early childhood practice when it is integrated into the environment, curriculum, and daily routines.

In 2019, the American Library Association announced the first recipients of the Excellence in Early Learning Digital Media (EELDM) Award which is given to the producer of the most distinguished digital media for an early learning audience, ages two to eight, produced in the United States during the preceding year. The award has recognized apps, podcasts, and children's programming on platforms such as YouTube and PBS Kids. Some of these award recipients are stories created specifically in digital form, others are adaptations of children's books, and many do not have a literature focus. Websites such as Common Sense Media offer reviews of book apps designed for children. There are also numerous sources that review reading apps. These apps are intended to teach reading skills rather than presenting a children's book in digital form.

When considering books that are available in an electronic format, such as e-books or apps, consider how sound, action, and interaction engage the child in a literary experience that brings the narrative to life. Be aware that an e-book will not contain features such as fold-out pages, die-cuts, or interactive elements like lift-the-flaps or pull tabs. Your purpose should guide you in the selection and sharing of an e-book or app. Perhaps you want to share a book with the whole class, but the book is so small that they could not see the illustrations. An e-book that can be projected on a screen or whiteboard will overcome this problem.

There are websites such as Storyline Online that feature various celebrities reading aloud popular children's books. On the internet, you'll also discover individuals such as teachers and librarians reading aloud stories. Always check the quality of these readings. Make sure the voices are clear and easily understood. The pages from the book should be distinct and in focus. Sound effects and music should help establish the mood of the story, not overpower it. Careful screening of these options will also support children for whom English is not their first language or children who are challenged by reading. Hearing stories read aloud either online or through audiobooks reinforces fluency and demonstrates how to read with expression. Having the book to read along with as children listen to the story is advisable as well. There is a wealth of options available online but it's important to review them in order to present the best available to children. The most important consideration with any format is the reading experience it provides for the child.

Instructional Strategy from the Field: Determining Word Meaning Using a Graphic Organizer

Nicole Noline teaches first grade in Window Rock, Arizona on the Navajo Nation. She uses the Frayer Model to support students in determining word meaning. This graphic organizer assists students in determining or clarifying the meaning of vocabulary words. It can be used before reading to activate background knowledge, during reading to monitor vocabulary, or after reading to assess vocabulary.

> Using the Frayer model helps students from a visual standpoint. It then allows them to verbally share ideas. Teachers can use this at all levels if they choose—Kindergarten and 1st grade can use it for phonics and the alphabet while 1st through 8th grade can use it for vocabulary and sight words. Here's how I use it with students:
>
> 1) Create the Vocabulary Square (I like to call it a diamond).
> 2) Write your topic or word in the middle.
> 3) Define your word (the word or topic should always be defined).
> 4) Decide for the remaining squares if you would like to do one of the following: a) synonyms, b) antonyms, c) pictures, d) words or phrases, e) write the word in sentences.

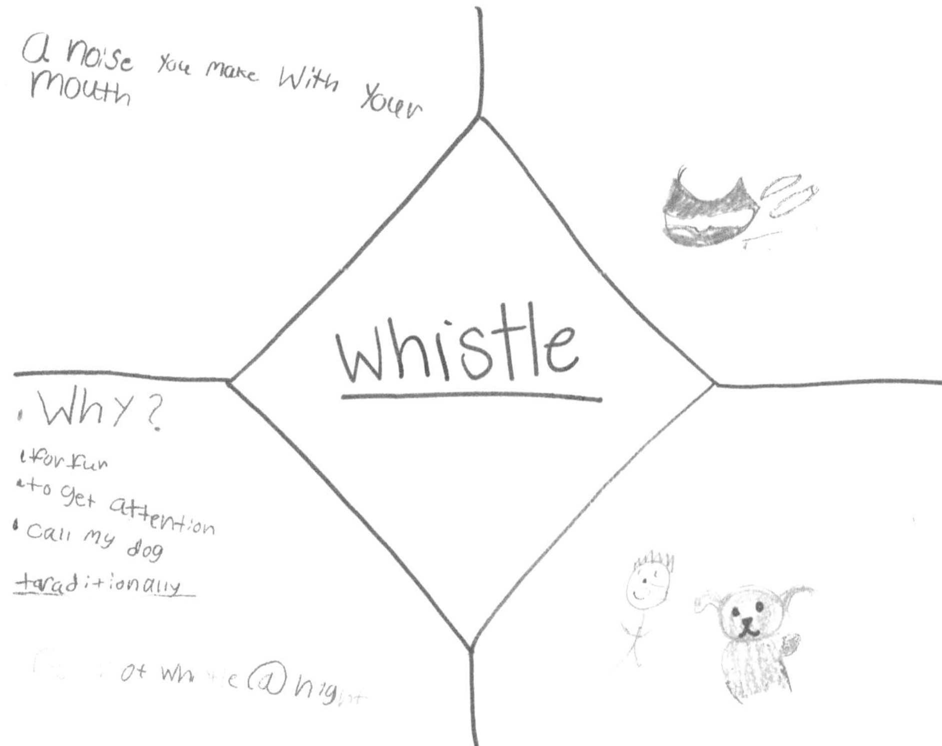

Cecelia

What is Peter's problem in the story?

RACE

Restate

Answer

Example

Peters problem is he can't whistle.

Do you have? O a sentence O?!. O Capital Letter at the beginning O Finger spaces

Prior to reading our story for the week, the writing prompt was about a character's problem. Cecelia didn't know what a whistle was. To break it down for her we used the Frayer model. I could have just told her but it was nice to hear her input and to see what she thought could be a whistle. I even learned more about her culture and how it ties into whistling.

Professional References Cited

American Academy of Pediatrics. (2016). *Media and Young Minds, 138*(5). https://publications.aap.org/pediatrics/article/138/5/e20162591/60503/Media-and-Young-Minds

Klassen, Jon. https://www.youtube.com/watch?v=4VPJp7chqH0

NAEYC & Fred Rogers Center. (2012). Technology and Interactive Media as Tools in Early Childhood Programs Serving Children from Birth though Age 8. https://www.naeyc.org/sites/default/files/globally-shared/downloads/PDFs/resources/position-statements/ps_technology.pdf

Only Picture Books: The Weekly Rumpus of Picture Book Things. (2019). Author Interview: Antoinette Portis. https://www.onlypicturebooks.com/2019/01/14/author-interview-antoinette-portis/

Serafini, F. (2014). *Reading the visual: An introduction to teaching multimodal literacy*. Teachers College Press.

Stewart, M. & Young, T. A. (Dec. 21, 2022). Understanding text structures in nonfiction. *School Library Journal*. Retrieved from https://www.slj.com/story/booklists/understanding-text-structures-in-childrens-nonfiction

Villarreal, A., Minton, S., & Martinez, M. (2015). Child illustrators: Making meaning through visual art in picture books. *The Reading Teacher*, *69*(3), 265–275.

Young, T. A., Moss, B., & Cornwell, L. (2007). The classroom library: A place for nonfiction, nonfiction in its place. *Reading Horizons*, *48*(1), 1–18.

Children's Literature Cited

Bernstein, Ariel. (2021). *We love fishing!* Ill. Marc Rosenthal. Simon & Schuster.

Biebow, Natascha. (2019). *The crayon man: The true story of the invention of Crayola crayons.* Ill. Steven Salerno. Houghton Mifflin Harcourt.

Falconer, Ian. (2000). *Olivia.* Simon & Schuster.

Fogliano, Julie. (2016). *When green becomes tomatoes: Poems for all seasons.* Ill. Julie Morstad. Roaring Brook Press.

Gibbons, Gail. (2022). *Volcanoes.* Holiday House.

Hale, Christy. (2018). *Water land: Land and water forms around the world.* Roaring Book Press.

Hepworth, Amelia. (2022). *How it works: Dinosaur.* Ill. David Semple. Tiger Tales.

Medina, Meg. (2020). *Evelyn Del Rey is moving away.* Ill. Sonia Sánchez. Candlewick Press.

Ormes, Jane. (2020). *Animal families: Forest.* Nosy Crow.

Pizzoli, Greg. (2022). *Pizza! A slice of history.* Penguin Random House.

Portis, Antoinette. (2019). *Hey, water!* Holiday House.

Sayre, April Pulley. (2020). *Being frog.* Beach Lane Books.

Schaefer, Lola M. (2002). *Lift, mix, fling! Machines can do anything.* Ill. James Yang. Greenwillow.

Taylor, Sean. (2023). *The dream train: Poems for bedtime.* Ill. Anuska Allepuz. Candlewick Press.

3

Creating a Literate Environment

> The fire of literacy is created by the emotional sparks between a child, a book, and the person reading. It isn't achieved by the book alone, nor by the child alone, nor by the adult who's reading aloud—it's the relationship winding between all three, bringing them together in easy harmony.
>
> (Mem Fox, 2001, p. 10)

When children read or are read to, it is hoped they will observe how one or more books connect to others. Children will also make personal connections to experiences similar to their own and literature related to the world around them. Having an opportunity to discuss books and respond to them in authentic ways allows stories to come alive for young children and provides a purpose for reading. How teachers, childcare providers, librarians, and parents share literature presents the possibilities and potential that books can offer.

Reading Aloud as Foundational

In 1983, the Commission on Reading, funded by the U.S. Department of Education, launched a study to examine school test scores. Based on the findings, reading was determined to be both the solution and the problem concerning declining test scores. When the final report, *Becoming a Nation of Readers: The Report of the Commission on Reading* (Anderson et al., 1985), was issued two

DOI: 10.4324/9781003367635-3

years later, one of the primary conclusions stated, "The single most important activity for eventual success in reading is reading aloud to children (p. 23)." The Commission determined there was conclusive evidence that reading aloud at home and in the classroom sowed the seeds of reading desire and subsequent success.

Reading aloud offers children the pleasure of books. Numerous research studies have supported the educational values of reading aloud (Casasola, 2016; Dunst et al., 2012; Duursma et al., 2008). The benefits of reading aloud include introducing vocabulary, modeling fluency, demonstrating expressive reading, supporting comprehension, and building background knowledge (Trelease & Giorgis, 2019). Reading aloud becomes the foundation on which reading and other areas of the curriculum are built.

Author, Mem Fox, has long been a passionate advocate of reading aloud to children. Her book for parents and educators, *Reading Magic: Why Reading Aloud to Our Children Will Change Their Lives Forever* (2001), details the many benefits of reading aloud and how this ongoing practice will impact children's ability to read. Fox discusses the emotional and intellectual impact of reading aloud and proposes that if a minimum of three stories a day were read to children then maybe we could eliminate illiteracy. Mem Fox's classic stories such as *Koala Lou* (1989) in which a child yearns to hear the words, "Koala Lou, I DO love you," or *Tough Boris* (1994) about a harsh swashbuckling pirate who succumbs to tears when his parrot dies, or *Wilfred Gordon McDonald Partridge* (1984) where the concept of memory is beautifully exhibited when a young boy attempts to help his elderly friend regain her memories, are all perfect for reading aloud. These and dozens of other books by Fox create emotional sparks and provide a memorable experience for the child and adult.

Reading Aloud with Infants

As parents and caregivers read to babies, a special bond is formed. Babies begin to associate reading and books with warmth and enjoyment. Even though babies are not yet speaking, they already understand 50 words or more, according to the KidsHealth website. As they listen to sounds, words, and rhymes, they coo, gurgle, and babble in response. Infants will want to grab the book and sometimes even chew on it, so cloth and board books are good choices for reading aloud.

As you read aloud to an infant, point to items on a page and describe what is happening. You can also ask the baby, "Where's the . . .?" or "What's that . . .?" In doing so, your voice will hint that the book has an exciting element. Begin by reading a couple of pages and then increase this amount over time. Also, be aware if the baby has lost interest. That might be the time to take part in fingerplays or to sing a song.

Reading Aloud with Toddlers

Children from 18 months to age three are starting to increase their vocabularies. Picture books have, on average, around 70 percent more unique words than conversations directed at children (Montag et al., 2015). Toddlers are also expanding their listening skills and attention spans. They are able to associate print with pictures and will start to favor books with stories about familiar topics or that contain repetitive rhymes and phrases.

While reading aloud to a toddler, engaging the child with the book is essential. In particular, ask them to turn the page, repeat words or phrases, or name items in the illustrations. Adding a bit of dramatic flair while reading to toddlers will enhance their interest. Take your time when reading to ensure meaning-making is occurring. Stop often to ask questions, look closely at the illustrations, and talk about how the book relates to the experiences of the child.

Reading Aloud with Preschoolers

Language development accelerates in children ages three and four. Preschoolers recognize words that rhyme and will notice sounds that are the same and different. Letters of the alphabet are becoming familiar, especially those in the child's name. A preschooler's knowledge base is also growing as books are read aloud that feature animals, vehicles, feelings, and more advanced concepts such as unusual shapes or secondary colors. Children at this age are curious and have vivid imaginations, making folktales, simple fantasies, and wordless stories an excellent choice for reading aloud.

When reading aloud with preschoolers, begin by sharing the author and illustrator's names and asking the child what the book might be about. As you read, run your finger under the text. Pause at the end of sentences so the preschool-aged child can see and hear the structure and craft of writing. Pause after a few pages and ask questions to ensure comprehension of the story is happening. Engage children in saying rhyming words or repetitive phrases—again, pointing to the words as they are read. After reading the book, children can be encouraged to talk, draw, or paint in response to the story.

Reading Aloud with Kindergarteners and Primary-Grade Children

Stories read aloud with kindergarteners and primary-grade children can continue to enhance language development. Children at this age generally have longer attention spans and can listen to multiple stories during one sitting or across the day. Books where characters may encounter a social or moral issue or dilemma will yield richer discussions under a skilled educator by asking questions such as, "What did you think about the story? How does the story make you feel? What do you wonder?" Literature can also serve as mentor texts as several writing styles and genres are shared. This is the time when children become independent readers but still enjoy hearing stories being read aloud. Primary-grade children enjoy hearing chapter books that contain well-developed characters, plot twists, and descriptive language.

As with all age groups, it is necessary to continue making reading a pleasurable experience. Some children may be challenged as they begin to read, so hearing a story read aloud provides them access to books they cannot read independently. Reading aloud can provide opportunities to develop the ability to comprehend a story. Literal questions and those that ask children to make inferences about the story can be asked. This is when children identify with characters in the story, make connections to other books they have heard read aloud, or even apply knowledge to events happening in their home, school, neighborhood, or the world. We often refer to these connections as text-to-self, text-to-text, and text-to-world.

When reading aloud to any age, let children be your guide. If they lose interest in a story, it might not be the right book. Honor children's enthusiasm for hearing a story read again. You'll notice that emergent readers will "pretend" to be reading as they retell the story while turning the pages of the book. As you read aloud, you also teach pre-reading skills such as demonstrating how a book is opened, supporting the understanding that text is read from left to right, and fostering the idea that letters make words. To offer the best experience in reading aloud with children, pre-read the book so that you can read the story with expression and anticipate where there are places to pause and savor the illustrations or ask a question.

In whatever setting you teach or care for young children, reading aloud should be a non-negotiable that is a valuable part of each day. Consider sharing a story as your gift to a child.

Choosing the Right Book

As you begin to select books and poems to share with children, consider several factors, including the quality of the material itself. Using the criteria presented in Chapter 2, assess the literary merit of the story, eliminating from consideration any books that do not meet that criterion.

Infants and toddlers should be "immersed in quality children's literature, especially books with rhyme, rhythm, and repetition, to give them a solid foundation in the sounds of language" (Towell et al., 2021, p. 323). Choose board books with large, colorful pictures on each page. Select books with familiar items such as shoes, dogs, or cows. Picture books should have a simple storyline with illustrations that capture the child's attention.

Books presenting basic concepts such as color or counting are also good choices for young children. These provide an opportunity to interact with the pages of the book as you point to a color and say "red" or count the objects on a page.

The purpose of reading to infants and toddlers may differ from that of reading aloud to preschoolers and primary-grade children. Suppose you are working with a group of three- and four-year-olds. It is the beginning of the school year, and you and the children are getting to know one another. You begin story time by reading stories you think they will have heard at home. You want the children to feel comfortable with you, and these stories will assist you in establishing rapport. You also want this experience to lead to sharing similar stories that children may not have heard.

To build from this notion of connecting home and school, you begin by reading *Brown Bear Brown Bear, What Do You See?* by Bill Martin Jr. (1967/1992). The 25th-anniversary edition of this classic story was published in 1992 and updated by illustrator Eric Carle using vivid colors and rich texture to help delineate animal bodies more sharply. This is a story often familiar to young children, prompting them to join in reading repetitive phrases. Another book by Bill Martin Jr. that invites interaction is *Chicka Chicka Boom Boom* (1989). In this lively alphabet rhyme, all the letters race up to the top of the coconut tree. "Will there be enough room? Chicka Chicka Boom! Boom!" Children who enjoy this toe-tapping story will also be eager to find the letter that begins their first name.

Brown Bear Brown Bear, What Do You See? and *Chicka Chicka Boom Boom* engage children immediately because of repetitive phrasing and active rhymes. Next, you might want to share a couple of Pete the Cat books. *Pete the Cat and His Four Groovy Buttons* (Litwin, 2012) can be read aloud first for children to hear the text. You can count the buttons as Pete loses each one. Follow up the read-aloud by listening to the Pete the Cat song, which can be found at various places on the internet, including www.petethecatbooks.com. *Pete the Cat: Rocking in My School Shoes* (Litwin, 2011) can be the next book to read and sing. Pete the Cat is rocking in his school shoes as he discovers the library, the lunch room, the playground, and other cool places at school.

Now that you have children singing and chiming in on repetitive phrasing, move to a selection of books about a topic they are now familiar with—school. Remember that young children enjoy books that rhyme, humorous stories, and those that have simple sentence structures or repetitive phrasing. A few good choices for preschoolers would be *Maisy Goes to Preschool* (Cousins, 2010), which will familiarize children with classroom routines, and *My Preschool* (Rockwell, 2008), which features a happy boy engaging in circle time, painting, and snack time. *Rosie Goes to Preschool* (Katz, 2015) is another option in which the main character, Rosie, introduces preschoolers to her cubby, the reading circle, and music class.

After the first week or two of school, you share books that invite children to create or mimic actions in response to a story. These books demonstrate that reading is fun and enjoyable. Eric Carle's *From Head to Toe* (1997) urges children to bend their necks like a giraffe, wave their hands like monkeys, and kick their legs like a donkey. *Don't Touch This Book* (Cotter, 2016) tells children, "Don't touch this book," but maybe they can with just *one* finger. This engaging, interactive adventure fuels children's imagination and is perfect for story time. *If You're Happy and You Know It* (Cabrera, 2019a) will have preschoolers clapping, flapping, and moving as you read aloud this picture book full of colorful jungle animals.

There is a progression of books you have selected and shared with children. You began by making connections to a familiar story, then moved to read about a relatable topic or experience, and then engaged children as they interacted with a story. All of the suggested books for preschoolers contained clear action, appealing language, and just a few characters. A similar progression could be done with kindergarten and primary-grade students using books that appeal to children ages five to eight. You'll find titles focused on many topics throughout the chapters in this textbook that would welcome children back to a new school year.

You have chosen literature carefully, keeping your purpose and the children's needs and interests in mind. You have also noted that the books you plan to share are large enough for a group of children to see the illustrations. If not, you should read the books with only one or two children at a time or project them larger for all children to see.

Creating a Positive Environment

You will want to share books in a way that welcomes children wholeheartedly into the experience. Orally reading well is fundamental to this. Always read the selected book aloud to yourself before sharing it with children of any age. Being familiar with the material will eliminate any stumbling over unusual words. It also permits you to rehearse any special voices you may want to use for different characters. If you have selected poetry, prior reading will allow you to plan where the breaks should be to keep the meaning intact.

It may be helpful to get feedback on your skill in reading aloud. There are numerous ways to create a video or recording of your reading. Ask several questions as you listen to this recording or watch the video. Am I enunciating clearly? That is, are my words distinct? Is the volume pleasant, loud enough to be heard without straining, yet not uncomfortably loud? Am I reading at a speed that allows the listener to comprehend easily? Does the expression in my voice move the story along and make it more interesting? If the answer to any of these is no, then perhaps you should practice the story several times, concentrating on areas to improve.

Another way to get feedback is to ask a friend or family member to observe you as you read to a group of children. Have them focus on the same questions you would ask yourself. In addition, have the observer tell you if you are looking up and making eye contact with the children as you read.

When you read aloud to infants, hold the book within the child's visual range and turn the pages slowly. As you read aloud to children 18 months and older, ensure they can see the illustrations. Some teachers accomplish this by holding the book to one side as they read. Others look down over the top of the book, reading the print upside down. Because text and illustrations together create meaning, you must read the text while simultaneously showing the illustrations. Otherwise, the meaning-making experience becomes disjointed and sometimes frustrating to young children who rely on visual images to engage them and enhance their understanding of the story.

Being familiar with the content of the book by previously reading it frees you to make more eye contact with the children and share in their enjoyment of the story. Also, it permits you to see children's responses—what amuses them, for example, or if any of them are becoming tired of listening.

After each reading, perhaps formally but usually informally, conduct a self-assessment. If all went well, remember what you did that contributed to the successful experience. If problems occurred, try to analyze why they happened and what you might do to avoid them in the future. For example, if the fire drill bell rang in the middle of the story, there is little you could have done to prevent it. But if the story was interrupted by one child kicking another, you might have seen the two poking at each other with increasing frequency if you had looked up more often. A look from you with a shake of your head or separating the children might have prevented the incident.

Whether for a small group or the entire class, plan the setting so that it will be as easy as possible for the children to pay attention. This means trying to find a quiet place to read. If there is extraneous noise, move so your voice and the noise are not competing, coming from the same direction. Place yourself so that children can focus on the book. Put their backs to any movement that may be distracting. If there is a strong light source, such as a window, have the children's backs to it. Light shining on you and the book will make both easily seen; light shining behind you may have children squinting at a silhouette.

If you know the children are likely to be restless, plan how you will help them calm down. Perhaps you can say a few poems together or have the children each tell one thing they like to eat or do two or three finger plays. Let children know your expectations. If story time is to be a quiet time for listening, praise such behavior. If you want children to hold their comments until the conclusion of the story, remind them of this when you begin reading aloud.

A set time for story hour, particularly for young children, lets them know it is an important part of the day. It also gives them control over the situation because they see the pattern or routine. You may want to have a rule that children may leave the story circle if they wish, but they are not to make noise, talk or distract those who are listening. Or you may want to establish a practice where all children stay for the entire story. For primary-grade children, you may want to have a set time for reading aloud but incorporate sharing books during other times that support the curriculum.

Think about the contingencies that may arise. A comment you are certain to hear at least once is, "I've heard this story before." Be prepared to respond with a statement such as, "See if you notice anything in the story this time that you didn't when you heard it before" or "Tell me what are two colors in the illustrations when I finish reading the story." This acknowledges the child's remark yet avoids a lengthy discussion about whether he or she wants to hear it again.

Plan how you will introduce the book. Some teachers give the title and author at the beginning; others do it at the end. At some time, however, children should be told the book title and names of the author and illustrator. This helps establish the idea that books are written by real people. In addition, this information assists children in making connections with other books that may have been written or illustrated by those individuals.

Helping Children Construct Meaning

There are many ways to build interest in and enhance the comprehension of a book you are about to read. You might ask the children to make predictions about the story from the title or the illustration on the cover. Before sharing *Pete the Cat and His Four Groovy Buttons* (Litwin, 2012), you point to the cover and ask what they think is happening to Pete's buttons. Introductory comments set the stage for the story and can be used to guide children's learning. Having them listen for particular details encourages careful listening. Children predicting what will happen fosters logical thinking about cause and effect.

Narrative Structure

Children develop a sense of story—an idea of how events are sequenced and interrelated. This comes partly from hearing many stories and from teachers and childcare providers who talk with children about what they have heard. Sipe (1998) found that first- and second-graders who responded to picture books read aloud engaged in five conceptual categories of response. First, the children talked about literary elements such as plot, characterization, and sequence and how the illustrations influenced their understanding. They compared the current story being read aloud with others they had heard. They connected the story to their own lives; some children used this as a basis for their creative activities.

Sipe also noted that the teachers exhibited scaffolding behavior—they engaged in practices that supported and encouraged children's understanding. They determined the pacing in reading aloud the story and added expression to their voices. The teachers described how to talk respectively with each other about a book in a way that elicited more discussion. They helped children make links between books and offered their opinions and wonderings about events in the stories. Finally, teachers were aware of and used the teachable moments, often taking children's comments to higher levels of abstraction.

Books read aloud provide the perfect time to discuss how stories are structured. This may come during the story reading. For many children, making a visual representation of the story structure, a flow chart of events, or a chart with arrows showing which events caused others is helpful. These visuals are usually most effective when constructed together by the children and teacher so that explanation and conversation accompany the charting. However, as with any strategy, this can be overused if done too frequently.

Visual Literacy

Visual literacy is the ability to gain meaning from visual images. For children viewing picture books, this means interpreting the non-textual elements—title page, illustrations, and end pages. John Stewig (1992) describes three steps in sharing books with children in a way that encourages the development of visual literacy. First, have children bring their own background to convey what they see. Have them tell what they notice and how it compares with their experiences. Second, have them pay attention to individual units within the larger unit; perhaps look at the use of color in an illustration or see how the end pages relate to the text. Third, ask the children to make aesthetic judgments about the relative merits of one picture book over another and give reasons for their conclusions. As you introduce children to a new book by conducting a picture walk, be sure the discussion includes delving deeper into illustrations beyond determining what the story might be about. "Reading" the illustrations enables children challenged by reading and multilingual learners to participate in the discussion and increase their skills in visual literacy.

Your discussions about books will most likely involve narrative structure and visual literacy because both contribute to meaning. If you are going to discuss a book, ask open-ended questions so children can understand that their personal connections to stories matter. You can also ask literal questions to assess their comprehension. If you plan extension activities, you need to have materials and directions ready. If you plan no follow-up, you may simply say, "I really liked reading about Pete the Cat and singing about his four groovy buttons. Would you like to hear another story about Pete the Cat?" If you ask children what they want to hear, be prepared to honor their responses. If they say yes, then plan to read what they want. If they say no, skip the book for now, even though you may know it is excellent literature.

Many teachers or caregiver providers display the book in a special place after they have finished reading. Children then know where to find the book if they want to read it themselves or look at the illustrations. This practice also allows the teacher to judge children's reactions to particular books. Some may sit unopened, while others may be in constant demand.

Box 3.1 Stories About Reading

The Book Hog (Greg Pizzoli; ill. Paul Bellantoni, 2019)
Dreamers (Yuyi Morales, 2018)
The Library Fish Learns to Read (Alyssa Satin Capucilli; ill. Gladys Jose, 2023)
Moose's Book Bus (Inga Moore, 2021)
The Oldest Student: How Mary Walker Learned to Read (Rita Lorraine Hubbard; ill. Oge Mora, 2020)
We Are in a Book!: An Elephant & Piggie Book (Mo Willems, 2010)

Storytelling

Storytelling provides both psychological and educational benefits for young children. These include enhanced imagination to help visualize spoken words, improved vocabulary, and more refined communication skills (Yabe et al., 2018). Storytelling also boosts listening skills. Storytelling uses props or visuals rather than printed materials, enabling the storyteller to make frequent contact with the audience. Becoming an effective teller of stories offers the opportunity to present stories in an interactive format.

Choosing the Right Story

In selecting a story to tell, either with or without visuals, you will use much of the same criteria to pick out books to read aloud. You want it to be good literature, and you want it to match the interest and understanding level of the audience. But there are other criteria to consider. The story should have a fairly compact plot that incorporates action. It should also have a strong beginning and a satisfying conclusion. Character dialogue will keep the story moving and add interest, although having too many characters speak can make a story difficult for both the teller and listener to follow. Because folktales originated in oral, rather than written, form, they are excellent for telling. Of course, they are not the only "tellable" tales but they are a logical place to begin.

Some qualities make a story better read than told. Examples include descriptive language integral to the story or exact dialogue essential to the meaning or mood. The storyteller tells the tale in his or her own words; so, if specific language is needed and it is difficult to memorize, the teller might be better off choosing another story.

The story that you choose should be one you like. If you spend time learning it, you will want to tell it more than once. It should be a story you think will appeal to many groups of children. You can build a repertoire of stories by learning three or four each year.

Storytelling for infants to two-year-olds encompasses rhymes and songs such as Itsy-Bitsy Spider or Pat-a-Cake. Children aged two to five are considered to be in the age of repetition. They enjoy stories that have repetitive plots, such as *The Three Little Pigs*, *The Gingerbread Boy*, or *The Little Red Hen*. Repeated lines keep children focused on the sequence of the story. Children also enjoy taking part in the telling themselves, saying the refrain with the storyteller, or engaging in motions to accompany the story. If you are working with preschool children, you might want to learn the story *We're Going on a Bear Hunt* (Rosen, 1989). Rosen demonstrates the motions for the story in an online video (https://www.youtube.com/watch?v=0gyI6ykDwds) that you can learn, and children can perform as the tale is being told. Other variations of this story are available on the internet as well.

Children aged five to eight exhibit a keen interest in fairy tales and are able to distinguish fantasy from reality. They can tolerate the violence sometimes present in traditional versions of the story because they know the story is make-believe. They expect the evil characters to be punished and the good to be rewarded, a pattern of justice that exists in most fairy tales. You may find that you know many fairy tales already. In this case, a quick review and practice might be all the preparation you need.

A classic, but still popular, visual aid used effectively by classroom and childcare storytellers is the felt or flannel board. This board or stiff cardboard is covered with cloth, usually felt or flannel. A variation of the classic felt board is a magnetic whiteboard with flat magnets on the back of the story pieces. Characters and bits of the setting are placed on the board as the story is told. To select stories for felt board storytelling, keep in mind the space on the board and how much you can manipulate at one time. There will not be room for a cast of hundreds. Consider if the characters appear randomly in the story or a patterned sequence. Identify stories that enable you to concentrate on the telling rather than trying to manage the manipulation of multiple characters. Multilingual learners benefit from the visual aspects of felt board stories because it connects a word with a visual image.

When first beginning to tell stories to toddlers, choose short stories they will know and invite their participation. Before presenting a complete story, start with familiar nursery rhymes such as "Hey, Diddle Diddle." The initial fascination with the flannel board is often the pieces themselves. Use large and simple pieces made out of washable materials, if possible. Tactile one-year-olds love to touch and "smooch" the pieces (Church, 2002). Once toddlers begin to understand the process of a story being told, then progress to fairy tales, especially those with repetitive phrases such as "Run, run as fast as you can. You can't catch me. I'm the Gingerbread Man."

For three- to five-year-olds, look for stories with a simple plot, perhaps cumulative or repetitive. Think about what can be used to give the essence of the story. Neither the setting nor the characters need to be exact in detail. The story should be simple enough to learn and has a straightforward plot with a limited number of characters. In sharing Eric Carle's *The Very Hungry Caterpillar* (1981), listeners hear how the caterpillar eats a variety of fruit until he eventually forms a cocoon. The sequence of the food items makes the story easy for children to follow, and the repetitive phrase engages them. Once the caterpillar eats through a piece of fruit, that storytelling piece no longer needs to be on the felt board.

Creating a Positive Environment

Children must be able to see the presenter in storytelling, as in reading aloud. One of the rewards of storytelling is that you maintain constant eye contact with the children and can adapt the story to their reactions. You can demonstrate that you find the tale amusing, sad, or poignant.

Some teachers and caregivers use a puppet to introduce stories they will tell. A hand puppet may come to the session, hidden in a pocket or a bag. The teacher or caregiver introduces the puppet, and the two may briefly discuss the story, or the puppet may talk directly to the children. This is one way of setting the stage for storytelling. The puppet is put away during the telling and perhaps recalled at the conclusion. This enables the focus to be on the story and not the puppet.

When using a felt board, decide whether you want it propped up on an easel or a chair. Think about where it will be in relation to the children's eye level. Will they be able to see it comfortably? Also, plan where you will stand or sit. It will need to be where you can reach the board, place the storytelling pieces, and see the children.

Preparing to tell a story usually takes more time than preparing to read a story. You may wonder where you will find the time to do this preparation or whether you have the talent to tell a story well. It may help to realize that your audience is not expecting a professional storyteller. You need not spend hours getting ready, nor should you expect to have a perfect presentation every time. Just do the best you can, improving as you gain experience.

Knowing how others learn a story and then adapt it to individual situations is beneficial. Few storytellers memorize a story word for word. Instead, most make note of the primary sequence of action—what happens when. They may memorize the opening and concluding sentences and any repeating refrains that are part of the story, but the rest they tell in their own words. They begin by reading the story several times, gaining a sense of it as a whole. Then they may list the action on paper or note cards. Storytellers use lists to set the action in their minds and to refresh their memories when they have not told that particular story for a while.

Some storytellers visualize the story, picturing the setting, characters, and how the action progresses. This visual picture helps them remember and is also helpful as they begin to describe the scene or tell about a character.

A story such as *If You Give a Mouse a Cookie* (Numeroff, 1985), which has straightforward action and easily learned text, is an excellent place to begin your storytelling. Stack the objects the mouse wants in order, then place them on the flannel board as you tell the story. Children will be able to participate in the storytelling (because they will surely know the story) and want to use the felt pieces to retell the story for themselves.

If the story is longer or has more action or characters, you might want to create brief notes that remind you of the story's action or the next character to appear. Some storytellers make a series of note cards denoting the essential activity of the story. The cards give the sequence of action but don't give the feeling of the story. Reading the story over and over does this. Keep in mind that sound and refrains enhance the story.

Now practice saying the story aloud. You will be able to identify any rough spots in the telling. Some teachers practice telling stories as they drive or do chores around the house. Once you have mastered the story, you can recall it by examining your note cards quickly and perhaps saying it once or twice to yourself.

Using a felt board to tell a story shortens one part of the preparation and lengthens another. Learning the story will probably take less time because by stacking the figures in the order they appear, you give yourself clues to the story's sequence. In particular, if you were telling *The Very Hungry Caterpillar* (Carle, 1981) with a felt board, you would see each food item in the order they appear. Some childcare providers keep the figures face up in a pile; others put them face down so the numbers that mark the sequence will show on the back. A brief synopsis of the story can be kept in a folder with the figures. This provides a quick review before each telling.

The preparation will be lengthened by making the figures themselves. They can either be cut from felt or made from paper with sandpaper or felt pieces glued to the back so they will adhere to the board. Using Velcro will help figures stick to the board. Many storytellers make characters from pellon, a type of interfacing available at fabric stores. Figures can be traced onto it and colored in with crayons, felt-tip markers, or liquid embroidery. Pellon figures tend to be more durable than those constructed from paper. Fortunately, many patterns for flannel board stories are available on the internet. The felt board itself is covered with cloth, generally a dark, solid color that provides a background for many stories. You can experiment with different backings and methods of making characters to find the ones that suit you best.

It is necessary to practice using the figures as you rehearse the story. Set the board up precisely as you plan to use it with children. Experiment with the angle of the board to ensure that the characters will not fall to the floor. Adjust the board or add more backing to the figures so the story can proceed smoothly when you tell it to children. If necessary, rough up the back of the characters with an emery board or fine sandpaper. Decide where to put the characters so children will not see them before placing them on the felt board. You may want to keep them in a box or behind the board.

After you complete the story, take a minute to evaluate your presentation. After you tell three or four stories to a group of children, you might ask them to tell which stories they liked best and why. Putting their impressions into words helps children compare stories to see how the tales are alike or different. It may also give you some insight into your own presentations. If they tell you they liked *Goldilocks and the Three Bears* because you used different voices for each of the bears, you know your expression and voice quality were effective. If they cannot remember any of the events of the story, then either the presentation or the selection of the tale for those children was a problem. Perhaps there were distractions, or the story was too complicated or too long for that group. Children may simply have lost interest and were unable to follow what was happening from the beginning. Analyzing past presentations will help you improve future storytelling.

Helping Children Construct Meaning

Telling stories well is key in helping children develop understanding. There are many similarities between reading and telling a story, but there are differences, also.

Narrative Structure

The requirements of storytelling to young children, especially when using a felt board, mean that sequence is a prime concern. Thus, it makes sense to focus on this area of story structure. Stories can be retold by having children engage in the storytelling by selecting the figure that should go next on the felt board or moving figures around. You might also have them listen to a story and then decide what characters would be needed to tell it as a felt-board story. Children are thus identifying the key characters.

Some stories may be told multiple times, allowing children to become familiar with the sequence and to master any refrains so they can say them with the teacher. The same is true as children learn motions to accompany the telling or if they sing during the telling as part of the story. If the children take turns participating in or retelling the story, let them know when the session is about to end. Comments such as, "Let's hear from two more people before we stop," or "Julia, we'll let you be the last one to tell our story for today" give children a sense of conclusion rather than an interruption.

Visual Literacy

As with looking at illustrations in picture books, children will view how the teacher or childcare provider has represented elements of the story visually if a felt board is used. Often, it will be less detailed, so rather than looking at the subtleties, as in an illustration, they will look at the symbolic nature of the representation. The children might suggest what objects are central to the plot and thus necessary for the retelling or how the setting could be indicated with only a few objects. If they were telling a cumulative tale, such as *The Bag I'm Taking to Grandma's* (Neitzel, 1998), it is clear which items—such as blue jeans, a baseball cap, a cuddly bunny, a pillow—the boy places in the bag to take to Grandma's house. The children will address the question of how visual elements contribute to understanding.

Box 3.2 Storytelling or Flannel Board Stories

Go Away Big Green Monster (Ed Emberley, 1993)
I'm the Biggest Thing in the Ocean (Kevin Sherry, 2007)
Lunch (Denise Fleming, 1996)
The Mitten (Jan Brett, 1989)
Mouse Paint (Ellen Stoll Walsh, 1995)
The Napping House (Audrey Wood, 1984)
(www.StorytimeKatie.com/flannelboards is a good resource for making flannel board stories)

Writing

Children begin writing at a very young age by creating drawings or marks on paper to represent their thoughts and ideas. While an adult may have difficulty deciphering this early writing, children can often tell you an elaborate story they have written. By doing so, they demonstrate their understanding that writing is a way of communicating.

Choosing the Right Literature

Over the decades, research has indicated a correlation between reading and writing (Fitzgerald & Shanahan, 2000; Reutzel et al., 2019; Wing, 1989). Oral language, concepts of print, phonological awareness, and alphabet knowledge also have significant scientifically based research support as predictors of early literacy success (Casbergue & Strickland, 2016). In considering young children's writing development, Norton-Meier and Whitmore suggest that it "is active and complex, and is contextualized in the rich physical and social spaces of their homes, neighborhoods, and school" (2015, p. 77). Literature serves as a model for writing by reading aloud stories and offering time for exploration of text and illustration.

Early writing, particularly for children around one to two years of age, generally consists of random scribbles, which may be horizontal or vertical lines or circular shapes. Young children are developing their fine motor skills, so jumbo, chunky crayons assist them in creating scribbles. Finger painting is another activity that engages hand–eye coordination. Around 12–18 months, children develop the hand and finger skills to grasp and control writing tools with enough coordination to make intentional marks on paper (Kid Sense, 2022). Reading aloud board and picture books provides the perfect opportunity to point to words as you say them. This action assists beginning writers in understanding those marks have meaning on the page.

In preschool, writing is about awareness and exploration (NAEYC & IRA, 2009). Three- to five-year-olds continue developing their writing skills. A framework for these emergent writing practices has been proposed by researchers and is composed of three domains: conceptual knowledge, procedural knowledge, and generative knowledge (Puranik & Lonigan, 2012). Conceptual knowledge relates to learning the function of writing and that print has meaning. For example, "Stop" is on the red street sign, and "McDonald's" is next to the golden arches (Byington & Kim, 2017). Share a book such as *Backseat A-B-See* (Van Lieshout, 2012) that displays familiar road signs that a child views from the backseat of a car.

Procedural knowledge involves the mechanics of letter and word writing. Children are learning the alphabetic code, including how to form letters and learning the sounds they make. Denise Fleming's *Alphabet Under Construction* (2002) stars a mouse hard at work constructing each letter of the alphabet, whether it's erasing the E or folding the F.

Finally, generative knowledge "describes children's abilities to write phrases and sentences that convey meaning" (Ray & Glover, 2008, p. 75). Children explore different ways of communicating through writing, such as stories, letters, lists, and messages. *The Thank You Letter* (Cabrera, 2019b) features letter writing and list-making in this story about gratitude.

In kindergarten and primary grades, children's writing development continues. Children are writing sentences and learning about capitalization, spacing, punctuation, and letter formation. Spelling sight words helps build confidence in writing. Word walls such as the ones described at the end of Chapter 5 assist in this regard. Invented spelling is also accepted so children can write expressively rather than being hampered by using only words they can spell. Writing throughout the day and across the curriculum is important and offers children the opportunity to engage in meaningful and purposeful writing. *How to Write a Story* (Messner, 2020) chronicles the process of writing within the context of a story.

As with all ages, reading aloud with children is critical to their writing development. As books are read and discussed, "teachers help young writers build understandings about texts, process, and what it means to be a writer" (Ray & Glover, 2008, p. 127). Selecting literature that furthers children's thinking about writing will also fuel their motivation for doing so.

Creating a Positive Writing Environment

Young children's writing development begins with scribbling, then making letter-like forms that soon result in strings of letters. While these strings do not create words, they demonstrate a child's understanding of writing. Invented and phonetic spelling occurs as children write stories and other forms of writing. Teachers and childcare providers play a decisive role in writing development as they recognize these stages and encourage children to express themselves through exploration.

Writing will take on meaning for children when it is purposeful. Generally, the first word that children learn to write is their name. In doing so, they are starting to demonstrate alphabetic knowledge, letting writing, and spelling. Teachers can provide a purpose for children to write their names by signing in on a whiteboard when they enter the classroom, or writing their name on a clipboard for which play area they want to go to that day. After a book is read aloud, children can brainstorm the names of the characters in the story that are then written on a chart or whiteboard by the teacher. Children could then write their names below the character name that was their favorite. Early in the year, children may only be able to write the first letter of their name. Additional letters are added as fine motor skills improve, and a child shows an interest in writing their complete name.

Children in preschool should observe evidence of writing in their classrooms. This may include nametags, labels, charts, simple messages, lists, and so on. Various writing materials such as markers, paint, chalk, pencils, crayons, whiteboards, journals, and sticky notes should be available for children to use. A learning center should always be available for children who want to write. Writing experiences should be spontaneous, as well as guided writing activities.

Writing activities may be tied to a current theme or topic of interest. Responding to literature through writing can elevate the style of writing or provide a new way of telling a story. However, not every read-aloud should result in children writing a response. Be purposeful in building off a piece of literature if using it as a mentor text.

Children should have opportunities to share their writing with others. This might be an "author's chair" where a few children share what they have written with the class or in a small group. In primary grades, children can also offer feedback to their peers by suggesting words or offering ideas for enhancing the story. A positive environment is created when children feel comfortable sharing their writing and are encouraged to do so.

Helping Children Construct Meaning

Literature provides immediate access to excellent examples of writing. Choose picture books as springboards for writing to assist in generating ideas of topics to write about, examining word choice, and exploring format.

Narrative Structure

Literature provides models of stories and how they are constructed. In reading aloud a book, a teacher might comment on the first sentence, such as in *Geraldine Pu and Her Cat Hat, Too!* (Chang, 2022) which begins, "Meet Geraldine Pu. Her last name rhymes with 'two' and 'moo'" (p. 7). You might say, "I like that the author immediately lets us know how to say Geraldine's last name, Pu." This Ready-to-Read book uses speech bubbles to share Geraldine's dialogue and her cat's thoughts. Children could similarly construct their stories. Books provide endless ideas for how to write. We refer to these as mentor texts.

What is a mentor text? The Iowa Reading Research Center defines mentor texts as written pieces that serve as exemplary models of writing. This writing provides an opportunity to study the craft or how an author uses words and structures the writing. A mentor text is explicitly chosen to highlight an aspect of writing, such as using energetic verbs or describing characters. It might be how the story is written, such as a first-person perspective or a persuasive argument. A book might also display how the font can be written in color to express an emotion or an increase in size to show a character is shouting.

In selecting mentor texts, consider different ways a story is told. How-to books such as Chris Raschka's *Everyone Can Learn to Ride a Bicycle* (2013) or *How to Have a Birthday* by Mary Lyn Ray (2021) offer a familiar experience and an explanation for "how to" do something. Children could choose their topic and explain how to make, build, or plan for a specific life experience. A how-to book might contain a fantasy scenario similar to the one in *How to Wash a Wooly Mammoth* (Robinson, 2014). All sorts of different animals could be selected to write about with detailed instructions for washing, feeding, or caring for that creature.

Another way to view mentor texts is to explore and examine multiple books by the same author or illustrator. In Chapter 4 of this text, an author study is described that focuses on the writing and art of Kevin Henkes. As children engage with the work of a single author, they recognize that writing isn't a one-time event but rather individuals write over time and write multiple stories (Ray & Glover, 2008). Children will also experience an author's writing style that enables them to contrast those stories with those from another author and even their own writing. A deep dive into an author study will yield student writing that may emulate a particular writing and illustration style. Children will understand that real people write books and understand the concept of authorship, which is essential to children's images of themselves as writers. "If children have had no experience with the kinds of people who make things with writing, they're not likely to imagine being writers themselves" (Ray & Glover, 2008, p. 129)

Second-grade teacher Megan Sloan, whose students' responses to literature are featured in the Instructional Strategy from the Field at the conclusion of Chapters 1 and 4, teaches mini-lessons using picture books as inspiration. She might select books such as *The Relatives Came* (Rylant, 2001) or *Daniel's Good Day* (Archer, 2019) to support "writing about heart and mind topics" (Sloan, 2009, p. 44). Another mini-lesson might highlight vivid verbs, and the books *Outside In* (Underwood, 2020) or *Bubbles . . . UP!* (Davies, 2021) could be read aloud and then revisited to talk about and list the verbs that were used. Books with interesting text features, such as *Scaredy Squirrel* (Watt, 2006) or *Hurricanes* (2019), a nonfiction picture book by Gail Gibbons, could be selected to further writing possibilities. Following the mini-lesson, Megan allows the children to practice the strategy with support from her and other students. Then she encourages them to "have-a-go" with their own writing. Megan also ensures students have access to the books she has shared.

While most books offer something interesting or unique in telling the story, not all books should be used as mentor texts. When you want to enhance children's writing in a particular area, such as energetic verbs, or showcase a story using a different format, select a book for that purpose. As you increase awareness about writing and illustration styles, children will begin to comment about their own word choice or design. They may also revisit a book that told a story in a way they want to emulate.

Box 3.3 Stories About Writing

Idea Jar (Adam Lehrhaupt; ill. Deb Pilutti, 2018)
One Day, The End: Short, Very Short, Shorter-Than-Ever Stories (Rebecca Kai Dotlich; ill. Fred Koehler, 2015)
The Panda Problem (Deborah Underwood; ill. Hannah Marks, 2019)
Rocket Writes a Story (Tad Hills, 2012)
The Story of a Story (Deborah Hopkinson; ill. Hadley Hooper, 2021)
Yours in Books (Julie Falatko; ill. Gabriel Alborozo, 2021)

Visual Literacy

As mentioned previously, the first stage of writing development is drawing. In wanting to tell a story, children will do so with images rather than words. They are demonstrating their understanding of communicating their thoughts and ideas through pictures. Asking children to tell about their drawings often results in an expressive story. There may be a tendency to write down what a child tells you and add words to the images. Allow the images to reflect the story to honor this form of writing and not push the child too quickly into thinking that words matter more than pictures.

Board books, picture books, beginning-to-read stories, and chapter books provide a model for composing and designing books children can create. Explain to children that speech bubbles share a character's words or thoughts, such as in *Geraldine Pu and Her Cat Hat, Too!*. Mo Willems's *Don't Let the Pigeon Drive the Bus!* (2003) uses speech bubbles of a very persuasive bird and his insistence on being able to drive the bus. Children may visit Willems's website to learn how to draw a pigeon to include in their versions of a story about the cantankerous character.

Select books that use font in unique ways. Toddlers and preschoolers will enjoy the board book, *How Do Dinosaurs Learn Their Colors?* (Yolen, 2006). Dinosaur colors start with a red fire truck stuck under the bed and a purple towel on the floor. Red and purple are written in their corresponding colors. *Arnie the Doughnut* (Keller, 2003) uses a colorful font to indicate who is speaking, words that are slanted to indicate motion, or increases in font size to express emotions.

Children could also view books such as David Wiesner's *Tuesday* (1991) or *Hike* by Pete Oswald (2020), which are told through framed and unframed vignettes on each page to show the progression of action through multiple scenes. Both books are also nearly wordless enabling children to write text for the scenes and actions. Provide sticky notes for children to write their story to add to the pages.

Creating a literate environment is one that is print- and story-rich furthering children's literacy development through reading, storytelling, and writing. How teachers, childcare providers, librarians, and parents share literature presents endless possibilities of what books can offer.

Instructional Strategy from the Field: Learning the Letter "C"

Sarah Lechner has served as a nanny to two-year-old Charlie since he was born. She reads aloud to Charlie on a regular basis and wanted to teach him the letter and sound for "C" since that begins his first name. Sarah decided that picture books would work well for this purpose.

Sharing Literature with Charlie

Day 1: Sarah knew that Charlie loved books about trucks and construction so she began by reading *Charlie's Very Own Trucks* which is a book written by Maia Haag that could be personalized with Charlie's name. Sarah pointed out to Charlie that his name was in the title but then focused only on reading aloud the story to him.

Day 2: Sarah read *Charlie's Very Own Trucks* to Charlie again but this time paused to point out the letter "C" at the beginning of words. Once she finished reading aloud the story, Sarah wrote the letter C on a whiteboard and exaggerated the motion she used to draw it.

Day 3: On the third day as Sarah read aloud *Charlie's Very Own Trucks,* Charlie began pointing to the letter C at the beginning of words.

Day 4: Sarah selected *The Very Hungry Caterpillar* (Carle, 1981) to read aloud to Charlie. He immediately recognized the letter C at the beginning of the word "caterpillar." On each page, he again pointed to "caterpillar" and was excited that he saw it on every page.

Day 5: Charlie selected his own book and chose *Construction Site Friends* (2021) which is a board book filled with different vehicles and items found on a construction site. As Sarah read, Charlie pointed out words that began with the letter C including crane, cement, and car.

By **Day 8,** Charlie wanted to write the letter C. So with assistance from Sarah guiding his hand, Charlie wrote C for the first time on the whiteboard. He then tried writing it over and over again.

Why This Strategy Worked!

Sarah shared: "Charlie always engaged with the read-aloud. When I introduced this new routine of learning the letter C, Charlie was eager to point to the letter on the different pages. After I wrote a large letter C on the whiteboard, Charlie wanted to write a C as well. First, we traced over the C several times with me guiding his hand. Charlie made a lot of circular motions with the marker to show me he was trying to write the letter C and not just scribbles. I was able to discover so much about Charlie and the way he learns when it comes to literacy development. Repetition and meaningful read-aloud were key to Charlie learning to identify the letter C!"

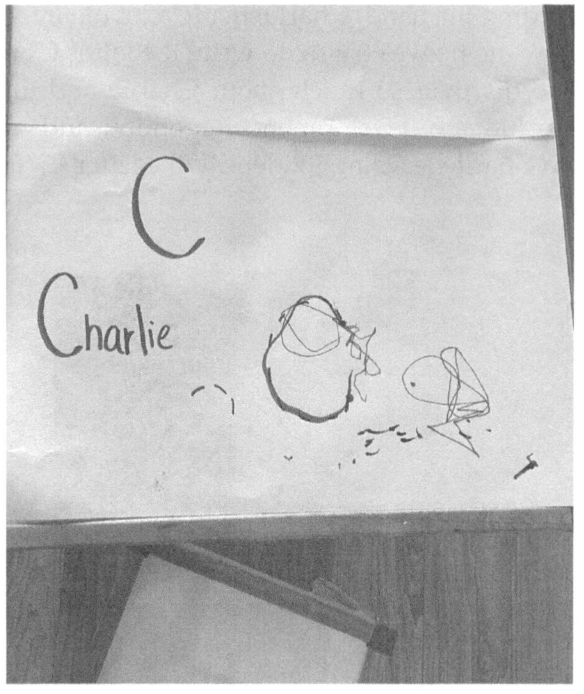
C
Charlie

Professional References Cited

Anderson, R. C., Hiebert, E. H., Scott, J. A., & Wilkinson, I. (1985). *Becoming a nation of readers: The report of the Commission on Reading*. U.S. Department of Education.

Byington, T. A. & Kim, Y. (2017). Promoting preschoolers' emergent writing. *Young Children, 72*(5), 74–82.

Casasola, M. (2016). Research sheds light on how babies learn and develop language. http://hdtoday.human.cornell/edu/2007/12/05/research-sheds-light-on-how-babies-learn-and-develop-language/

Casbergue, R. M. & Strickland, D. S. (2016). *Reading and writing in preschool: Teaching the essentials*. Guilford Press.

Church, E. B. (2002). Flannel board fun. *Scholastic Early Childhood Today, 16*(4), 52–53.

Dunst, C. J., Simkus, A., & Hamby, D. W. (2012). Effects of reading to infants and toddlers on their early language development. *Center for Early Literacy Learning Reviews, 5*(4), 1–4.

Duursma, E., Augustyn, M., & Zuckerman, B. (2008). Reading aloud to children: The evidence. *Archives of Disease in Childhood, 93*(7), 554–557.

Fitzgerald, J. & Shanahan, T. (2000). Reading and writing relations and their development. *Educational Psychologist, 35*(1), 39–50.

Fox, M. (2001). *Reading magic: Why reading aloud to our children will change their lives forever*. Harvest/Harcourt.

Haag, Maia. (n.d.). *My very own personalized storybook*. Ill. Jez Tuya. I See Me! Inc.

Iowa Reading Research Center. https://iowareadingresearch.org/blog/mentor-texts-student-writing#:~:text=Mentor%20texts%20are%20written%20pieces, in%20crafting%20their%20own%20piece

Kid Sense. (2022). Writing readiness: Prewriting skills. https://childdevelopment.com.au/areas-of-concern/writing/writing-readiness-prewriting-skills/

KidsHealth. *Reading milestones*. https://kidshealth.org/en/parents/milestones.html

Montag, J. L., Jones, M. N., & Smith, L. B. (2015). The words children hear: Picture books and the statistics of language learning. *Psychological Science, 26*(9), 1489–1496.

NAEYC & IRA. (2009). Where we stand on learning to read and write. https://www.naeyc.org/sites/default/files/globally-shared/downloads/PDFs/resources/position-statements/WWSSLearningToReadAndWriteEnglish.pdf

Norton-Meier, L. & Whitmore, K. F. (2015). Toddlers through grade 2 developmental moments: Teacher decision making to support young writers. *Young Children, 70*(4), 76–83.

Puranik, C. S. & Lonigan, C. J. (2012). Name-writing proficiency, not length of name, is associated with preschool children's emergent literacy skills. *Early Childhood Research Quarterly, 27*(2), 284–294.

Ray, K. W. & Glover, M. (2008). *Already ready: Nurturing writers in preschool and kindergarten*. Heinemann.

Reutzel, P., Mohr, K., & Jones, C. D. (2019). Exploring the relationship between letter recognition and handwriting in early literacy development. *Journal of Early Childhood Literacy, 19*(3), 349–374.

Sipe, L. (1998). The construction of literary understanding by first and second graders in response to picture storybook read-alouds. *Reading Research Quarterly, 33*(4), 376–378.

Sloan, M. S. (2009). *Into writing: The primary teacher's guide to writing workshop*. Heinemann.

Stewig, J. (1992). Reading pictures, reading texts: Some similarities. *The New Advocate, 5*(1), 11–22.

Towell, J. L., Bartram, L., Morrow, S., & Brown, S. L. (2021). Reading to babies: Exploring the beginnings of literacy. *Journal of Early Childhood Literacy, 21*(3), 321–337.

Trelease, J. & Giorgis, C. (2019). *Jim Trelease's Read-Aloud Handbook*. 8th ed. Penguin.

Wing, L. A. (1989). The influence of preschool teachers' beliefs on young children's conceptions of reading and writing. *Early Childhood Research Quarterly, 4*(1), 61–74.

Yabe, M., Oshima, S., Eifuku, S., Taira, M., Kobayaski, K., Yabe, H., & Niwa, S. (2018). Effects of storytelling on the childhood brain: Near-infrared spectroscopic comparison with the effects of picture-book reading. *Fukushima Journal of Medical Science, 64*(3), 125–132.

Children's Literature Cited

Archer, Micha. (2019). *Daniel's good day*. Nancy Paulsen Books.

Cabrera, Jane. (2019a). *If you're happy and you know it*. Holiday House.

Cabrera, Jane. (2019b). *The thank you letter*. Holiday House.

Carle, Eric. (1981). *The very hungry caterpillar*. Philomel.

Carle, Eric. (1997). *From head to toe*. HarperCollins.

Chang, Maggie P. (2022). *Geraldine Pu and her cat hat, too!* Simon Spotlight.

Construction site friends. (2021). Little Hippo Books.

Cotter, Bill. (2016). *Don't touch this book*. Sourcebooks Jabberwocky.
Cousins, Lucy. (2010). *Maisy goes to preschool*. Candlewick Press.
Davies, Jacqueline. (2021). *Bubbles . . . UP!* Ill. Sonia Sánchez. Katherine Tegen Books.
Fleming, Denise. (2002). *Alphabet under construction*. Henry Holt.
Fox, Mem. (1984). *Wilfred Gordon McDonald Partridge*. Ill. Julie Vivas. Turtleback Books.
Fox, Mem. (1989). *Koala Lou*. Ill. Pamela Lofts. Clarion.
Fox, Mem. (1994). *Tough Boris*. Ill. Kathryn Brown. Houghton Mifflin Harcourt.
Gibbons, Gail. (2019). *Hurricanes*. Holiday House.
Katz, Karen. (2015). *Rosie goes to preschool*. Schwartz & Wade.
Keller, Laurie. (2003). *Arnie the doughnut*. Henry Holt.
Litwin, Eric. (2011). *Pete the Cat: Rocking in my school shoes*. HarperCollins.
Litwin, Eric. (2012). *Pete the Cat and his four groovy buttons*. HarperCollins.
Martin, Bill Jr. (1967/1992). *Brown bear brown bear, what do you see?* Ill. Eric Carle. Henry Holt.
Martin, Bill Jr. & Archambault, John. (1989). *Chicka chicka boom boom*. Ill. Lois Ehlert. Henry Holt.
Messner, Kate. (2020). *How to write a story*. Ill. Mark Siegel. Chronicle Books.
Neitzel, Shirley. (1998). *The bag I'm taking to Grandma's*. Ill. Nancy Winslow Parker. Greenwillow.
Numeroff, Laura Joffe. (1985). *If you give a mouse a cookie*. Ill. Felicia Bond. HarperCollins.
Oswald, Pete. (2020). *Hike*. Candlewick Press.
Raschka, Chris. (2013). *Everyone can learn to ride a bicycle*. Schwartz & Wade.
Ray, Mary Lyn. (2021). *How to have a birthday*. Ill. Cindy Derby. Candlewick Press.
Robinson, Michelle. (2014). *How to wash a wooly mammoth*. Ill. Kate Hindley. Henry Holt.
Rockwell, Anne. (2008). *My preschool*. Henry Holt.
Rosen, Michael. (1989). *We're going on a bear hunt*. Ill. Helen Oxenbury. Simon & Schuster.
Rylant, Cynthia. (2001). *The relatives came*. Ill. Stephen Gammell. Atheneum.
Underwood, Deborah. (2020). *Outside in*. Ill. Cindy Derby. Clarion Books.
Van Lieshout, Maria. (2012). *Backseat a-b-see*. Chronicle Books.
Watt, Mélanie. (2006). *Scaredy squirrel*. Kids Can Press.
Wiesner, David. (1991). *Tuesday*. Clarion Books.
Willems, Mo. (2003). *Don't let the pigeon drive the bus!* Hyperion Books.
Yolen, Jane. (2006). *How do dinosaurs learn their colors?* Ill. Mark Teague. Scholastic Press.

4

Partnering with Literature

> When I was a kid, much like Iris, I would escape into my imaginative worlds when I needed to process things (actually, I still do). So, I think it's helpful for us to remember that escaping into our imaginations is often more than just a flight of fancy—it can also be a necessary and productive journey.
>
> (Minh Lê, author of *Lift*, in Sondheimer, 2020)

Longtime children's literature advocate Charlotte Huck recognized the power of literature in children's lives. She emphasized that literature has the capability to develop and enlarge the imagination in helping to entertain ideas previously not considered and to interpret and translate experiences that expand, rather than limit, children's creative potential (Huck et al., 1987). Authors of children's literature, such as Minh Lê, delve deeply into their own imaginative worlds to write stories that in turn entertain, inspire, and stimulate children's imagination. An example of Lê's creative and imaginative world is depicted in the story *Lift* (2020), which is featured later in this chapter.

Developing the Imagination

Listening to children talk freely about a story they have heard read aloud, or a book they have read independently, offers evidence that literature plays a key role in developing imaginations. Understanding imagination as both a cognitive and affective endeavor is crucial for parents and educators in order to promote creative and imaginative thinking in formal and informal

DOI: 10.4324/9781003367635-4

learning environments (Eckhoff & Urbach, 2008). Participating in the literary experience is an imaginative endeavor because readers project themselves into a story. They often see worlds they could not—or would not choose to—experience themselves. The confrontation with lives both better and worse and with experiences quite different than their own, refine their sensibilities and broaden their perspectives.

Literature exposes readers to other people's basic wants and needs and the problems, values, and attitudes that underlie their decision-making. Readers are forced to look at their own values—and biases—more objectively. Stories present children with a more structured picture of life than actual experience. Authors select for presentation those events that have the most relevance to characters' actions and those feelings that most epitomize the characters' personalities. They impose an order or mode of presentation designed to help the readers grasp the significance of the total happening. Literature aids children in interpreting experiences by narrowing the range of events discussed.

A fundamental goal of partnering with literature is enhancing children's imaginations. By listening to a broad spectrum of literature, children participate in the imaginative experiences of many authors and illustrators and begin to see that all literature is part of a body of interrelated works. Childcare providers and teachers of young children contribute to this goal by involving children with literature in ways that establish positive attitudes toward it and by grouping books and structuring presentations so that children begin to perceive the interrelatedness of literature.

Promoting Positive Attitudes

Because literature is experienced more than taught, if children are to become deeply involved with it, they must choose to do so. They become involved when literature is a satisfying experience for them. You can assist children in being engaged and developing positive attitudes toward literature through regular reading and careful selection of fiction, nonfiction, and poetry and by involving children in activities that extend books in a pleasurable manner.

As presented in the previous chapter, reading aloud to children is imperative in offering the gift of literature to all children. Even after children have begun to read independently, the teacher, caregiver, or parent should continue to share literature orally on a daily basis—preferably multiple times during the day. Many books and poems that are appropriate for young children are still too difficult for them to read independently. Stories are more enjoyable when presented by a skilled reader than when deciphered on a word-by-word basis. Adults have the opportunity to present to children how effectively language can be used and what enjoyment it can bring.

Selecting Literature

As suggested in Chapter 1, you need to know the children and their backgrounds as you select books to read to them. Most young children like humor. They respond to exaggeration in words and illustrations and enjoy being in on the pranks and jokes played on fictional characters. Therefore, humorous books should be a standard part of your literature curriculum. So, too, should books with content that appeals to many young children with topics such as friendship, birthdays, family, neighborhood, and pets.

Children tend to prefer poetry that rhymes. This includes individual poems and narrative stories told in rhyme. Poems about familiar experiences involving children or animals are also preferred. Children tend to like poems they have heard before, so it's essential to revisit poetry that may have been enjoyed previously.

Keeping in mind the general preferences of young children, you also need to assess the difficulty of the book or poem you are considering. Children dislike what they do not understand. If the literature is beyond their comprehension, you are likely wasting your time and theirs by reading it. Don't misinterpret this statement to mean that if the poem or story has a few unfamiliar or unique words, it shouldn't be selected. Remember that a child's listening ability is three times above their reading ability. Exposure to new words is what increases children's vocabulary. However, be sure you pause to define an unknown word or ask children to determine the meaning by using context clues.

In selecting literature, consider the style of writing, the approach to the content, and the complexity of the theme. Style of writing includes, among other aspects, the choice of vocabulary, sentence length, and structure. Reading and listening comprehension are related to these items. The Theodor Seuss Geisel Award-winning *I Did It!* by Michael Emberley (2022) contains an all-dialogue text featuring a character in striped pajamas attempting various tasks and challenges. Building a tower of blocks results in "I can do it!" but when the tower collapses, a frustrated cry erupts, "I can't do it." Scaling a rope, playing baseball, and climbing a tree also yield limited success. The final challenge is trying to ride a bike. After several unsuccessful attempts, his friends encourage him to keep trying, and soon the pajama-clad character finally exclaims, "I did it!"

The text in *I Did It!* is limited but, simultaneously, will invite children to repeat the sentences and possibly learn a few sight words. The activities the character is attempting should also be familiar to most children. *I Did It!* is labeled as an "I Like to Read Comics" series intended to support emergent readers with comprehension while instilling confidence and the joy of reading. You can follow up the reading of *I Did It!* with *Let's Go!* (Emberley, 2023), which features the same pajama-wearing protagonist.

Knight Owl by Christopher Denise (2022) is a 2023 Caldecott Honor book. Ever since he was hatched, Owl has wanted to be a knight. His opportunity arises when knights begin disappearing from the castle. Applications to Knight School are distributed, and Owl is accepted. Owl is an exemplary student but does have a few problems with the bulk of the sword and shield. Staying awake during the day also proves to be challenging. But Owl graduates with honors and is assigned to the Knight Night Watch. This job is perfect for Owl until the night he hears the "whoosh, whoosh!" of a ravenous flying dragon. Owl tries to convince the terrifying dragon that he is more feather and fluff than a meal, but the dragon remains undeterred. When the clever Owl offers the dragon an alternative, "It turned out that the dragon loved pizza." The two become friends, and coincidentally no more knights disappear. The vocabulary in *Knight Owl* includes words such as "trembled," "midnight," "mouthful," and "patrolled." The sentences are not lengthy but are appropriate for the listening level of kindergarten and primary-grade children. There is wordplay, such as Knight Night Watch, and humor infused, such as Owl's habit of nodding off during the day. Some children will quickly comprehend the cleverness of the text, but if not they will still enjoy the story.

The storylines in *I Did It!* and *Knight Owl* lend themselves to children predicting possible outcomes and discussing how characters react when a problem arises. Even though one story has a realistic plot and the other is based on fantasy, they both contain story elements that children can comprehend. The stories are entertaining and will prompt children to ask to hear them read again. Repeated readings will also enhance learning the sight words in *I Did It!* and becoming familiar with new vocabulary in *Knight Owl.*

Writing style, vocabulary, and content make *Knight Owl* a book appropriate for children aged five or six, whereas *I Did It!* can be shared with children ages three or four. However, these two books would appeal to both age groups. Use your judgment about the difficulty of a book, then watch children's reactions as you read and listen to their comments. Their responses will indicate how well you match their comprehension and enjoyment levels.

Grouping Books for Instruction

Guiding children to perceive literature as a body of work rather than as separate and unrelated stories and poems is important. If you group books for instruction, you set the stage for children to see the relationships among stories and to notice the recurring structural patterns of literature. In addition, this provides children with a database from which they can make their own generalizations about literature.

One role of the preschool and primary-grade teacher is to guide an emerging realization that fiction presents possible alternatives, which is of the imaginative world. Children develop a sense of story as they mature intellectually. Realizing the world of literature is an imaginative way of learning, and knowing is a gradual process.

As you share books with children, tell them the author and illustrator's names. Giving them the information that stories were created by people will take on meaning when they are ready to fit it into their schemata for organizing their world. Provide examples of many types of stories, with diverse settings and varied characters, so that children have the data to generalize broadly about story conventions. Grouping stories helps children see that certain events, images, or story shapes occur repeatedly. They can observe how stories with different characters, settings, and plots may still offer the same theme. Children may view one animal character and one human character that may occupy the same role in different stories as each leaves home for an adventure, is successful, and returns home. There are many ways of grouping books. During one school year, you should vary your approach to grouping. At times you may group only two books for comparison; other times, you may create a unit using several books or generate a graphic organizer to build multiple topics off of one piece of literature.

Book Comparison

Questions about stories usually focus on only a few of the many responses to literature. Some questions help children identify with the characters; others stimulate creative thought. Still, others guide children in their literary understanding. It is beneficial to discuss more than one book at a time if the discussion aims to sharpen children's awareness of the interrelatedness of literature. Book comparisons demonstrate that certain patterns, themes, and types of characters appear in many stories. Further, they show that the elements of stories work together, which is the core of all literature.

Suppose you read *Ruby Finds a Worry* (Percival, 2018) to a group of first graders. Ruby was perfectly happy until one day she discovered a Worry. At first, it wasn't a big worry, but then it began to grow. The Worry appeared everywhere—at breakfast staring at Ruby over the cereal box, and at night when she brushed her teeth. The more Ruby worried about the Worry, the more it consumed every part of her life. Ruby was concerned the Worry would be with her forever. Then, one day, Ruby saw a boy sitting on a bench with his own Worry. When Ruby asked the boy what was on his mind, his Worry began to shrink. As Ruby talked about her Worry, it soon disappeared as well. Before reading aloud *Ruby Finds a Worry*, engage in a before, during, and after reading strategy. Pre-reading the book is imperative, so you know when to pause and ask a question. Be sure not to pause too often as this will disrupt the story and impact students' comprehension. Here is an example of what type of questions you might ask.

Before Reading

Ask children to notice the cover illustration. How do they think Ruby is feeling? What clue(s) do they have for their response? What is the yellow image on the cover? What else is that color?

Set a purpose by saying, "Today we are going to read a story about a girl who has a worry. What is a worry? Turn and talk to the person next to you and share what you worry about. (Have a few children share their worries.) As I read this story, think about what Ruby did to deal with her worry."

During Reading

Pause at the page that states, "Each day it got a little bigger." How does Ruby feel about her worry? Why do you think it is getting bigger?

Stop at the page showing Ruby in her classroom and ask, "Why can't anyone else see Ruby's worry?"

Read the page, "The Worry became the only thing that Ruby could think about, and it seemed like she would never feel happy again." Then ask, "Have you ever felt this way? Why do you think Ruby tries to ignore her worry?"

After Reading

At the story's conclusion, ask the children why the boy was willing to share his worry with Ruby.

Ask, "Do you think by talking about a worry that it will go away? Why or why not?"

Response Strategy

Here are a few activities children can do in response to the book:

1. Draw what a worry looks like for them.
2. Write or draw what happened first in the story, next, and at the end.
3. As a class or in small groups, have children brainstorm words that describe Ruby throughout the story.
4. Discuss cause and effect relating to the story. You could present the cause and then have children provide the effect, or you can write each cause and effect on separate puzzle pieces and have them match the cause with the effect.

   Cause: The Worry was all Ruby could think about. Effect: The Worry grew and grew.

Cause: Ruby saw a boy alone in the park with his own worry. Effect: Ruby asked the boy to talk to her.
Cause: Ruby talked about her Worry. Effect: The Worry became smaller.

When asking children questions, be sure they explain using their own words to demonstrate understanding of the story. Ask them also to expand on their responses. If children answer with only yes or no, they miss the opportunity to develop their ideas, and the adult and other children won't hear the child's reasoning for the answer. Rephrase a question if a child has difficulty with it so the response requires less information or fewer inferences but still permits the child to explain fully. Sometimes a question such as the last one under the "During reading" heading can be broken down into two or more questions, so children aren't overwhelmed with remembering numerous things being asked at once.

After reading *Ruby Finds a Worry*, spend time examining the illustrations and how Tom Percival used color, or lack of it, throughout the story. This book also lends itself to dramatization for students to retell the story or even to create a readers' theater script for the book.

Reading a second book on a similar theme about a similar situation, or of the same genre, or contrasting a second book with the first provides more information for children to process—information for how literature works. For instance, the next day after reading *Ruby Finds a Worry,* read a book about a similar issue, such as *Catching Thoughts* (Clark, 2020). A young girl has a thought that shows up on a bad day. At first, it is a "teeny, tiny, little thought," but then it starts to follow her everywhere. The only thing the girl can think about is the horrible thought in her head. As the girl takes a deep breath and looks at the thought, she realizes it isn't that big. A small and beautiful thought emerges, and the girl decides she will be catching new thoughts that are hopeful and positive.

Ruby Finds a Worry and *Catching Thoughts* are imaginative in how the worry or thought is depicted in the illustrations. Both books also focus on social and emotional well-being. These stories provide realistic situations with reasonable solutions. A few before, during, and after strategies related to *Catching Thoughts* include:

Before Reading

Notice the cover illustration. The girl clutches some colorful balloons, but a dark gray balloon is behind her. What do you think the different colors of the balloons mean?

What is a welcome thought? Give me an example. What is an unwelcome thought?

During Reading

After reading the first page, ask, "What do you see in this illustration?"

The girl says, "I had to do something." What can the girl do to get rid of the one horrible thought that is following her everywhere?

Pause after a few pages showing the girl catching positive thoughts. Ask, "Why do you think the balloons are now different colors?"

After Reading

If we look at the illustrations, the gray balloon, which is a horrible thought, is still there. Do you think the girl will have another horrible thought? Why or why not?

What words did the girl use to describe the different types of thoughts she wanted to gather?

Response Strategy

1. Give each child a balloon cut-out and have them write a good thought on it. Display them around the room.
2. Use the following sentence starters to share welcome thoughts:
   I can . . .   I will . . .   I am . . .
3. Make a chart of different colors and the emotions they signify.

After reading both stories, compare and contrast them using a Venn diagram or bubble map. Discuss how color was used in each story. Or write down each character's emotions at the story's beginning, middle, and end. Consider how the characters resolved their problems. You can also have children compare how the Worry and the horrible thought were each depicted in the stories.

Having compared books under your guidance, children can then begin to compare them on their own. Tom Percival has published several books focused on emotions that can be read and compared with *Ruby Finds a Worry.* Other books featured in Chapter 8 address social and emotional well-being that could be used in conjunction with these two stories as well.

Box 4.1 Supporting Reading Comprehension

All children are readers but may be at various points in their reading development. Here are a few strategies to assist them with comprehension:

- Write sentences from stories on separate pieces of paper. Engage in echo reading whereby the teacher reads the sentence and then the student echoes by reading the same sentence.

- Activate prior knowledge of students so they can apply this knowledge to their reading.
- Conduct picture walks before reading to focus attention on important aspects and details of the story.
- Model think-alouds to demonstrate the process that active readers use as they comprehend the story plot.
- Write down interesting and new vocabulary from a story either on a class chart or in children's reading journals.

Units of Study

Grouping books with common characteristics can be formed into units of study that focus on a single topic, describe similar content, represent the literature of a particular genre, or are written or illustrated by a specific author or illustrator. When you plan a unit of study, consider a variety of titles, but narrow the selection to those that best fit your purpose and include only those you plan to use. Prepare the sequence of books and activities in advance, although modifications may be made based on children's reactions.

Thematic Unit: Author Study

If you are working with three- and four-year-olds or kindergarteners, the literature you select will generally be simpler than what you would choose for children in grades first through third. Your plan will involve children in the stories' language, content, and feelings. You'll want to select visually appealing books to prompt discussion of the illustrations.

In preschool, thematic units focus on topics such as community helpers, holidays, seasons, vehicles, farms, or dinosaurs. Thematic units generally last one week and involve a series of integrated lessons across content areas, including reading, writing, math, science, and social studies. Part of the goal of thematic units is for children to learn more about themselves and the world around them. They also center on the goals of early childhood programs, which focus on social, emotional, personality, physical, aesthetic, and intellectual development.

Another type of thematic unit that can be created for young children is an author and/or illustrator study. These studies support children in focusing on a single author or illustrator while gaining a richer understanding of that individual's writing and illustration style. Meacham et al. (2017) suggest author-illustrator studies may include the following: engaging children in active conversation during read-aloud to expand talk about text and illustrations; responding to visual elements of different books; finding visual motifs among books; comparing and contrasting books; and drawing, painting, or writing like the author-illustrator.

By saying the names of the authors and illustrators of the books you read aloud, you have already created an interest in that individual's work. Selecting an author or illustrator whose storylines and illustrations will appeal to young children is essential. When you partner with authors and illustrators, you invite children into that individual's work.

The author-illustrator chosen for this unit is Kevin Henkes. Begin by reading aloud ***Kitten's First Full Moon*** (2004). Explain to children that Kevin Henkes received an award called the Caldecott Medal for his illustrations in this book. He also wrote the story. In *Kitten's First Full Moon*, Kitten spies a huge moon in the sky and thinks it's a bowl of milk. She can't wait to taste it, so she sets off on a search. When she spies the moon's reflection in a pond, she jumps in, thinking it is the bowl of milk. Every attempt to reach the bowl of milk fails, so the discouraged Kitten returns home only to find a big bowl of milk waiting for her on the porch. After the first page of text, be sure children understand it is the moon the kitten sees and not a bowl of milk. Read the book through in its entirety. Then ask, "Why do you think Kevin Henkes illustrated this book in black and white?" The story has a repetitive phrase, "Still, there was a little bowl of milk, just waiting." Have children practice saying this sentence. Then when you read the story a second time the next day, have the children echo you as you read that repeating sentence, pointing to each word as it is said. When you revisit this book a third time, conduct a picture walk and ask children to describe the emotions of the kitten. Write these words on a piece of paper or the whiteboard.

Next, you select ***A Parade of Elephants*** (2018). This delightful story features five elephants marching up and down, over and under, in and out, until the end of the day when they yawn and stretch and then lift their trunks and trumpet. Before reading, ask children if they have ever seen an elephant at a zoo or on television. How do elephants move? Have children stand up, clasp their hands together to form an elephant's trunk, and have them show how an elephant would march. The first page says, "Look! Elephants!" On the next page, a chart-like illustration counts from one to five. Have children count the elephants with you. Do they notice the elephants are different colors? Name the colors. Tell children to watch the elephants carefully as they march through the pages. On the page with the sentence phrase "Up, down," have them demonstrate that movement with their hands. At the end of the story, check that the children know what "trumpet" means. If possible, locate a video on the internet of an elephant as it trumpets. You could build off this story by matching numerals with number words or discussing what is "big and round" in the classroom or other big and round animals like elephants. Finally, survey children which is their favorite elephant in the book and make a chart with the results.

Following the reading of *A Parade of Elephants*, next read ***Egg*** (2017). There are four eggs, blue, pink, yellow, and green. Three eggs hatch, revealing a bird the same color as the egg. But why hasn't the green egg hatched? The little birds give it a little help with a "peck, peck, peck." When the egg cracks open, a baby alligator emerges. The birds immediately fly away, leaving the alligator "alone, sad, lonely, and miserable." Soon the birds return and befriend the alligator. The format of *Egg* is unique in that it uses a graphic layout of boxes with text and illustrations. Prior to the green egg cracking open, ask the children to predict what is inside. Discuss the words, alone, sad, lonely, and miserable, and have them demonstrate that emotion. Place *A Parade of Elephants* and *Egg* side by side and ask children what they notice about the illustrations (both books are illustrated in similar pastel colors).

The World and Everything in It (2023) is the next book you select. This book focuses on the different sizes of things around us. "There are big things and little things in the world." The story lists little things, such as animals, tiny flowers, and pebbles, and big things, like the sea, the sun, and the moon. The little things can be held or touched, while the big things can be experienced in a way such as the moon shining through a window. After reading the story, have children draw a picture of a little thing or a big thing. Then have the children share their drawings and hang them under the appropriate label you have made. Add the item's name on the picture so children have the word and the visual.

A House (2021) is another book by Kevin Henkes selected for the author study. *A House* uses a different format in the posing of questions. "Where is the door? What color is it?" The story then shows the house during different seasons of the year and asks, "Where are the clouds? Which one is the smallest?" The final illustration shows a family coming home to the house. This interactive book addresses colors, shapes, counting, directionality, and size. After reading *A House*, have children discuss if this book is like any other by Kevin Henkes. Remove the book jacket to show a different illustration on the book casing. Revisit the other books you have shared and do the same thing to discover the "treasure" (a different illustration) beneath the jacket. To understand the media of watercolor that Henkes uses for his illustrations, have children draw a picture of where they live and paint it using watercolors.

As a final activity, have children compare and contrast the five books you have shared. Create different categories, such as the book's subject, colors used in the illustrations, and the format. During the school year, share other books by Kevin Henkes that have longer text and engaging storylines, such as *Lilly's Purple Plastic Purse* (1996), *Owen* (1993), and *Chrysanthemum* (1991).

You could also share the *Penny* series of beginning readers later in the school year. The intent is to learn about an author-illustrator and continue to revisit and build on this knowledge. Also, be sure to access Kevin Henkes's website at https://kevinhenkes.com to view book trailers and download activities to accompany a variety of his books.

Other author-illustrator studies that work well at the preschool level include Eric Carle, Tomie dePaola, Denise Fleming, Sandra Boynton, Jan Thomas, and Donald Crews.

Thematic Unit: Imagination

Focusing a unit on a specific theme, topic, or author allows children to engage in authentic literacy experiences. In primary grades, there is an opportunity to expand the notion of a theme and thematic unit. You could use themes like kindness, friendship, hope, or courage. The possibilities of partnering with literature are endless, as are the potential themes. Imagination is not only developed through reading children's literature; it can also serve as a theme encompassing a range of literature and ways to respond. Books fitting the theme of imagination can be read in any order with suggested before, during, and after reading questions. Possible student response activities for each story and ideas for collectively exploring these titles are suggested in the explanation of this unit on imagination.

This Is Sadie by Sara O'Leary; Illustrated by Julie Morstad

Sadie has a big imagination. Whether she is living under the sea, has wings that take her anywhere, or is talking to birds in treetops. All of these adventures stem from the pages of a book she is reading. Sadie likes stories because her imagination can offer her incredible experiences and then bring her home again. The world found in books is full of possibilities. *This Is Sadie* is the ideal story to begin the unit of study on imagination because it demonstrates the power and potential of literature.

Before Reading

Ask children to share what they see on the cover illustration. Why do they think Sadie is wearing a mask?

During Reading

Pause after reading aloud the first few pages to ensure children understand Sadie is using her imagination.

After reading "So many things to make and do and be," ask the children where they think Sadie gets her imagination.

After Reading

Sadie has many adventures that stem from the pages of a book. Have children share the adventures they have experienced through a story.

Response Strategy

Brainstorm with children books they have enjoyed. Write their responses on a chart so other titles can be added later.

What If . . . by Samantha Berger; Illustrated by Mike Curato

A young girl imagines how she could express herself artistically if her pencil disappeared one day. She hypothesizes all the different materials she could use and locations where she could create art. Her imagination lies in the way she views herself and her creative ability.

Before Reading

Look at the cover illustration. "Let's open the book wide to see both the front and back covers. What do you notice?"

Finish the sentence that begins, "What if . . . ?"

During Reading

Pause before reading the page, "I could still shape the leaves." Ask, "Where is the girl now? What is she making?"

Ask what the phrase means, "If I had nothing, but still had my mind . . ."

What do you see on the back end page that differs from the front?

After Reading

Why do you think there is a double-page fold-out when the girl talks about imagination and her mind? Why are the girl's eyes closed?

What do you think is the most important idea from this book?

Response Strategy

Brainstorm with the children all the materials they could use to create things. Then, make a list on chart paper.

Collect various materials children can use to explore their creativity and imagination. Leave the parameters open as to how they approach and complete the task. Or you can provide materials such as leaves, paper, pipe cleaners, flowers, sand, and so on, and have them create something using one material and their imaginations.

The Adventures of Beekle: The Unimaginary Friend by Dan Santat

This fantasy story begins with an imaginary friend born on an island. He patiently waits for his turn to be chosen by a real child but is repeatedly overlooked. So, he does the unimaginable and journeys to the real world to meet the child he dreams about. When he arrives at the bustling city, he is dismayed that children aren't eating cake, people aren't stopping to listen to the music, and no one notices him. Finally, he meets his perfect match and, at long last, is given his memorable name—Beekle.

Before Reading

What do you see on the cover? Does anyone notice Beekle?

Think about the title. What is an imaginary friend? What would an unimaginary friend be?

During Reading

After reading the page, "But his turn never came," ask, "How do you think he is feeling? What makes you think that is his emotion?" (Point out Beekle's expression, the lack of other characters, and the use of empty space surrounding him.)

Pause after reading the pages, "Then he finally saw something familiar. So he followed." Turn and talk to the person next to you and share what you have seen on these past few pages.

When the text says, "But no one came," ask students to predict if he will find his friend.

After Reading

Say, "Let's conduct a picture walk. I'm going to pause on the first page where all the imaginary friends are gathered. As I turn the pages, raise your hand when you see any of these imaginary friends." (Place a sticky note on the pages that are identified so they can be revisited for another activity.)

Share with children that you hoped they noticed the use of color during the picture walk. Walk through the book again and tell the children to think about how Dan Santat used color throughout the story.

Revisit the three pages when Beekle first meets Alice. Say, "Pay attention to the piece of paper on these pages and then let's discuss who you think drew this picture."

The following website offers an excellent analysis of these pages, https://www.slaphappylarry.com/adventures-beekle-dan-santat/, and states:

> The piece of paper is a drawing of himself [Beekle] handing Alice a picture—a naive rendering of the professional illustration by Santat.

> Look carefully at the previous two spreads and you'll notice that piece of paper. It has blown on the wind and lodged itself on a spike of the tree. The illustration has been drawn by Alice. Yet it's Beekle who hands the paper to Alice, so who really imagined who up?

The final page says, "And together they did the unimaginable." What do you think this means? What kind of experiences and adventures do you think Alice and Beekle might have?

Response Strategy

1. Character traits: Either as a class, in small groups, or individually, have children list the traits of each character. Brainstorm a few traits first, so children understand the task.
2. Compare and contrast the imaginary world with the real one.
3. Draw your own imaginary friend and write about what you would do with that friend.

Lift by Minh Lê; Illustrated by Dan Santat

Iris loves to push the elevator button. That's *her* job until one day when her little brother pushes it, which makes Iris very upset. When the repairman throws away an old button after fixing the "out of service" elevator, Iris stashes it in her backpack and later tapes it to her wall. Now when she pushes the magical button, she is transported to other worlds. Soon, Iris decides that sharing these adventures with her little brother is much better than doing it alone.

Before Reading

The author of *Lift* is Minh Lê, and the illustrator is Dan Santat. Do you remember another book that Dan Santat illustrated?

What do you see on the cover? What do you think this story is about? Think about the title before sharing your answer.

During Reading

On the title page, tell me what is happening.

After reading the page that says "Betrayal," pause and have children turn and talk to the person nearest to them and discuss the story so far.

When the repairman has thrown away the old elevator button, ask, "Who can share what is happening in each of the panels on these two pages? How do you think Iris is feeling now?"

Pause on the page that says "Finally," then ask, "How does Iris feel about her little brother? What illustrations support your answer?"

After Reading

At the end of the story, Iris says, "After all, everyone can use a lift sometimes." Explain what you see in this illustration and what Iris meant by that statement.

Let's look at the front end pages and the back end pages. How are they different, and why?

There is a different illustration on the book jacket than on the book casing when we remove the jacket. How do they differ? Why do you think Dan Santat made two different illustrations?

Response Strategy

1. Minh Lê and Dan Santat use real and imagined events in the story. As you conduct a picture walk, mark the pages with real events with a pink sticky note and those with imagined events with a green sticky note. Have children explain their reasons for why they think an event is real or imagined.
2. Have children compare and contrast the illustrations in *The Adventures of Beekle* with *Lift* in small groups.
3. If you had a magical button, write or draw where the elevator would take you.

***Milo Imagines the World* by Matt de la Peña; illustrated by Christian Robinson**

As Milo and his sister ride the subway, he studies the people around him. Based on their appearance, he imagines what their lives might be like. There is a woman wearing a wedding dress whom Milo imagines getting married in a grand cathedral ceremony and then being whisked away in a hot-air balloon. He imagines the whiskered businessman climbing the stairs to his apartment, where cats and parakeets greet him. A boy in a suit boards the subway train, and Milo imagines a horse-drawn carriage will take him to his castle, where a butler and a chef serving crust-free sandwiches greet him. When Milo and his sister arrive at their destination to visit their incarcerated mother, he is surprised the boy in the suit is there as well. "Maybe you can't really know anyone just by looking at their face." The best picture of all is the one Milo gives to his mother showing her at home and the three of them eating ice cream.

Before Reading

Look at the cover illustration. "Which parts of the picture are real, and which are imaginary?"

As you open *Milo Imagines the World*, ask, "Did you notice this design on the end pages matching something on the front cover? Let's take a look."

During Reading

After reading the page that begins, "These monthly Sunday subway rides are never-ending, and as usual, Milo is a shook-up soda," ask the children to discuss how Milo is feeling.

Talk about how the text describes and depicts people in Milo's pictures. Then, ask, "Can you know about people just by looking at them?"

Ask, "Where did Milo and his sister visit their mother? Why do you think he was surprised to see the boy in the suit standing in line?"

After Reading

Discuss with children the differences between Milo's drawings and people's real lives. Does he know what real life is for everyone he drew?

"What did Milo learn about himself? Is imagination a good thing in this story?"

Response Strategy

1. Have children work in small groups. Have each group draw a picture of what happened early in the story, the middle, and the end. Then have the groups share their drawings. Display them together under the headings, beginning, middle, and end.
2. Locate another book illustrated by Christian Robinson, such as You Matter (2020) or *Another* (2019). Have children study the illustrations and discuss how Robinson shows the characters' emotions. What else do they notice in his art?

Additional response strategies for all the books in the thematic unit on imagination might include:

1. Have children examine the books you have read aloud related to imagination. What do they see? How do they feel? What are they wondering?
2. Remove the book jacket from the books. Each book has a different illustration on the hard casing than on the book jacket. Why do they think the illustrator chose to create two different cover illustrations?
3. Compare and contrast the books. Children could consider the colors of each book and why they were used. A chart could be generated showing the main character's traits in each story. How did the characters use their imaginations? Discuss the style of writing and how the story is told in each.

Sharing these books should be the initial step. This unit of study could be revisited multiple times during the school year by rereading the books or sharing new ones. Provide access to books or display stories that build off the imagination theme. If children continue to connect to other books regarding imagination, add to the charts you have created. Also, try to weave this theme into other areas of the curriculum, such as science, social studies, and art.

Box 4.2 Supporting Multilingual Learners' Reading Comprehension

- Provide as many language clues as possible through visuals, gestures, voice tone, expressions, and repetitive phrases.
- Print sentences from a story on strips of paper. Have small groups of children read the sentences. Then place them in sequential order.
- Rephrase or simplify your question if a child does not appear to understand. However, never talk down to a child.
- Begin with what a child knows and expand on his/her English language acquisition and comprehension skills.

Cornerstone Text

Another strategy for partnering with literature is to generate curriculum based on a cornerstone text. One way to do this is to use a graphic organizer such as a spider map, tree chart, idea web, or cluster web to think through the potential within a single book or the possible ways of developing a single topic through literature. Graphic organizers differ from units of study in that they show far more ideas than will be used and do not show sequence. They are a form of brainstorming. Think of all the possible extensions of a book or all the aspects of a topic. Jot them down around the main heading, categorizing them as you go. After you have finished, you will have many ideas you might pursue with children. Graphic organizers can help you remain flexible because they encourage the exploration of many facets of a book or topic. This way, you can emphasize one aspect of the book or topic with one group of children and another with a different group.

The book selected as a cornerstone text needs to have a lot of "meat on its bones," meaning there are various themes and sub-themes that authentically build off of the story and illustrations. A picture book fitting this criterion is Molly Beth Griffin's *Ten Beautiful Things* (2021), illustrated by Maribel Lechuga. Lily goes to live with Gram in the middle of nowhere in empty old Iowa. As they begin their road trip, Gram suggests they find ten beautiful things along the way. As Lily looks out the car window, she is not convinced that anything could be beautiful. Just at that moment, the sun burst over the horizon, making that number one. As the trip continues, Gram and Lily spy more beautiful things, such as a windmill farm, a red-winged blackbird, a cloud shaped like a swan, and a little brown calf. When they arrive at the farmhouse, only nine beautiful things have been counted. "We're ten," Gram tells Lily with a hug. While the transition won't be easy for Lily, she understands she belongs with Gram now.

Ten Beautiful Things is a poignant story that touches on the experience of some children living with a grandparent or having to move. This book also lends itself to examining other topics within literature. Here are a few ideas for creating curriculum using *Ten Beautiful Things* as a cornerstone text. Each set of books could be read, discussed, and responded to by a small group of children and then shared with the whole class. The books could then be made available for other children to explore.

The books listed under each heading are picture books unless otherwise noted.

Grandparents

Before reading the suggested books about grandparents, brainstorm with children about the traits and characteristics of grandparents. Be aware that some children may not have grandparents in their lives while others may live with them, like Lily.

Castillo, Lauren. (2014). *Nana in the City*. Clarion.

Juster, Norton. (2005). *The Hello, Goodbye Window*. Ill. Chris Raschka. Hyperion.

McElroy, Clint. (2022). *Goldie's Guide to Grandchilding*. Ill. Eliza Kinkz. First Second.

Medina, Meg. (2015). *Mango, Abuela, and Me*. Ill. Angela Dominguez. Candlewick Press.

Yum, Hyewon. (2021). *Grandpa Across the Ocean*. Abrams.

Farm

Ask children what they know about farms. Write down their responses. Following the reading of these books, write down what they have learned about farms and farming.

Blackall, Sophie. (2022). *Farmhouse*. Little, Brown and Company.

Doyle, Eugenie. (2016). *Sleep Tight Farm: A Farm Prepares for Winter*. Ill. Becca Stadtlander. Chronicle Books.

Ehlenberger, Sabrina. (2022). *Morning on the Farm*. Ill. Shalie Miller. Warren Publishing. (illustrated song)

Elliott, David. (2008). *On the Farm*. Ill. Holly Meade. Candlewick Press. (poetry)

Vamos, Samantha R. (2019). *The Piñata That the Farm Maiden Hung*. Ill. Sebastiá Serra. Charlesbridge. (based on a traditional folktale)

Moving

As each book is read, have children discuss and then write about the emotions felt by the child who is moving or from the perspective of the child whose friend is moving.

Ledyard, Stephanie Parsley. (2019). *Home is a Window*. Ill. Chris Sasaki. Holiday House.

Marcero, Deborah. (2020). *In a Jar*. Putnam.

Medina, Meg. (2020). *Evelyn Del Rey is Moving Away*. Ill. Sonia Sánchez. Candlewick Press.

Percival, Tom. (2014). *Herman's Letter*. Bloomsbury.

Wild, Margaret. (2021). *Goodbye, Old House*. Ill. Ann James. Blue Dot Kids Press.

Positive Attitude

Create a chart with three columns: How did the character feel at the beginning of the book? What did the character do, and how did they feel at the end of the book? What ideas did the book give you for creating your own positive attitude?

Archer, Micha. (2019). *Daniel's Good Day*. Nancy Paulsen Books.

de la Peña, Matt. (2015). *Last Stop on Market Street*. Ill. Christian Robinson. Putnam.

Eggers, Dave. (2019). *Tomorrow Most Likely*. Ill. Lane Smith. Chronicle Books.

Gorman, Amanda. (2021). *Change Sings: A Children's Anthem*. Ill. Loren Long. Viking. (poetry)

Stein, David Ezra. (2012). *Because Amelia Smiled*. Candlewick Press.

Books Written by Molly Beth Griffin

Compare and contrast books written by Molly Beth Griffin. Learn more about this author by viewing her website, www.mollybethgriffin.com. After reading her books, identify wondrous words in her stories. What topics does she write about?

Griffin, Molly Beth. (2011). *Loon Baby*. Ill. Anne Hunter. Houghton Mifflin Harcourt.

Griffin, Molly Beth. (2014). *Rhoda's Rock Hunt*. Ill. Jennifer A. Bell. MHS Press.

Griffin, Molly Beth. (2019a). *A New Year (School Sidekicks)*. Ill. Colin Jack. Picture Window Books. (early chapter book)

Griffin, Molly Beth. (2019b). *Plans Gone Wrong*. Ill. Colin Jack. Picture Window Books. (early chapter book)

Griffin, Molly Beth. (2022). *The Big Leaf Leap*. Ill. Meleck Davis. Minnesota Historical Society Press.

Partnering with literature using a cornerstone text offers endless possibilities for extending the book, creating topics, and providing a spectrum of books and activities that can be accessed over a period of time. After reading *Ten Beautiful Things* to children, they may generate additional topics that emerged as they listened to and discussed the story. Locate books to support the topics you have generated. Select one or two books to either be read aloud by you or a book buddy, presented through audiobooks, experienced in small groups or independently, or to take home and share with a parent.

Partnering with Literature Across the Curriculum

You can integrate literature with other curriculum areas in a variety of ways. Combining literature with other sources of knowledge to broaden the story of a topic in science, social studies, mathematics, or the arts enhances and extends those areas. Select books that include up-to-date information, give a broader view of a topic, and provide for the interests and capabilities of a diverse group of children. The key concepts come from the subject area.

For example, you might read *Two Dogs on a Trike* (Snyder, 2020) to promote number concepts and word recognition. A spotted pooch wearing striped leggings and a colorful scarf takes advantage of an open gate to make a getaway with a trike-riding poodle. The vigilant family cat spies the getaway and is soon in hot pursuit. The dogs increase in number while the mode of transportation changes to accommodate them—three dogs on a scooter, four on a bike, five on a trolley, and so forth. When the number of dogs reaches ten in a rocket, they realize they are not alone—the cat is now among them. Panicked, the dogs backtrack, and the original troublemaker is now behind the locked gate. A hilarious ending shows two cats on a trike, and the chase is on with a mouse following close behind. The text includes the numeral and the names of numerous forms of transportation, including a hot-air balloon, a plane, and a ferry. The illustrations show the pups' fur-raising adventures and the cat tailing behind with the same or different type of transport. A sticky note could be used to write each number and then placed on the corresponding page with that numeral.

Box 4.3 Books Featuring Mathematics

The Boy Who Loved Math: The Improbable Life of Paul Erdös (Deborah Heiligman; ill. LeUyen Pham, 2013)
A Computer Called Katherine: How Katherine Johnson Helped Put America on the Moon (Suzanne Slade; ill. Veronica Miller Jamison, 2019)
Five Minutes: That's a Lot of Time. No It's Not. Yes It Is. (Liz Garton Scanlon & Audrey Vernick; ill. Olivier Tallec, 2019)
Leo + Lea (Monica Wesolowska; ill. Kenard Pak, 2022)
Now What?: A Math Tale (Robie H. Harris; ill. Chris Chatterton, 2019)
Snowman – Cold = Puddle: Spring Equations (Laura Purdie Salas; ill. Micha Archer, 2019)
We Are One: How the World Adds Up (Susan Hood; ill. Linda Yan, 2021)

Prairie Days by Patricia MacLachlan (2020) celebrates life on the Wyoming prairie in the 1940s, where cool summer mornings begin with the rose orange sun and the smell of earth. There are wagon rides, farm dogs, trips into town, penny candy, and games of kick the can. *Prairie Days* is a good choice for social studies in viewing what life was like years ago when television and cell phones were not present. Micha Archer's mixed-media illustrations combine acrylics, ink, and textured papers that could be examined in exploring different media used to create art.

Protecting natural resources such as our water is explored in *We Are Water Protectors* (Lindstrom, 2020) and would enhance the science curriculum. This lyrical picture book was inspired by the many Indigenous-led movements across North America to safeguard the earth's water from harm and corruption. It is also a recipient of the Caldecott Medal.

Literature and Literacy for Young Children: Envisioning Possiblities in Early Childhood Education for Ages 0–8 utilizes an organizing principle that highlights how books can stimulate and support children's growth in five different areas of development. These areas cut across infant, toddler, preschool, and primary years and are important in themselves. Some of the possibilities in sharing literature correlate with the goals and standards of particular academic areas. For example, observing and classifying as part of intellectual development are also related to science and art education. Learning to see from the viewpoint of another, an objective for social and moral development is also a goal of many social studies programs. And certainly, language development addresses many areas of language arts. Partnering with literature extends all areas of the curriculum and supports the ongoing development of reading and writing.

Instructional Strategy from the Field: Author-Illustrator Study—Sydney Smith

As part of an author-illustrator study, Megan Sloan and her fellow second-grade teachers read and responded to several of Sydney Smith's books. The first was *I Talk Like a River* written by Jordan Scott and based on the author's experiences as a child who stuttered. Lyrical and figurative language piqued children's interest while drawing on their compassion for a young boy whose loving father tells him that he talks like a river. While reading *I Talk Like a River*, illustrated by Sydney Smith, students noticed the words Scott used to describe the movement of the water (*bubbling*, *whirling*, *churning*, *crashing*). They were also captivated by Smith's eye-catching watercolor paintings. Students brainstormed other words to describe the movement of water. Then they used watercolor and paint, like Smith, to create their own art with shades of blue and purple followed by the addition of white paint after the watercolors had dried.

The next book read was *Small in the City*, written and illustrated by Sydney Smith, about a child giving advice to a special friend in need. As the second-graders immersed themselves in the text and art, they noted the places in the city the child passed and discussed what was seen, heard, smelled, and felt. Afterward, students listened to recordings of the sounds of the city. They

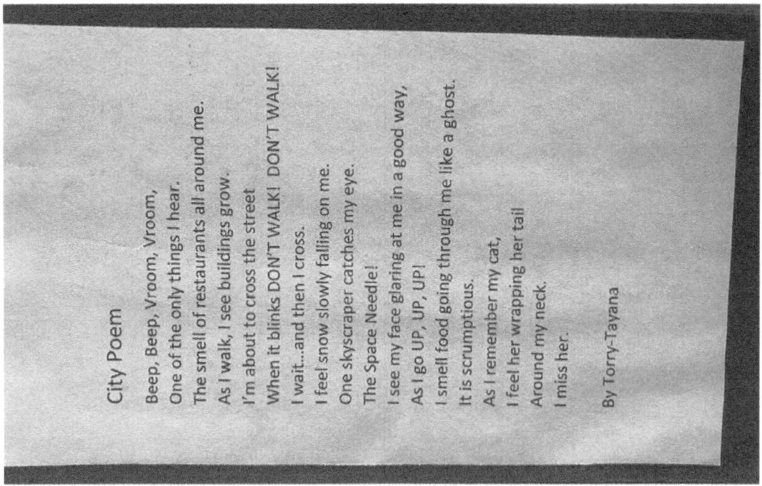

City Poem

Beep, Beep, Vroom, Vroom,
One of the only things I hear.
The smell of restaurants all around me.
As I walk, I see buildings grow.
I'm about to cross the street
When it blinks DON'T WALK! DON'T WALK!
I wait…and then I cross.
I feel snow slowly falling on me.
One skyscraper catches my eye.
The Space Needle!
I see my face glaring at me in a good way,
As I go UP, UP, UP!
I smell food going through me like a ghost.
It is scrumptious.
As I remember my cat,
I feel her wrapping her tail
Around my neck.
I miss her.

By Torry-Tayana

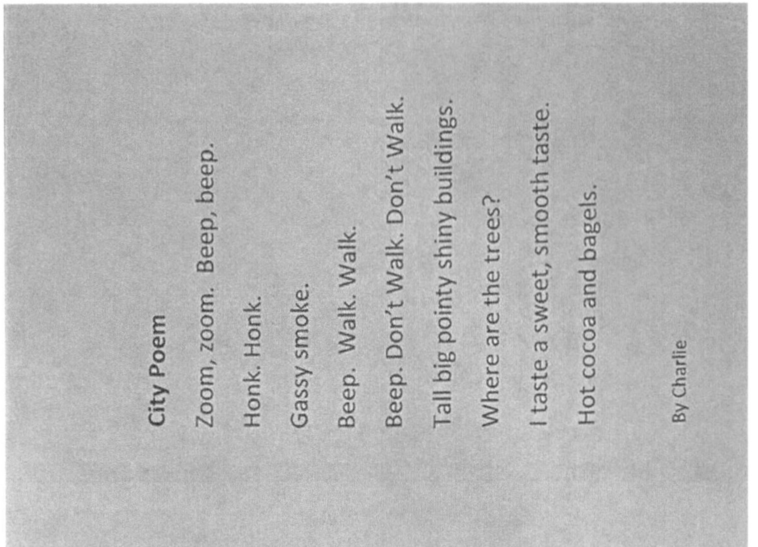

City Poem

Zoom, zoom. Beep, beep.

Honk. Honk.

Gassy smoke.

Beep. Walk. Walk.

Beep. Don't Walk. Don't Walk.

Tall big pointy shiny buildings.

Where are the trees?

I taste a sweet, smooth taste.

Hot cocoa and bagels.

By Charlie

were inspired to participate in an exercise to write a sensory poem. Students then created a picture of the city, as they imagined it, with marker and crayon.

Books Written and/or Illustrated by Sydney Smith

I Talk Like a River written by Jordan Scott; ill. Sydney Smith, 2020.
My Baba's Garden written by Jordan Scott; ill. Sydney Smith, 2023.
Sidewalk Flowers written by JonArno Lawson; ill. Sydney Smith, 2015.
Small in the City written and illustrated by Sydney Smith, 2019.
Town Is by the Sea written by Joanne Schwartz; ill. Sydney Smith, 2017.

Professional References Cited

Eckhoff, A. & Urbach, J. (2008). Understanding imaginative thinking during childhood: Sociocultural conceptions of creativity and imaginative thought. *Early Childhood Education Journal*, *36*(2), 179–185.

Huck, C., Hepler, S., & Hickman, J. (1987). *Children's literature in the elementary school*. Holt, Rinehart & Winston.

Meacham, S., Meacham, S., Kirland-Holmes, G., & Han, M. (2017). Preschoolers' Author-Illustrator Study of Donald Crews. *The Reading Teacher*, *70*(6), 741–746.

Sondheimer, S. W. (April 27, 2020). Explore the power of *Lift* with Minh Lê and Dan Santat. https://theroarbots.com/explore-the-power-of-lift-with-minh-le-and-dan-santat/

Children's Literature Cited

Berger, Samantha. (2018). *What if . . .* Ill. Mike Curato. Little, Brown and Company.

Clark, Bonnie. (2020). *Catching thoughts*. Ill. Summer Macon. Beaming Books.

de la Peña, Matt. (2021). *Milo imagines the world*. Ill. Christian Robinson. Putnam.

Denise, Christopher. (2022). *Knight Owl*. Little, Brown and Company.

Emberley, Michael. (2022). *I did it!* Holiday House.

Emberley, Michael. (2023). *Let's go!* Holiday House.

Griffin, Molly Beth. (2021). *Ten beautiful things*. Ill. Maribel Lechuga. Charlesbridge.

Henkes, Kevin. (1991). *Chrysanthemum*. Greenwillow.

Henkes, Kevin. (1993). *Owen*. Greenwillow.

Henkes, Kevin. (1996). *Lilly's purple plastic purse*. Greenwillow.
Henkes, Kevin. (2004). *Kitten's first full moon*. Greenwillow.
Henkes, Kevin. (2017). *Egg*. Greenwillow.
Henkes, Kevin. (2018). *A parade of elephants*. Greenwillow.
Henkes, Kevin. (2021). *A house*. Greenwillow.
Henkes, Kevin. (2023). *The world and everything in it*. Greenwillow.
Lê, Minh. (2020). *Lift*. Ill. Dan Santat. Disney Hyperion.
Lindstrom, Carole. (2020). *We are water protectors*. Ill. Michaela Goade. Roaring Brook Press.
MacLachlan, Patricia. (2020). *Prairie days*. Ill. Micha Archer. Simon & Schuster.
O'Leary, Sara. (2015). *This is Sadie*. Ill. Julie Morstad. Tundra Books.
Percival, Tom. (2018). *Ruby finds a worry*. Bloomsburg Children's Books.
Robinson, Christian. (2019). *Another*. Atheneum.
Robinson, Christian. (2020). *You matter*. Atheneum.
Santat, Dan. (2014). *The adventures of Beekle: The unimaginary friend*. Little, Brown and Company.
Snyder, Gabi. (2020). *Two dogs on a trike*. Ill. Robin Rosenthal. Abrams Appleseed.

5

Promoting Young Children's Language Development

> The more words he knew, the more clearly he could share with the world what he was thinking, feeling, and dreaming.
>
> (*The Word Collector* by Peter H. Reynolds, 2018)

Many of us collect words that may come in the form of a text sharing exciting news from a friend, a loving note written on a card, or a gripping story from a recent novel that continues to resonate. In *The Word Collector* (Reynolds, 2018), Jerome loves collecting words that he hears, sees, and reads. He fills scrapbooks full of words written on strips of paper and organized into various categories such as dreamy, sad, or action. When Jerome slips while carrying his scrapbooks, the words fly everywhere. As Jerome sorts through the jumbled words, he realizes they are more powerful when not in categories but arranged as poems, songs, and conversations with others. Jerome recognizes he needs to share his words and scatters them to the wind where they are happily collected by others. "Jerome had no words to describe how happy that made him."

Words have power as Jerome discovered in both collecting and scattering words. This textbook is largely based on that belief. Literature offers words arranged in a way that touches the hearts and minds of young children. Stories also play a critical role in the language development of infants, toddlers, preschoolers, and primary-age children.

DOI: 10.4324/9781003367635-5

Language Development in Young Children

Essa and Burnham (2020) state, "The ability to communicate is a complex process that begins very early in life" (p. 314). Children are born with "communication intent" but not with language (Gonzalez-Mena & Eyer, 2018). Language is a necessary skill for children in order to participate in everyday life. Development in literacy as well as in the areas of intellectual, social-emotional, and personality can be impacted by a child's language acquisition and growth. From the moment a human voice is heard, the capacities for listening and later cooing, babbling, and producing other vocal sounds are developing (Visser-Bochane et al., 2020).

Communication skills grow in the first year of an infant's life. Learning how to express themselves often results in babbling and combining vowels and consonants such as "ga ga" or "ba ba." By five months, a baby copies gestures such as waving or starts to make sounds at different pitches and volumes. As you play pat-a-cake or Itsy Bitsy Spider, a nine-month-old will try to combine sounds with rhythm and tone. Essentially, a baby listens to words spoken and the gestures made in an attempt to imitate them.

Words for everyday objects such as shoes or tummy are understood by a child's first birthday. Toddlers might be asked to point to their nose, for example. By 18 months, simple instructions can be followed. Toddlers will also begin to put words together, such as "me go." Language development begins to accelerate during this time as young children repeat what they hear as they try on new words for size. Lawhon and Cobb (2002) state, "Infants and toddlers gain a substantial amount of knowledge about language development" (p. 114) that is done through talking, reading, playing, singing, smiling, and other forms of interaction that are mutually enjoyable stimulators that enhance language.

As children reach preschool age, they begin using longer sentences to tell stories or share their feelings (www.raisingchildren.net.au). As their vocabulary increases, engaging in conversation with a preschooler becomes possible. Children around ages four or five will use past and future tenses as they speak. They can follow directions that contain multiple actions, such as, "Go to the closet and get your blue coat." From birth through preschool, children's language development grows tremendously. The number of words children hear and the quality of language is important. Exposing young children to a vast range of words becomes essential by speaking to them and sharing the rich vocabulary found in books.

How Children Become Literate

Literacy growth, including reading, writing, speaking, viewing, and listening, is a lifelong process. Reading to infants and young children is a powerful way to enhance early literacy and language development. Through sharing literature, parents, caregivers, and teachers boost pre-reading skills, increase attention spans, and support word comprehension while instilling a sense of pleasure in reading.

As stories are read to infants, they may listen to the book, attempt to turn the pages, and sometimes chew on the book itself. Any interaction infants have with books will place them on the path to literacy. An adult sharing books with a toddler will observe the child's growing concept of print as the child listener no longer covers the words and stops turning pages rapidly when there is print but no picture. These actions show the child knows the print offers portions of the story that the illustrations do not. The child may engage in reading-like behavior, providing some of the text of stories they have heard before or repeating a phrase immediately after it has been read. Many toddlers absorb a story so thoroughly that they can "read" the book by looking at the illustrations, often maintaining most of the story language but at times using their own language while retaining the meaning. As preschoolers, children begin to associate the print with the exact words. They go through a phase when the number of words appearing on a page does not match the number of words they use, mainly if they think of each syllable as a word. Knowing a story by heart allows them to go back again and again to a page, work on the problem, and teach themselves that long words have more than one syllable.

Adults can nurture young children's language learning in two basic ways: (1) provide rich, varied, and abundant samples of both oral and written language; and (2) give children regular opportunities to use their language.

Hearing Rich Language

Babies start with a remarkable aptitude for learning language. A three-month-old infant coos and makes noises when talked to. From six to 11 months, infants babble, try to repeat sounds, and utter their first word (www.stanfordchildrens.org). By age 18 months to two years, a toddler has a vocabulary of approximately 50 words, makes animal sounds such as "moo," and uses two-word phrases. Preschoolers begin to use descriptive words such as "big" or "happy," can answer simple questions, know some spatial concepts such as "in" or "on," and use question inflection to ask for something such as "my ball?" For young children to develop these language skills, they need to hear rich language because this is the database from which they generalize rules for how language works. It is also an essential source of vocabulary. Adults are more helpful to children's language growth if they use mature syntax than limit their speech to what they perceive to be the child's level. Research has demonstrated that toddlers with frequent verbal interactions with adults are likelier to make early language sounds, matching their language to what they hear (Hannon, n.d.).

Literature provides a source of mature and expressive language. Children listening to stories read aloud are exposed to language that often is more complex than what they hear in ordinary conversations. They hear new sentence patterns and vocabulary. A seminal study by Noam Chomsky (1972) found a positive correlation between children's linguistic development and the average complexity of the books each had encountered, the number of books named familiar, and the received numerical score based on having been read to in earlier years. This positive relationship between linguistic development and exposure to literature was true for pre-readers who had listened to books and for older children who had read the books themselves. The prereaders in the high linguistic stages had heard more books each week, were read to by more people, and had heard more stories at higher complexity levels than those children at lower linguistic stages.

Hearing books read aloud also increases children's competence in other language areas. Sipe (2002) studied responses from first- and second-graders during the reading aloud of picture books and determined that children engaged in text and visual analysis, formed links with other texts, connected text with their own lives, and playfully manipulated the story for their creative purposes. Sipe's study also indicated it was important for children to occasionally talk during the read-aloud to offer their initial responses and support their comprehension of the story.

Using Language

In addition to presenting abundant samples of language, adults can nurture young children's language growth by providing opportunities for them to use language. Children form hypotheses about grammar and must then test them. This testing by using language provides direct feedback. Children can judge whether or not they have communicated effectively. They may also refine their definitions of particular words as they gather more information about the concept named by the word. For example, they no longer use "car" for any four-wheeled vehicle such as a truck or a riding mower but apply it to only one type of vehicle.

As childcare providers, parents, or teachers, you should offer children opportunities to use language in conversations, singing, spontaneous dramatics, and writing. Immersion in literature helps children make sense of written language and also helps create a positive attitude toward learning to read. Reading becomes desirable because there are things to be learned and stories to be enjoyed. Children are intrigued by the sounds of language, from its poetic beauty to its lighthearted nonsense. A three-year-old often repeats pairs of rhymed words and enjoys playing games with repetition and rhyme. Thus, literature builds on and expands this fascination with language.

Introducing Vocabulary in Context

Vocabulary expands as children learn new concepts and the words that denote them. Children can determine meanings when new words are shown in context. When this happens, they are less likely to forget the word than if its meaning had been explained to them in isolation.

Literature presents words to children in the context of a complete story or poem. When you call attention to a particular word, look carefully at the section where it appears to determine if the context needed is the entire story, one or two paragraphs, or just one sentence. In *Not Friends* (Bender, 2017), Giraffe and Bird are definitely *not* friends. The bird makes funny faces at the giraffe, and the giraffe responds by sticking out his long tongue. Getting along proved to be very difficult to the point that giraffe simply "can't abide" the bird while his feathered friend "can't stand" the giraffe. Of course, being not friends sometimes results in discovering that friendship runs deeper than annoying behavior. Context clues within the text and illustrations offer hints about the meaning of words such as invade, prunes, swats, and pecks.

Author Kate Messner uses sensory language to describe what is happening *Up in the Garden and Down in the Dirt* (2015). A girl and her grandmother plant, cultivate, and harvest fruits and vegetables up in their garden while down in the dirt is a busy world of ants gathering, earthworms digging, snakes hunting, and skunks burrowing. The lyrical, repetitive phrasing of "Up in the garden/Down in the dirt" engages listeners and offers a structure for their writing. Context clues and illustrations assist in understanding what the girl is seeing, hearing, and feeling. Words and phrases such as "pumpkins blush orange," "wind whistles," and "wilt in the sun" all connect to the senses and offer examples of descriptive language.

Sometimes the explanation of a word is developed through many examples. *Hurty Feelings* (Lester, 2004) tells the story of Fragility, a hippopotamus whose feelings are easily hurt. After hearing her constant whining and wailing of, "You hurt my *feelings*!" her friends begin to avoid her. Although the word fragility is never defined directly, children can determine its meaning through both text and actions of this high-strung hippo.

If you plan to ask children to hypothesize about the meaning of a word, make sure there is a context that is explanatory from the text or illustrations. For instance, Bear "fusses and fidgets," "frets and fiddles," and "wiggles and twiddles" in *Bear Can't Wait* (Wilson, 2021). As all the animals gather, bringing cake, presents, confetti, berries, and flowers, Bear becomes increasingly impatient. After initially determining the meaning of "fusses and fidgets," children will be able to understand the other phrases. This is also a good book to use for predicting the big event the animals are planning.

There are opportunities to evaluate and reinforce children's comprehension of words that may be new to them. You can ask them to tell what happened in the story or use phrases from the story to elicit personal responses. For *Bear Can't Wait*, children can physically demonstrate what "wiggles and twiddles" means or what happens when the girl "wilts in the sun" in *Up in the Garden and Down in the Dirt*.

Unless you are positive the story will be misunderstood without fully discussing the meaning of the word or phrase, wait until the book is completed before talking with children about the word, or give them only a brief explanation and continue reading. If it is necessary to explain several words for children to make sense of the story, the book is probably too difficult.

Encouraging Language Play

If you listen to young children as they play, you will find that they seem to have a natural enjoyment of language. They repeat nonsense words just for the fun of listening to the sounds; they use jump rope rhymes and other chants in their games; they repeat the lyrics of songs they have heard. So naturally, literature that exudes this same delight in language appeals to them, and often their favorite books capitalize on the sound of language.

Using literature demonstrating how others have played with language has several benefits for children. First, they enjoy it and thus develop positive attitudes toward literature. It sets the stage for the enjoyment of poetry, with its reliance on rhythm, rhyme, and patterns in language. And it shows children the tone and feel of a word contribute to its meaning—that words connote and denote. Finally, it stimulates them to reflect on the language itself with the understanding that words and sentences can have more than one meaning.

Language play takes on a variety of forms. It may center on the sound of the language, the patterns within the language, the appearance of written language, or the meanings of words or phrases. In addition, children's books can stimulate children to engage in wordplay themselves.

Playing with the Sounds of Language

Playing with the sounds of language may take many forms, but in children's books those appearing most frequently are rhythm, rhyme, alliteration, and onomatopoeia. Infants and toddlers often bounce to the rhythm of a Mother Goose rhyme such as pat-a-cake, or I'm a little teapot. Preschoolers respond to the toe-tapping rhythm and rhyme of *Pete the Cat: I Love My White Shoes* (Litwin, 2008). Pete the Cat loves his new white shoes until he steps in a large pile of strawberries, turning his shoes red. Subsequent encounters with blueberries and mud turn his shoes blue and then brown. Pete never cried but continued singing until he washed his shoes, and they were white again. The song and a printable Pete the Cat template can be found on the internet. Another rollicking rhythm and rhyme is in the classic favorite *Chicka Chicka Boom Boom* (Martin & Archambault, 1989). The letters of the alphabet race to the coconut tree top, only to weigh it down so much that they all tumble to the ground.

Language can elicit giggles from children when a topic such as *Chicken Cheeks* (Black, 2009) provides all sorts of names for animal derrieres. A bear is motivated to create a tower of animals to claim honey from a tree. From turkey tushy to penguin patootie to moose caboose, as the tower of 16 animals grows, so does the list of terms relating to the animals' rear ends. Instead of telling young children to sit with their legs crossed on the floor, they could sit on their toucan can or their bumblebee bums. This book is also great to share with multilingual learners and emergent readers to demonstrate that learning initial consonants or rhyming words can be fun.

Wordplay in books engages children and stimulates a love of language. Wordplay also promotes learning new vocabulary and inspires writing. The more you expose children to rich language, the more their vocabulary increases. *Hornswoggled!: A Wacky Words Whodunit* (Crute, 2021) incorporates fun words such as "skunked," "bamboozled," "buffaloed," and "outfoxed" as various animals discover something missing and another item left in its place— deer is missing his antler, the buffalo's lucky boots have been replaced with swim fins, and the detective who offers to assist them in their search has had his thinking cap swapped with a piece of cherry pie. This hilarious story has a range of wacky words that may find their way into children's vocabulary. Bridget Heos's *Stegothesaurus* (2018) offers a variety of synonyms within a story about a clever dinosaur with a huge vocabulary of descriptive words.

Rhyming is a skill that takes time for young children to learn. Books such as *The Cat, the Rat and the Hat* (Lynas, 2021) feature a cat that sits, plays, and sleeps on a mat. When a rat arrives with a big hat, the cat says, "I want that HAT!" So the cat and the rat go back and forth wearing the hat. That is until a bat flies by wearing a fancy cravat. The rhyming words are presented in large, black font as the hilarity continues over wearing the hat and cravat.

Numerous authors of books for young children write narratives in rhyme. Their work may be lighthearted and humorous, like *The Cat and the Rat and the Hat*, or a serious, thoughtful mood, like *Granny and Bean* (Hesse, 2022). Granny and her grandchild delight in the sounds of the seashore and the treasures they discover. The rhyming, simple text contains memorable vocabulary such as "scuttered," "trilled," and "chafed." While these words may not be heard in daily conversations, they will enhance and enrich children's vocabulary. If you are working with toddlers, preschoolers, or kindergarteners, look for the books of Sandra Boynton, Atinuke, Rosemary Wells, Jan Thomas, Jabari Asim, and Denise Fleming. If you are working with primary-grade children, share picture books by Julia Donaldson, Angela Joy, Jez Alborough, Oge Mora, Julie Fogliano, and Andrea Beaty. These will provide you with a standard of excellent writing by which you can measure other rhyming narratives for children.

Along with rhyming narratives, poetry plays with the sound of language in various ways. Laura Purdie Salas has published numerous books of poetry for children. *A Leaf Can Be . . .* (2012), *Water Can Be . . .* (2014), and *A Rock Can Be . . .* (2015) each contains a single beautifully illustrated poem. In addition, Salas includes back matter with additional facts about each topic to share with primary-grade children. Other poets with books to read to a wide range of ages include J. Patrick Lewis, Nikki Giovanni, Pat Mora, Douglas Florian, April Pulley Sayre, and Lee Bennett Hopkins. These poets have published collections of poetry as well as single illustrated poems.

Alliteration is a writing technique in which initial consonant sounds repeat at close intervals. Children gain a sense of the sound of the initial consonant and enjoy a delightful story. Soil, sprinkle, scarecrow, sizzle, swirl, and smell describe the actions of planting vegetables, preparing them to eat, and sitting down to enjoy a *Summer Supper* (Pfeffer, 2018) with family. Alliteration is found not only in the brief text but also in the illustrations. Alphabet books also contain alliteration. For example, *B is for Baby* (Atinuke, 2019), and "B" is for bicycle, banana, big, bumpy, and baboon. A few words are not pure "B," such as brother and bridge, but plenty of other words will have toddlers and preschoolers saying the "B" sound. *B is for Baby* is available in board-book and hardcover editions.

Onomatopoeia, using words whose sound suggests their meaning, is another element of writing that is popular with children and invites interaction. "Bang-a-shudder! Clang-a-judder!" are sounds that machines make that *Dig, Dump, Roll* (Sutton, 2019). This board book features a variety of sounds along with rhyming text that will have toddlers exclaiming, "Wham-a-hammer!" Gabi Snyder's (2021) *Listen* contains words such as beep, woof, vroom, slap-slap-slap, and crunch, all highlighted in red. These are sounds heard when someone slows down to listen to the world around them. The book *R is for Robot: A Noisy Alphabet* (Watkins, 2014) pairs letters of the alphabet with different sounds such as hiss for H, kapow for K, and tick-tock for T.

Children hear how others have used language to describe sounds. Just as the young girl demonstrated in *Listen*, children can listen to sounds on the playground, in the lunchroom, or in their classroom. Or, try having children take a walk to listen to the sounds that machines make in their homes or the sounds of people and animals in the neighborhood. What word could they make up for each sound? What sound does a vacuum cleaner make? A washing machine? A blow dryer? A car horn? A bird chirping? Make a list of those sounds on a chart or individual cards. Pause at different times during the day to do a "sound check" of the words they created.

Box 5.1 Single Illustrated Poems

All the World (Liz Garton Scanlon; ill. Marla Frazee, 2009)
Crown: Ode to the Fresh Cut (Derrick Barnes; ill. Gordon C. James, 2017)

Daniel Finds a Poem (Micha Archer, 2016)
A House that Once Was (Julie Fogliano; ill. Lane Smith, 2018)
Me, I Am! (Jack Prelutsky; ill. Christine Davenier, 2007)
My Heart (Corinna Luyken, 2019)
A Stone Sat Still (Brendan Wenzel, 2019)

Exploring Patterns of Language

Books that feature language patterns, sequences, and connections are defined as predictable books. These books have repetitive lines, plots, refrains, rhythms, or phrases. Predictable books allow children to engage directly with the story, embrace early reading practices, and gain confidence in themselves as a reader.

The use of repetitive refrains invites children to join in with the teacher as the story is being read. Eric Carle's (1969) classic *The Very Hungry Caterpillar* uses the refrain of "But he was still hungry" even though the insect eats through apples, pears, plums, strawberries, and oranges. This story is available in hardcover and board-book formats. The hardcover version is preferred to share the full volume of the items munched by the caterpillar. *Thank You, Omu* (Mora, 2018) is what everyone in the neighborhood says after tasting Omu's delectable stew. The repeating question asked by those knocking on Omu's door after catching a whiff of a delicious smell is, "What is it?" with the response of, "Thick red stew." Soon, the pot is empty, and Omu is left with no meal for herself—or is she?

Cumulative stories are another type of predictable book that uses patterned language. The structure used for cumulative stories is when a new event or character is added, all the earlier ones are repeated. Preparations are being made for birthday party festivities in *The Piñata that the Farm Maiden Hung* (Vamos, 2019). As a young girl embarks on errands, the farm maiden prepares a piñata with help from a boy, horse, goose, cat, sheep, and farmer. In this delightful cumulative story with a similar cadence as "The House That Jack Built," Spanish words are featured in bolded capital letters and supported with lively, colorful illustrations. Back matter includes a glossary of Spanish words and directions for making a piñata.

Chicken Story Time by Sandy Asher (2016) is a cumulative story that uses a somewhat different structure where the action repeats and builds as the story progresses. Story time at the library is always an exciting event. "One librarian. One Story. Children. And a chicken." Apparently, both the children and the chicken enjoy story time so much that they invite others. Soon story time is overrun with children *and* chickens. What's a librarian to do? Like most librarians, she is a problem solver, and so each child is handed a book to read to small groups of chickens. There is repetitive phrasing, "One week later. Story time at the library," as the action unfolds and the number of participants expands.

Another type of predictable story uses a question-and-answer format that encourages listening and making predictions. *Brown Bear Brown Bear, What Do You See?* (Martin, 1967) poses that question and then answers, "I see a _____ looking at me." The bear sees a red bird, a yellow duck, a blue horse, and many more colorful animals. In addition to being a predictable book, this classic story also teaches colors and animals. Elisha Cooper's *Yes & No* (2021) showcases the differences between dogs and cats. The owner of the two pets asks a series of questions. The dog answers "yes," and the cat responds with a firm "no." But even predictable stories change course, which is true for the dog who decides that he doesn't want to go to bed after all. Several wordless double-page spreads in *Yes & No* offer opportunities for children to predict where the duo is going and what will happen next.

Finally, circular stories also have a predictable structure. A circular or chain story begins and ends in the same place. Two familiar examples are *If You Give a Mouse a Cookie* (Numeroff, 1985) and *Where the Wild Things Are* (Sendak, 1963). The circular structure isn't as common as others discussed, but they are excellent examples of predictability in storytelling.

Playing with the Appearance of Language

Most books present vocabulary as part of the story, as a tool needed to convey the content. Some books, however, work directly with vocabulary through the appearance of the text or typography. *Mister Kitty is Lost!* (Pizzoli, 2023) and the girl in the story asks the reader to help look for him. She describes the different attributes of Mister Kitty, such as yellow spots, orange paws, and a pink nose. The text is written in the appropriate color to accompany the die-cut shapes on each page.

Laughter will erupt when reading aloud *The Book with No Pictures* by B. J. Novak (2014). The reader is warned that all words in the book must be read. Silly words such as BLORK or BLUURF, along with goofy sounds such as BLAGGITY BLAGGITY and GLIBBITY GLOBBITY, are written in large, colorful letters. This book continues to be a favorite in preschool and primary-age classrooms.

Laura Vaccaro Seeger's *Bully* (2013) has spare text presented as a speech-balloon dialogue between the bull(y) and other animals. The bully's words grow larger as he calls the animals hurtful and cruel names. As the word "bully" increases in size, children will recognize it should be said louder until the end when the bully quietly says, "Sorry."

Typography, or the arrangement and design of words on the page (Lambert, 2015), is a "basic tenet of early literacy" (p. 38). Remember to pay attention to the words and how they are visually represented through color, size, shape, and design.

Exploring Other Languages

Dual-language books are being published in an increasing number. This genre of children's literature offers stories written in English as well as a second language (Leland et al., 2023). There are also traditional and recent stories translated into a language other than English that gives teachers and child-care providers a wider selection of literature from which to choose. Many of these books introduce children to aspects of a culture in which the language is spoken.

Vocabulary from languages other than English may be introduced in context, either with or without explanation. Author and illustrator Raúl the Third has created several picture books that depict Little Lobo and Bernabé, his dog. *¡Vamos! Let's Go Eat* (2020) is about the food Little Lobo must deliver to the luchadores before the big match. "¡Tortas de milanesa!" "¡Churros!" "¡Elotes!" The area around el Coliseo is frantically busy with food trucks, some—like "Taco Tuesday Everyday"—in the shape of the foods they offer, and Little Lobo knows them all. The images, the dazzling colors, and the delightful Mexican food trucks make this story utterly distinctive. Several phrases are written in Spanish with the English translation below, while others are woven effortlessly into the dialogue spoken by merchants and luchadores. A food glossary completes this delicious story.

Still, other books give the complete text in both English and another language. Leo Lionni is a familiar author to young children. *Let's Play / Vamos a jugar* (1993/2021) is a Spanish–English-language board-book edition about two mice friends who are looking for something fun to do. Dual text is presented on each page: "We could read a book. / Podemos leer un libro." The colorful collage illustrations offer clues as to the potential activity the mice might do. Lionni's book is perfect for young children to learn new words in English and in Spanish. The most common language for dual-language books has been Spanish. Still, publishers are beginning to recognize the value and need for books that feature other languages and cultures, such as Swahili, Cherokee, Tagalog, Hebrew, Japanese, Vietnamese, and Mandarin.

Illustrations offer context clues for *Luli and the Language of Tea* (Wang, 2022). None of the children in the playroom speak English, so they play alone while their parents attend an English as a second-language class in the room next door. The last time Luli was in the playroom, she played by herself, too. But this time, she has a plan. After Luli pulls a thermos, a fat-bellied teapot, and a stack of cups out of her backpack, she calls out *Cha!* (tea in Chinese). Immediately, all the children begin to say tea in their language—Russian, Hindi, Turkish, Persian, Arabic, Spanish, and others. As the children speak in their own languages, it is apparent the word they are saying is "tea." While sharing tea, they also share smiles. Next, Luli pulls out a box and says, "Cookie?" An author's note and additional information about tea in various countries highlight that language may be different, but shared knowledge brings about new experiences.

Kanzi and her family have just moved from Egypt to America. On her first day of school, Kanzi desperately wants to fit in at her new school. However, when she forgets (on purpose) to take the kofta sandwich her mother made for lunch, she regrets that action after her mother arrives at school with the sandwich and wearing a hijab. When classmates overhear Kanzi's mother calling her daughter "Habibti" (dear one), they laugh at the sound of the term. In *The Arabic Quilt: An Immigrant Story* (Khalil, 2020), Kanzi realizes that being bilingual is beautiful, especially when her teacher creates a class quilt featuring the students' names written in Arabic. A glossary of Arabic words completes this story about acceptance of self and others.

Linguistically and Culturally Diverse Learners

In addition to sharing dual-language stories, children's literature can also promote cultural awareness and appreciation. One way of promoting this awareness is by selecting and sharing diverse literature. Diverse literature "helps children to identify with their own culture, exposes children to other cultures, and opens the dialogue on issues regarding diversity" (Colby &

Lyon, 2004, p. 24). Through literature, children realize that while "people are different and differences should be recognized and celebrated, they share similar feelings and thoughts with people from other backgrounds" (Kiefstad & Martinez, 2013, p. 75).

There are high-quality picture books that depict culture in the United States. In *All Are Welcome* (Penfold, 2018), children from all backgrounds learn from and celebrate each other's traditions. It's a school where everyone is welcomed with open arms. Other times, school isn't quite as welcoming when Faizah's older sister, Asiya, wears her first-day hijab of beautiful blue cloth and is made fun of by a bully in the schoolyard. *The Proudest Blue: A Story of Hijab and Family* (2019) was written by Olympic medalist Ibtihaj Muhammad so that "children of color, Muslims, and those who are both (like me) know they aren't alone."

Cultures from around the world are also celebrated in picture books. Travel to Zanzibar, where there is *Room for Everyone* (Khan, 2021) on the daladala. As Musa and Dada drive to the beach, they offer a ride to numerous individuals along the way. "Do you need a ride? Come in, there's room for everyone!" Along with wiggles and giggles, as one stop becomes ten, everyone becomes smushed like sardines in a tin. This bouncy, joyous tale in rhyme offers a glimpse into Zanzibar's colorful clothing, food, and much more. Celebrate the Lunar New Year by sharing Michelle Sterling's (2022) *A Sweet New Year for Ren*. Ren hopes this year she will get to help make pineapple cakes which are her favorite. Instead, Ren is told she is still too little and must watch her family members roll out the dough and make other preparations for the new year. An author's note and a recipe for pineapple cakes celebrate family and traditions.

In selecting diverse books to share with young children, choose stories that enable children to better understand their culture and the culture of others. Be sure to provide time for children to savor and discuss stories to further knowledge and to possibly discover connections with books and each other.

Box 5.2 Diverse Children's Literature

Berry Song (Michaela Goade, 2022)
Besos for Baby: A Little Book of Kisses (Jen Arena; ill. Blanca Gómez, 2014)
Danbi Leads the School Parade (Anna Kim, 2020)
My Two Border Towns (David Bowles; ill. Erika Meza, 2021)
Strollercoaster (Matt Ringler; ill. Raúl the Third, 2021)
Watercress (Andrea Wang; ill. Jason Chin, 2021)
We Are Grateful: Otsaliheliga (Traci Sorell; ill. Frane Lessac, 2018)
We Are Here (Tami Charles; ill. Bryan Collier, 2023)

Attentive, Critical, and Appreciative Listening Skills and Language Development

Educators use various terms to describe and categorize types of listening skills. One system classifies listening as either marginal, attentive, critical, or appreciative. The listening that occurs when a child is not paying attention but does respond if their name is called or a sound such as a siren intrudes is often termed *marginal* or *passive* listening. Sharing literature with children is seldom concerned with this type of listening.

Building Attentive Listening Skills

Attentive listening occurs when children can decipher the literal meaning of what is heard, recall sequence, and follow directions. It requires listeners to attend to what is presented and understand the meaning directly conveyed by the words. One way literature can build listening skills is for the teacher to involve children with the story during the reading. This can be accomplished by having children repeat refrains in pattern or cumulative stories such as those highlighted earlier in the chapter.

Assigning children specific parts in the telling of a story containing a repetitive refrain or sound requires that they must listen for their time to participate. Read a story through once so children see and hear the pattern. Then, reread the story so children can provide the repetitive phrase or generate a specific sound. Many teachers find it helpful to use a hand signal for children to recognize when sound effects or musical instruments are to be used. For example, teach children that when you lift your hand in the air, the sound is to begin, and when you lower it, the sound is to end. The higher your hand, the louder the sound; the lower your hand, the softer the sound. This allows you to orchestrate the effects and lets you and the children work together.

Another technique for helping children become attentive listeners is to have a specific purpose for listening. Most people listen more carefully when they need or want to know the information being given. Before reading an informational book, ask children to listen for the answer to specific questions or one new bit of information. Or there might be a word repeated in the book that children can listen for and raise their hands when they hear it. These strategies help to create a focus and set a purpose for listening.

Building Critical Listening Skills

The types of questions you ask about a book determine the kind of listening children are likely to do. If you ask only questions that require direct recall, then children will form the habit of listening for detail only. To encourage critical listening, you must develop a pattern of asking questions and providing activities beyond memory. Critical listening, sometimes called analytical listening, requires the listener to go beyond the information as stated directly. The listener interprets facts, makes generalizations and inferences, and evaluates the material. The listener engages in critical thinking about what has been heard.

If following the reading of Seeger's *Bully* (2013), you asked, "Why do you think the bull called the turtle, 'Slow poke?' you would reinforce habits of attentive listening that require thinking beyond the text and using prior knowledge about turtles to respond to the question. Another question is, "What happened after the goat called the bull, 'Bully!'" In general, memory-type questions and activities do not lead children to explore the more important aspects of literature. Questions that further analytical listening often begin with "Why?" Try to go beyond the literal level of asking questions with answers directly from the text and engage children in critical listening and thinking.

Building Appreciative Listening Skills

The next type of listening, appreciative, leads to aesthetic enjoyment. This is the kind of listening that occurs when attending a concert, hearing poetry, or enjoying the humor in a story. You can encourage appreciative listening by showing that you value it. Asking open-ended questions such as "What do you think? How do you feel? or What do you wonder?" associate appreciative listening with pleasure. These are times when children can relax and enjoy hearing a wonderful story, and they can choose to respond or not. Another way to foster appreciative listening is to seek out resources such as internet sites where authors and poets are reading their own stories, music is available that accompanies a book, or a book is dramatized using different voices. Remember that reading a story purely for pleasure and not associated with a lesson should always be an option.

For all types of listening, help children develop skills by rereading a story after a discussion—especially if it's a story that children want to hear again. Children who are good listeners are often successful in speaking, communicating, and socializing with others.

Leading Naturally to Reading

The best preparation for reading is instilling the desire to read. Literature shared orally helps motivate children because they learn that books give interesting information and contain enjoyable stories and poems. In addition, those who have listened to a variety of stories have been introduced to many new words and sentence patterns they may encounter when they begin to read.

Observing the Reading Process

The oral sharing of literature can be structured in such a way that it helps children understand the process of reading. By watching the adult turn the page and "tell" a story from it, children will realize the print on the page conveys meaning. They learn the book remains constant when they hear the same story several times. If they watch the print as the adult reads, they associate specific segments of print with segments of speech. At first, this may be the entire sentence or phrase; later, it will be separate words and, eventually, the correspondence between letters and sounds.

Reading aloud provides an opportunity to support children who are challenged by reading. In listening to stories, children become aware of phonemes, or the sound of language. Whether the language is English, Spanish, Mandarin, or another, infants and toddlers begin to discern differences in sounds that lay the foundation for speaking, reading, listening, and writing. As the adult points to the words on each page, this practice models that active readers do not skip words; if they do, they stop and self-correct. When an interesting word is in the text, especially one that is not easy to determine phonetically, the adult can stop, point to the word, repeat it, and have the child say it. This brings attention to the word and presents an opportunity to introduce a strategy for decoding an unfamiliar word.

To assist in gaining these understandings, you must provide ways for children to hear a story more than once. This may be accomplished by reading it to a group when many request it again or rereading the story only for an individual who requests it. Have parents willing to help or classroom aides set up an area for reading where a child can come to have a special book read again and again. It is through repetition that children can begin to generalize about print and speech. Additionally, the adult can point to words as they are read, reinforce the left-to-right progression demonstrated in reading, explain any words that might not be familiar, and allow the child to turn the page, and talk about ideas or words.

Big books published in a format large enough for children to see the print clearly when sitting in a group serve this purpose well. This is one of the reasons why big books are so popular in preschool. Children watch as the print is read, and because so many of these books have predictable stories and language patterns, children can begin to read a book with the teacher, often after hearing only part of the story.

Some teachers invite fourth- or fifth-grade students to their kindergarten and primary classes to read to individual children as book buddies. This can be a valuable experience for older as well as younger children. Older children can improve their oral reading skills, get feedback on how well they are doing, and build self-confidence. Younger children get attention and individual help with reading. It may be necessary, however, for you to provide some instruction on oral reading for older children as well as parents and aides. This is especially true if you want them to involve children in the story through discussion and pointing out words and phrases. Please don't assume that because someone knows how to read, they are knowledgeable about how to read to children. An expressive reader can elevate a child's enjoyment of the book while helping them to experience the magic of stories.

Listening centers can easily be set up at home or in the classroom. A listening center offers one more way for children to hear stories that will assist in developing reading fluency, expression, and comprehension skills. Numerous stories are available online, featured on www.youtube.com or through sites such as EPIC! or www.StorylineOnline.com. Stories can be uploaded for listening later or retrieved directly on the internet. Donated or used laptop computers or tablets allow children to listen to stories anywhere in the classroom or at home. Purchase or ask each child to bring an inexpensive pair of earbuds and develop a storage system to retrieve them easily. A listening center can be a regular option for children as they make work choices or as you assign tasks.

Providing Time for Reading

Whether you are working in a childcare center, preschool, kindergarten, or primary grades, the day may be structured in various ways. You should provide time regularly for children to read and look at books. Do this through sustained silent reading, as work chosen for the children such as a listening center, or while others work in small groups with the teacher.

Children should have opportunities to select books themselves. Begin early to help them become responsible for their choices, and let them know that reading is also for personal enjoyment. They need not read every story aloud, discuss it with an adult, or complete a worksheet for every story they listen to. Particularly in sustained silent reading, children choose books independently and are not responsible for reporting on their reading. Children who are not yet reading text also need the opportunity to look at books, enjoy and "read" the illustrations, and think of themselves as "readers" from the start.

Responding to Books Orally

Activities frequently involve more than one aspect of language development, even though only one may be emphasized. To illustrate, while some children are speaking, others are listening. What one child writes, another reads. Oral activities for children can help both the speakers and the listeners; speakers become more fluent and lucid, and listeners become more attentive and analytical. Most oral activities either naturally involve listening activities, or you can structure them so that they do.

A significant reading skill is comprehension. Retelling a story or part of one assists not only with language development but also indicates whether a child has understood the story. Children can tell parts of stories they liked to classmates, with a time following in which they can be asked questions. They can record their opinions on particular books and put the Flipgrid recording, podcast or audio recording in the listening center for other children to hear. Children can retell a story using a felt board or puppets. They can engage in book discussions. Art activities based on books can be created and then shared.

Wordless picture books offer many opportunities for children to tell a story. Select books that provide a relatable story and plenty of opportunity to interpret the characters' actions. *A Ball for Daisy* (Raschka, 2011) illustrates the story of an adorable dog who has a favorite toy. When it is destroyed, the emotions of loss and sadness are visible in the engaging illustrations. Children can write or dictate sentences to be written on a sticky note and placed on respective pages. One child can respond to the entire book, or a group can select a few pages for their response. Later, read aloud the story that has been created. Children might also tell the story by passing the book around a group of four children, each orally telling about a page. As you listen to children's descriptions, you will learn about their comprehension of the story and gain insight into their language development.

As you preview books and poems, look for those that lend themselves to choral speaking. Books with refrains invite class participation. Short poems can be spoken in unison or divided so that groups within the class say different lines. Find opportunities to lead children in echo reading where you say the phrase first, and then they repeat it, such as with *Brown Bear Brown Bear, What Do You See?* (Martin, 1967). This allows the teacher to model, and then the children follow as they demonstrate volume, speed, and phrasing.

Finally, give children time to talk with one another as they work on projects that are book related. These informal conversations provide language practice in a realistic situation and allow many children to speak if they are working in pairs or small groups. Their turn to talk comes often, and they actively engage in listening.

Masks and Puppets

Children who are somewhat reticent to speak are sometimes more verbal if they use a mask or puppets. When responding orally to books, it becomes less about them and more about the characters who are speaking. Children can make masks to represent characters and hold them in front of their faces as they speak—just not too close to their mouths so they can still be clearly understood. Reproducible literature-related masks can also be found online and may have a space cut out for the child's face or eyes. Author and illustrator Jan Brett provides masks for several of her books, such as *The Mitten* (2009) and *The Hat* (1997), on her website (www.janbrett.com) that can be printed out for children to use. Puppets can also be constructed from objects attached to a stick or dowel to be manipulated by moving the rod. There are videos for producing paper plate puppets for stories like *The Very Hungry Caterpillar* (Carle, 1969). The critical thing to remember in making puppets is that children can manipulate them easily. That way, they can concentrate on the action, dialogue, and interaction among the characters.

Engaging Children in Writing Activities

In a discussion of writing activities, it is necessary to remember that there is a strong connection between reading and writing. Oral and written aspects of language develop simultaneously and are linked in that both engage the child in actively making meaning of the world. Talking about their topic, both before they write and while they write, helps some children to write in a more focused manner. They may share their writing while the piece is in progress, getting feedback from an audience of their peers.

Children select their topics to write about and may record thoughts and feelings in a daily response journal. There are times, however, when you may want to provide an idea or prompt for their writing. Sometimes books seem to lead directly to writing activities. Books written in a letter format naturally encourage writing. *Can I Be Your Dog?* (Cummings, 2018) features a homeless pup that wants to find a home. Arfy writes letters to homeowners, the butcher, the fire station, the junkyard guy, and even to an abandoned house. No one seems to want or have room for a dog. Then Arfy receives an unexpected letter from a person seeking a dog, and the tail-wagging pooch has a job and a new owner. Children could select another animal seeking a home or be a person looking for a pet.

Letter writing is one format that prompts writing and language development. Books with dialogue are another structure to encourage oral and written stories. Mo Willems's pigeon books have become a hit with children of all ages. *The Pigeon Will Ride the Roller Coaster!* (Willems, 2022) is the newest in the series. Pigeon is excited to ride his first roller coaster. He has his ticket, understands he'll need patience while waiting in line, and expects to be a little dizzy because it *is* a roller coaster. Speech balloons communicate Pigeon's thoughts and emotions about the big ride. Children can use this story or one of the other books in the series to generate dialogue for the pigeon or create their own pigeon story.

Content and format will suggest writing activities. This includes books in graphic formats for young children. Children who read comics will be familiar with this format. Books told through graphic design are ideal for children who are multilingual learners or are challenged as readers because there is minimal text with a reliance on art to assist in telling the story.

TOON Books was one of the first publishers who created books for young children in a graphic format. *Wordplay* (Brunetti, 2017) has fun with language while highlighting word stems throughout the book. Sergio Ruzzier's Fox + Chick series utilizes a graphic format for beginning readers using a brief, three-chapter format. The fourth book in the series, *Up and Down and Other Stories* (2022), highlights Chick's panic as he cannot climb down from a tree. In the second chapter, Chick impatiently counts each snowflake in anticipation of sledding, while the final chapter finds Chick unsure of what to do with a book gifted by Fox. Ruzzier uses a pastel-colored palette, large panels, easy-to-read font, and spacious speech bubbles that enable early readers to follow the sequence of events effortlessly. Publisher Simon & Schuster has created Simon Spotlight Ready-to-Read Graphics, including *Figgy & Boone: Best Brother Ever* (Trasler, 2022), about two friends, a mouse and a rat, who believe they are more like family than rodents. *Geraldine Pu and Her Lucky Pencil, Too!* (Chang, 2022) is in graphic format and tells about collecting family memories. Both books contain three brief chapters, colorful illustrations, and easy-to-read text.

Building Ideas from Types of Writing

Using a category system as a stimulus to find writing activities that will extend children's responses to literature may be helpful. One such category system is based on the type of writing: narrative, expository, persuasive, or descriptive. Narrative writing tells a story and has a plot. *Hair Love* by Matthew A. Cherry (2019) tells of the special relationship between father and daughter. When Zuri wants the perfect hairstyle for a particular day, her dad steps up to help with a few unsuccessful results. This book also received an Oscar for best animated short film.

Expository writing explains how something is done or provides information on a topic. *Our Planet! There's No Place Like Earth* (McAnulty, 2022) describes climate change so even the youngest readers can understand. The brief text offers information and facts, such as the earth is 98 million miles from the sun. Nonfiction books feature expository writing and are great for reading aloud to support learning about a topic or teaching a unit on a specific subject.

Persuasive writing is designed to influence people or to be convincing. In *The Day the Crayons Quit* (Daywalt, 2013), Duncan wants to color, but the crayons have decided they have had enough. Red crayon is a persuasive narrator who tells how overworked he is while advocating for his fellow crayons. The crayons display an emotional language that adds to the persuasiveness and the humor. Children can take on a persona of an inanimate object or write a persuasive letter to their parents, teacher, or classmate to try and get them to change their mind about an issue or topic. They can dictate or write reviews of their favorite books using language that highlights all the good points of the books and makes them sound appealing to others. Young writers may draft a letter defending a book character, such as Mo Willems's pigeon series of books mentioned previously.

Descriptive writing portrays a character or situation. It describes how an object appears to the senses, how someone feels, or what a scene is like. In Deborah Marcero's (2020) *In a Jar*, we meet Llewellyn, a collector. Llewellyn likes to gather ordinary things like feathers and heart-shaped stones and extraordinary items like rainbows, the sound of the ocean, and the tart cherry syrup color of the sunset. Evelyn soon becomes a collector herself, and the two "collected the wonders of winter . . . the newness of spring . . . and the long days and shadows of summer." When Evelyn moves away, the two friends find they can still share their special memories that are placed in a jar. The descriptive language found *In a Jar* highlights how seemingly everyday objects and events can be described with colorful, vibrant, and descriptive phrases. In addition to describing their surroundings, children can write descriptions of book characters without including their names. The descriptions can be placed on display as part of a riddle game. Children read the descriptions and attempt to guess who the characters are.

Providing children with various types of writing in literature will serve as mentor texts as they begin writing their own stories. That is one of the many reasons why children should be introduced to stories told in various ways using wondrous words that enhance language development.

Helping Children to Write Well

As you plan writing activities related to literature, you will want to do all you can to make the writing experience successful for children. Generally, you should engage children in a discussion before they begin writing. During this time, children exchange ideas and think through their responses so that when they start to compose, they have some notion of what they want to say. In a good writing program, children write daily, taking responsibility for choosing most of their topics and having regular conferences with the teacher during the writing process. Children should also have the opportunity to share their writing with others. These procedures will carry over when children write about literature.

It's imperative to be flexible about how much writing a child produces. Some responses to books may take the form of lists or one-word answers. Other children may write a paragraph or more, developing an idea fully. A special writing corner, a writers' club, and access to a computer often encourage children to write. Having an adult who can write down children's ideas or stories is also motivating when they can read the stories they created without having to write them physically. Orally telling a story that can be transcribed is another option. Often children who struggle with reading are also challenged by writing. Having children dictate and transcribe a story allows them to feel successful as beginning writers and provides time to reread the story they have created. So, too, will writing and illustrating their own books. Once the books are stapled or bound, place them in the classroom library where other children may read them.

Literature provides myriad opportunities for children to engage in oral, written, and visual language. Story interpretations and improvisations, use of masks and puppets, written responses to books, character studies, and making one's own books enhance children's appreciation of literature and strengthens their language development and communication skills.

Instructional Strategy from the Field: Word Walls

Daria Nalborczyk is a kindergarten teacher at Oakbrook Elementary School in Wood Dale, Illinois. She grew up speaking Polish and was born in the United States to immigrant parents from Poland. Daria's classroom has 16 students with diverse backgrounds and needs. Nine students have been identified as ELLs and are participating in a Transitional Bilingual Program. Daria supports students who speak Polish, Russian, Ukrainian, Spanish, and Urdu.

"I use a word wall to teach high-frequency words and vocabulary, I always start with what students know. We explore how letters look—if they are tall, short, or falling letters. I circle the letters with corresponding colors and keep that consistent throughout the year. During the year, we begin to differentiate between consonants and vowels, using blue to symbolize consonants and red to symbolize vowels. After teaching the words, I focus on finding songs or chants that go with high-frequency words to make them easier to remember. I also pair a visual to go with each word. At the beginning of the year, we learn each other's names before we begin learning any high-frequency words. I follow the same steps of identifying the various shapes of letters, consonants, and vowels, finding letters that are repeating, and placing a picture next to the corresponding student. When I teach vocabulary, I use pictures and examples so students can make connections between new words and vocabulary."

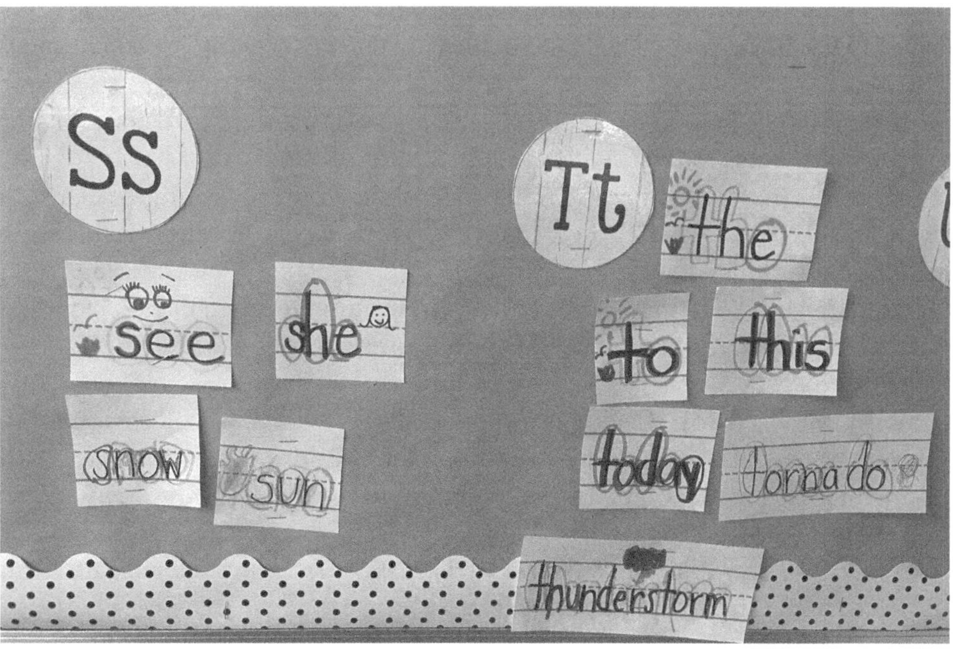

Literature Word Wall

A word wall is often prominently displayed in many preschool and primary-grade classrooms such as Daria's and contains a collection of words the teacher or children have identified as important in building a rich resource for vocabulary. A literature word wall focuses on words that come from a story or could be used to describe a book and might be descriptive (helps to see, smell, feel, taste, or hear something in the story), poetic, lyrical, or words that rhyme, humorous or silly sounding, onomatopoeic or words that are fun to say, or are memorable or important words from the story.

At times, a collection of words might be visually overwhelming for young children. A variation could be writing the word(s) from a book on a sticky note and placing them inside the front cover or even directly on the page in the book where it is found. That way, children can focus on a few words from a story and use context clues to assist in determining meaning.

Professional References Cited

Australian Parenting Website. www.raisingchildren.net.au

Chomsky, N. (1972). Stages in language development and reading exposure. *Harvard Educational Review*, *42*, 124–128.

Colby, S. & Lyon, A. 2004. Heightening awareness about the importance of using multicultural literature. *Multicultural Education*, *11*(3), 24–28.

Essa, E. L. & Burnham, M. M. (2020). *Introduction to Early Childhood Education*. Sage.

Gonzalez-Mena, J. & Eyer, D. W. (2018). Assessing infant and toddler play environments. *Young Children*, *68*(4), 22–25.

Hannon, C. (n.d.) Reinforcing language skills for our youngest learners. NAEYC. https://www.naeyc.org/our-work/families/reinforcing-language-skills

Kiefstad, J. M. & Martinez, K. C. (2013). Promoting young children's cultural awareness and appreciation through multicultural books. *Young Children*, *68*(5), 74–81.

Lambert, M. D. (2015). *Reading picture books with children*. Charlesbridge.

Lawhon, T. & Cobb, J. B. (2002). Routines that build emergent literacy skills in infants, toddlers, and preschoolers. *Early Childhood Education Journal*, *30*(2), 113–118.

Leland, C. H., Lewison, M., & Harste, J. C. (2023). *Teaching children's literature: It's critical*. (3rd ed.). Routledge.

Sipe, L. (2002). Talking back and taking over: Young children's expressive engagement during storybook read-alouds. *The Reading Teacher, 55*(5), 476–483.

Stanford Children's Health. (n.d.). Age Appropriate Speech and Language Milestones. https://www.stanfordchildrens.org/en/topic/default?id=age-appropriate-speech-and-language-milestones-90-P02170

Visser-Bochane, M. I., Reijneveld, S. A., Krijnen, W. P., van der Schans, C. P., & Luinge, M. R. (2020). Identifying milestones in language development for young children ages 1 to 6 years. *Academic Pediatrics, 20*(3), 421–429.

Children's Books Cited

Asher, Sandy. (2016). *Chicken story time*. Ill. Mark Fearing. Dial Books for Young Readers.

Atinuke. (2019). *B is for baby*. Ill. Angela Brooksbank. Walker.

Bender, Rebecca. (2017). *Not friends*. Pajama Press.

Black, Michael Ian. (2009). *Chicken cheeks*. Ill. Kevin Hawkes. Simon & Schuster.

Brett, Jan. (1997). *The hat*. Putnam.

Brett, Jan. (2009). *The mitten*. Putnam.

Brunetti, Ivan. (2017). *Wordplay*. TOON Books.

Carle, Eric. (1969). *The very hungry caterpillar*. World Publishing.

Chang, Maggie P. (2022). *Geraldine Pu and her lucky pencil, too!* Simon Spotlight.

Cherry, Matthew A. (2019). *Hair love*. Ill. Vashti Harrison. Kokila.

Cooper, Elisha. (2021). *Yes & no*. Roaring Brook Press.

Crute, Josh. (2021). *Hornswoggled!: A wacky words whodunit*. Ill. Jenn Harney. Page Street Books.

Cummings, Troy. (2018). *Can I be your dog?* Random House.

Daywalt, Drew. (2013). *The day the crayons quit*. Ill. Oliver Jeffers. Philomel.

Heos, Bridget. (2018). *Stegothesaurus*. Ill. T. L. McBeth. Henry Holt.

Hesse, Karen. (2022). *Granny and Bean*. Ill. Charlotte Voake. Candlewick Press.

Khalil, Aya. (2020). *The Arabic quilt: An immigrant story*. Ill. Anait Semirdzhyan. Tilbury House.

Khan, Naaz. (2021). *Room for everyone*. Ill. Mercé López. Atheneum.

Lester, Helen. (2004). *Hurty feelings*. Ill. Lynn Munsinger. Houghton Mifflin.

Lionni, Leo. (1993/2021). *Let's play / Vamos a jugar*. Knopf.

Litwin, Eric. (2008). *Pete the Cat: I love my white shoes*. Ill. James Dean. HarperCollins.

Lynas, Em. (2021). *The cat and the rat and the hat*. Ill. Matt Hunt. Nosy Crow.

Marcero, Deborah. (2020). *In a jar*. Putnam.

Martin, Bill Jr. (1967). *Brown bear brown bear, what do you see?* Henry Holt.

Martin, Bill Jr. & Archambault, John. (1989). *Chicka chicka boom boom*. Ill. Lois Ehlert. Simon & Schuster.
McAnulty, Stacy. (2022). *Our planet! There's no place like earth*. Ill. David Litchfield. Henry Holt.
Messner, Kate. (2015). *Up in the garden and down in the dirt*. Ill. Christopher Silas Neal. Chronicle Books.
Mora, Oge. (2018). *Thank you, Omu*. Little, Brown and Company.
Muhammad, Ibtihaj. (2019). *The proudest blue: A story of hijab and family*. Ill. Hatem Aly. Little, Brown and Company.
Novak, B. J. (2014). *The book with no pictures*. Rocky Pond Books.
Numeroff, Laura. (1985). *If you give a mouse a cookie*. Harper & Row.
Penfold, Alexandra. (2018). *All are welcome*. Ill. Suzanne Kaufman. Knopf.
Pfeffer, Rubin. (2018). *Summer supper*. Ill. Mike Austin. Random House.
Pizzoli, Greg. (2023). *Mister Kitty is lost!* Little, Brown and Company.
Raschka, Chris. (2011). *A ball for Daisy*. Random House.
Raúl the Third. (2020). *¡Vamos! Let's go eat*. Versify/Houghton Mifflin Harcourt.
Reynolds, Peter H. (2018). *The word collector*. Orchard Books.
Ruzzier, Sergio. (2022). *Fox + Chick: Up and down and other stories*. Chronicle Books.
Salas, Laura Purdie. (2012). *A leaf can be . . .* Millbrook Press.
Salas, Laura Purdie. (2014). *Water can be . . .* Millbrook Press.
Salas, Laura Purdie. (2015). *A rock can be . . .* Millbrook Press.
Seeger, Laura Vaccaro. (2013). *Bully*. Roaring Brook Press.
Sendak, Maurice. (1963). *Where the wild things are*. Harper & Row.
Snyder, Gabi. (2021). *Listen*. Ill. Stephanie Graegin. Simon & Schuster.
Sterling, Michelle. (2022). *A sweet new year for Ren*. Ill. Dung Ho. Simon & Schuster.
Sutton, Sally. (2019). *Dig, dump, roll*. Ill. Brian Lovelock. Candlewick Press.
Trasler, Janee. (2022). *Figgy & Boone: Best brother ever!* Simon Spotlight.
Vamos, Samantha R. (2019). *The piñata that the farm maiden hung*. Ill. Sebastiá Serra. Charlesbridge.
Wang, Andrea. (2022). *Luli and the language of tea*. Illus. Hyewon Yum. Neal Porter Books/Holiday House.
Watkins, Adam F. (2014). *R is for robot: A noisy alphabet*. Price Stern Sloan.
Willems, Mo. (2022). *The pigeon will ride the roller coaster!* Union Square Kids.
Wilson, Karma. (2021). *Bear can't wait*. Ill. Jane Chapman. McElderry Books.

6

Nurturing Children's Intellectual Development

> If I sit down at my drawing table and say, "I need to make something funny," I would kill every ounce of my creativity. Instead, I say, "I'm going to make some marks on my paper and see what happens."
>
> (Cindy Derby, author-illustrator, in Hohl, 2021)

There are a variety of thinking processes related to children's intellectual development including observing, classifying, organizing, and applying. Author and illustrator Cindy Derby draws on many of these in order to write humorous stories such as *How to Walk an Ant* (2019) which offers detailed instructions for becoming an ant walker, or *Blurp's Book of Manners* (2022) which features an unruly and messy creature that causes disruptions in Ms. Picklepop's etiquette class. Derby's "marks" on the paper not only provide a feast of visual humor but also draw on the "what if" curiosities that fuel children's intellectual processes.

Children's interactions with their environment and with people in their lives such as family members, peers, teachers, and caregivers assist in the development of intellect (Lynch & Warner, 2013). This dynamic process is further enhanced by children's natural curiosity and eagerness to learn. Whether it is intentional or by chance, adults serve a key role in encouraging children's cognitive growth. Introducing basic skills and facts, or concepts, to young children, fosters independence and understanding of the world around them.

DOI: 10.4324/9781003367635-6

Intellectual Development in Young Children

A concept is an idea that represents a class of objects or events. Consider concepts as "big ideas" children learn as they engage in a range of experiences. Concepts embody many images and memories that blend to make a meaningful whole. The advantage of developing a system of concepts is that it allows children to process new information by fitting it into an existing framework. Each impression, object, or event need not be assessed and remembered separately. When children have seen several round objects and have been told that each is a ball, they generalize so that new examples fit into their concept of a ball—if it's round then it's a ball. When they hear the term *heavy* used to describe a box that is difficult to lift, a desk that their father cannot move, or a large animal such as an elephant, they begin to develop a concept of heavy. This learning of concepts is termed *concept formation* and begins in infancy. Using their sense of touch, smell, sight, hearing, and taste, children take in information (Charlesworth & Lind, 2010). Consider babies who grab things to touch or put objects in their mouths to taste. They are trying to make sense of their world through these experiences.

The changing and enlarging of concepts as new events are experienced and where new insights are gained is a continual process. For example, researchers have found young children may have misconceptions about the world around them, particularly in the area of science (Anderson et al., 2014). Limited information may have been provided about plants and plant growth that narrowed children's understanding at an early age about what exactly is a plant (Barman et al., 2006). In a seminal study by Bell (1981), children did not consider trees to be a plant and that a plant had to have a flowering structure. This finding was also demonstrated in a later study in which children typically drew a flower when asked to draw a plant (McNair & Stein, 2001). Taking the time to offer correct information to children can assist in their understanding of scientific and other content as they begin to acquire basic knowledge about the world around them.

One task of the childcare provider or teacher is to assist young children to form accurate concepts. Teachers supply materials for children to manipulate, bring information to the classroom or center, take children on trips around the school or community, and encourage children to discuss what they have seen. In other words, they provide the raw data from which children can construct their own concepts. Through questioning, teachers guide children to think about and order what they have experienced.

Young children engage in thinking processes that are fundamental in concept formation. The function of concepts is to organize experiences efficiently.

Children associate ideas, classify, generalize, and reach logical conclusions (Papalia & Martorell, 2021). A qualitative change in children's concepts evolves over time with major shifts between four and seven years (Gelman, 1996). Until they are seven or eight years of age, children rely more on sensory data than on logic to reach conclusions regarding physical objects. Almost all four-year-olds will look at two short, wide glasses of water equally filled and report that both glasses have the same amount of water. After watching the water from one of these glasses being poured into a tall, narrow container, the children will report that the tall glass has more than the short one, or vice versa. The logic that no water has been added or taken away is secondary to the sensory data that after the water is poured from one glass into a taller container, it looks as if the amounts are different. Around the age of seven, children begin to rely on the logic of the situation and will report that the quantities of water remain equal. At this time, they are also able to keep more than one attribute in mind, looking at both the height and width of the containers.

After the age of seven, children are more likely to use the standard forms of logical reasoning. They will use deductive reasoning, which goes from general to particular. All collies are dogs. This is a collie. Therefore, it is a dog. They will also use inductive reasoning, which goes from the particular to the general. Collies, spaniels, boxers, beagles, and terriers all have hair, and four legs, and make a barking sound. They are dogs. It is likely that all dogs have hair, and four legs and make a barking sound.

Piaget's Theory of Cognitive Development

The Swiss psychologist Jean Piaget concluded that the order in which children's thinking matures is the same for all children, but the pace varies from child to child (Piaget & Inhelder, 1969). Piaget was interested in how organisms adapt to their environment and described two processes individuals engage in: assimilation and accommodation. Assimilation occurs when an individual attempts to make new information or experience fit into an existing concept or schema. Accommodation takes place when the "schema is modified or a new concept is formed to incorporate the new information or experience" (Essa & Burnham, 2020, p. 102).

Piaget characterized four stages of cognitive development (Huitt & Hummel, 2003):

- Sensorimotor (Birth 0 to 2 years)
  - Differentiates self from objects

- Recognizes self as agent of action and begins to act intentionally (shakes a rattle to make noise)
- Achieves object permanence in realizing things continue to exist even when no longer present

- Pre-operational (2 to 7 years)
  - Learns to use language and to represent objects by words and images
  - Thinking is still egocentric; has difficulty taking the viewpoint of others
  - Classifies objects by a single feature (groups together objects by color)
- Concrete Operational (7 to 11 years)
  - Can think logically about objects and events
  - Achieves conversation of number, mass, and weight
  - Classifies objects according to several features and can order them in a series along a single dimension such as size
- Formal Operational (11 and up)
  - Can engage in abstract thinking and logical reasoning abilities

Adults working with young children should recognize and understand the characteristics of each stage of cognitive development. In doing so, they are better able to design instruction and activities that facilitate and promote children's intellectual development.

Developmental Goals and Cognitive Abilities

Literature contributes to the achievement of goals that align with Piaget's stages of cognitive development. In addition, Lev Vygotsky, a Russian psychologist, describes what he called the zone of proximal development as the range beyond the independent level, but within the child's potential (1978). Working with guidance from others helps children reach this potential. When teachers provide support, or scaffolding, it encourages children's intellectual growth.

Goals for intellectual growth can be categorized as long-term developmental goals, general goals for an age or grade level, and specific goals for individual children. Long-term goals are behavior or competencies that are developed over time and considered desired patterns of behavior. A long-term goal for intellectual development is that children will continue to acquire new concepts and refine old ones. Teachers and childcare providers will assist children in attaining this goal throughout the toddler, preschool, and primary-grade years.

Assisting in the Acquisition and Refinement of Concepts

Young children have many concrete experiences that aid them in the process of developing and refining concepts. Books, both fiction and nonfiction, are a source of information from which children gather data necessary for generalizing and through which they assess the accuracy of concepts already held.

Giving Information

Literature often provides information that children could not discover through their own manipulations and observations of the environment. Some are in the form of naming what they observed. Children may see there are three different kinds of fish in the aquarium, but no amount of watching will teach them what the fish are called. You may want to read books to children that will provide this information, or leave the books for them to browse themselves. If preschoolers are learning about water, the Robert F. Sibert Honor Award book *Hey, Water!* (Portis, 2019) shows a young girl exploring her surroundings and realizing that water is everywhere. However, it doesn't always look or feel the same. Water can be a lake, a dewdrop, a tear, a cloud, an iceberg, or snow. Limited text and eye-catching illustrations incorporating various hues of blue make this a perfect book for preschoolers. Lyrical language is utilized in *All the Water in the World* (Lyon, 2011) which also explores the concept of water and is appropriate for preschoolers or primary-grade students. *A Drop of Water* (Wick, 1997) provides more detailed information about water and would work well in primary-grade classrooms.

Books may offer information about a topic that is familiar to children but present new facts about that topic. Many children have been to a zoo or have seen zoo animals on television or on the internet. What do they know about the many jobs there are at the zoo? Before reading Steve Jenkins and Robin Page's *What Do You Do If You Work at the Zoo?* (2020), brainstorm with children what jobs there might be at the zoo. Then read the story and discover that someone's job is to brush the hippo's teeth or shine a tortoise's shell. The information is presented in short paragraphs and accompanied by textured collage illustrations.

When books about familiar topics are shared with children, they can compare the information in the book to their own knowledge. It is always interesting to hear what children "know" about water or zoos based on their own observations or what others have told them. As a class or individually, additional research can be done to determine if what they know is fact or fiction.

Reinforcing Concepts

Just as some books can be used to introduce ideas, others serve to reinforce concepts or to add further information to a topic children have already explored through direct experience. The concept book *Shape by Shape* (MacDonald, 2009) presents a variety of shapes such as circles, squares, and triangles as well as less common shapes like diamonds, crescents, and semicircles. Children will be thrilled by what results by combining the shapes that are slowly revealed through the die-cuts on each page. One preschool teacher created a felt-board activity where the children could make their own creatures using shapes following the reading of *Shape by Shape*.

A book to pair with *Shape by Shape* is Joyce Hesselberth's *Shape Shift* (2016). Vibrant illustrations utilize nine different shapes as two children play a game to see what they can make by putting two or more shapes together. There is a video by Hesselberth on www.youtube.com as she uses two shapes to draw a variety of pictures. An app is also available from Hesselberth for a nominal fee called PrestoBingo Shapes. A more sophisticated approach to shapes is found in *Circle Under Berry* (Higgins, 2021). A rhythmic text and rich language explore shapes, colors, and prepositions. Shapes such as octagon, heart, and trapezoid along with rectangle, circle, and square are described using the color words green, orange, and red, along with magenta, emerald, and goldenrod. *Circle Under Berry* adds to color and shape recognition and spurs imagination in creating new configurations.

Another book that reinforces prepositional phrases is the classic *We're Going on a Bear Hunt* (Rosen, 2009), presented in a delightful and entertaining manner with illustrations by Helen Oxenbury. "We can't go over it. We can't go under it. We've got to go through it!" reinforces the concepts of *over*, *under*, and *through*. To further the understanding of these words, children can engage in creating movements to go along with the story. *We're Going on a Bear Hunt* is available in board-book, picture-book, and sound-book versions which makes it an excellent choice to share with one young child or a group of children.

Box 6.1 Concept Books: Opposites

Big Bear, Small Mouse (Karma Wilson; ill. Jane Chapman, 2016)
Kitty + Cat: Opposites Attract (Mirka Hokkanen, 2023)
Opposites (Sandra Boynton, 1982) board book
Perros! Perros! / Dogs! Dogs! (Ginger Foglesong Guy; ill. Sharon Glick, 2006)
Web Opposites (Rob Hodgson, 2021)
Yummy Yucky (Leslie Patricelli, 2003) board book

Books as Teaching Partners

Some books have qualities that make them visual aids and teaching partners, as described in Chapter 4, in exploring the alphabet, counting, colors, and other concepts. Alphabet books can be used by children individually or in small groups to recognize letter sounds. Children can take turns opening the book, seeing the letter, naming its sound, and the object pictured. In selecting books for this purpose, be sure that the name of the object is a pure rather than blended sound. *We're Going on a Bear Hunt: My First ABC* (2020) contains each letter of the alphabet coupled with a familiar object. Children can use their fingers to trace the shape of each letter that is recessed into the board-book pages. Atinuke's (2019) *B is for Baby* explores one specific letter by showing different items that start with the letter "B" such as banana and bus, as well as unique words like bumpy and baboon. As children become familiar with letters and sounds, books such as *A is for Axolotl* (Macorol, 2022) introduces fascinating animals like the gerenuk, kiwi, and pangolin. A totally twisted take on the alphabet can be found in *The Alphabet's Alphabet* (Harris, 2020). "A is an H that just won't stand up right. A B is a D with its belt on too tight." Hilarious illustrations by Dan Santat invite children in for a second look and laugh.

In selecting counting books, the number of objects on a page should match the numeral. *We're Going on a Bear Hunt: My First 1 2 3* (2020) follows the same board-book format as the ABC book in showing familiar animals accompanied by traceable numerals. Anita Lobel's *Ducks on the Road: A Counting Adventure* (2021) follows Mama and Papa duck as they lead their ten ducklings along the road with one after the other turning back to quack. *10 Hungry Rabbits* (Lobel, 2012/2022) features bunnies gathering fruits and vegetables that are made into a delicious soup.

Finally, concept books about color are often bright and vivid. Matthew Reinhart's *Colors: My First Pop-Up!* (2021) is filled with color words along with names of colors and objects. "My favorite color is blue. It's popsicles and sails, oceans and . . ." The final rhyming object is found by pulling a tab or lifting a flap. *Freight Train* (Crews, 1978) is a classic that features color concepts. This book is available in various formats and in Spanish. Each train car is a different color with a matching print. There are strong possibilities for vocabulary development and information about trains as children learn color words.

Developing Skills in a Variety of Thinking Processes

Books provide an opportunity for children to engage in many thinking processes. Obviously, almost any picture book you select could be shared to assist children in improving their observational skills. However, some are better than others.

Observing

If you want children to become aware of detail, you might select a wordless book that relies upon the reader to look carefully at the illustrations in order to interpret the story. Matthew Cordell's Caldecott Medal-winning *Wolf in the Snow* (2017) begins with several pages of illustrations with the first depicting a young girl in a house with her parents and dog. The next double-page spread shows the girl dressed in a red jacket walking away and waving goodbye as her dog barks. As you turn the page, you see the girl walking alone on the left-hand side while on the right there is an illustration showing a pack of wolves. These illustrations all appear prior to the title page. The story continues as the girl is shown leaving school as a snowstorm makes it more difficult to see. A corresponding story shows a wolf pup who has lost its way. The girl scoops up the pup and tries to make her way through the snow as she encounters various animals and sounds. She follows the sound of howling and eventually comes eye-to-eye with the mother wolf. After mother and pup are reunited, the girl begins the arduous journey home but becomes lost and exhausted. Who should come to her rescue? The wolves, including mother and pup, who howl until the girl's parents and dog locate and carry her home. There are many aspects of this story that require a keen eye to catch the various nuances Cordell has incorporated into his illustrations. *Explorers* (2019) by Cordell is also wordless and follows a family's trip to a local museum. Both are excellent for honing observational skills particularly because every aspect of the book from the book jacket to the casing, to the end pages, to the initial illustrations, are all part of the story being told.

When you share books such as *Wolf in the Snow* or *Explorers*, be certain that children can easily see the illustrations. This might mean working with a few children at a time or using a device that projects images onto a screen. This way you can show a particular illustration to more students. Wordless picture books also support multilingual learners and emergent readers because they enable children to read a story by interpreting visual images rather than reading text.

Some books are observational guessing games. Infants and toddlers will enjoy *Where's the Kangaroo?* (Arrhenius, 2019) and *Where's the Fire Truck?* (Arrhenius, 2021). Each page in these board books asks the question, "Where's the [animal name]?" or "Where's the [vehicle name]?" The corresponding page has a felt flap that is covering a picture of that animal or vehicle with the sentence, "Here it is!" At the conclusion of each book, the question is asked, "And where are you?" This time a felt flap covers a mirror and the statement, "There you are!"

Who Am I?: An Animal Guessing Game (Jenkins & Page, 2017) shows different parts of an animal and then asks, "Who am I?" If you share this book with one child, you might then ask the child to choose a friend and play the guessing game again. One child can look at an illustration and tell about something he or she spies on the pages and then try to guess what the animal might be. Children who have observed animals like frogs or rabbits can offer additional clues about the animal before turning the page.

A book for a little older child that requires careful observation and searching the pages is *Where's the Penguin?* (Schrey, 2017). A family of ten penguins has escaped from the city zoo and is trying to get back to Antarctica. Along the way, they stumble upon a birthday celebration, spend some time relaxing at a lake, and even stop by a bowling alley. The double-page spreads contain the ten penguins that children will need to find. In addition to locating the wayward penguins, children can observe various settings and people. For further observational fun, provide a magnifying glass to use in locating the penguins.

Is it a duck or is it a rabbit? Two unseen characters debate the identity of the creature in *Duck! Rabbit!* (Rosenthal, 2009). It's all about perspective because the creature could, in fact, be either. Just as the characters determine that both could be right, the duck/rabbit runs away and they see an anteater. Or is it a brachiosaurus? This simple, yet clever, story is a wonderful interactive read-aloud that will have children expressing their opinion while providing an opportunity to discuss how points of view can differ based on what is observed.

You may want children to observe the action in a story or the reactions of characters. Keep in mind the maturity level and experience of the children as you select books for practice in observing. The four-year-old needs less complex books with clearer illustrations than does the seven-year-old. *This Is a Dog* (Collins, 2020) was titled "My First Animal Book" until an energetic dog crossed it out and wrote his own title. Each page shows a different animal—cat, monkey, rabbit, squirrel, crocodile, and others, as well as the dog. His encounters with each animal, particularly the giraffe, elephant, and bear, become more annoying until finally the animals have had enough and a chase ensues. Fortunately, the devilish dog has one more trick up his paw.

A little older reader will need to slow down and read the text and carefully observe the illustrations in *Lift* (Lê, 2020). This picture book, featured in Chapter 4, is about a girl who loves pushing the elevator buttons in her apartment building. When she acquires her own button that transports her to other worlds, she is delighted. Author Minh Lê's dynamic storytelling is the perfect complement to Dan Santat's comic style and cinematic illustrations. This book works well as a read-aloud or for independent reading because both listener and reader can elevate their imaginations and immerse themselves in this visually, delightful story. Observant children and adults will also notice the illustration on the hardcover book casing and the end pages.

Hypothesizing

Children can be guided to hypothesize about any book you are sharing with them. They may look at the cover or listen to the title and make reasonable guesses about the book's content. Taking a "picture walk" through the book before reading will offer children an opportunity to tell what they think a character will do or what might happen next based on the illustrations. Teach children that hypothesizing means taking into account the information one already has in order to make predictions. Be sure to encourage them to give reasons for their conjectures. Teach children that hypothesizing is a logical process and is not simply telling what they would like to happen or what they think would be interesting. Their guesses may prove to be exactly what the author has done with the plot, but it may turn out to be quite different though still reasonable. The object is to suggest logical possibilities, not to match exactly the author's choice.

Some books have plots that naturally invite hypothesizing, especially when the story is about a beloved character with whom they are familiar. They see the character's feelings and reactions and use these, as well as their own understanding of the emotions, for anticipated actions. The "Pigeon" series of books by Mo Willems *Don't Let the Pigeon Drive the Bus!* (2003), *The Pigeon Wants a Puppy!* (2008), *The Pigeon HAS to Go to School!* (2019), and *The Pigeon Will Ride the Roller Coaster!* (2022) feature a dynamic and emotionally expressive character. The text is varied and coupled with the appropriate punctuation, to show how the words should be read. The illustrations leave no doubt as to how the Pigeon is reacting to the particular problem. There is always a punchline of sorts at the conclusion of the book. Before it is revealed, children can hypothesize what may happen that changes the Pigeon's mind or what will be the focus of the next book.

Other books have such strong characterization that this becomes the basis for children's hypotheses about what will happen next. One of the many benefits of series books, in both picture-book and chapter-book form, is that readers come to know the characters and can predict what may happen as well as how the issue is resolved. Picture books for very young children that fill the bill are *Maisy* by Lucy Cousins and *Pete the Cat* by Eric Litwin. Other enjoyable picture-book characters include *No, David!* by David Shannon, *Llama, Llama* by Anna Dewdney, and *Duck and Goose* by Tad Hills. Beginning-to-read series most memorable characters are *Elephant and Piggie* by Mo Willems, *Fly Guy* by Tedd Arnold, *Mercy Watson* by Kate DiCamillo, and *Penny* by Kevin Henkes. Early chapter-book favorites include *Ivy and Bean* by Annie Barrows, *Horrible Harry* by Suzy Kline, and *Katie Woo* by Fran Manushkin.

Still, other books have an identifiable pattern to the actions within them. Folktales such as *The Gingerbread Boy* or *The House that Jack Built* have cumulative or repetitive plots. Children may use the generalizations they make about the literary form itself to suggest what will happen.

Comparing

Literature offers the opportunity for children to engage in structured comparisons. When you group books in pairs, units, or using graphic organizers, you set the stage for children to compare and contrast one work of literature with another.

Fairy tales provide numerous possibilities to compare and contrast stories. Often we assume children are familiar with different fairy tales, but sadly that may not be the case. One second-grade student thought Walt Disney wrote *Cinderella* and *Snow White* because the only fairy tales she had been exposed to were movies produced by Disney. Although Disney presents one version of the classic tales, there are more from many cultures than can be shared with young children.

Begin by sharing traditional versions of *Goldilocks and the Three Bears* by James Marshall (1988) or a similar retelling by Caralyn Buehner and Mark Buehner (2007). After reading each story, choose one illustration from each book depicting a similar action or event and have students compare and contrast them. Initially, it is better to begin with one illustration rather than overwhelming children by comparing and contrasting the entire story. When working with multilingual learners, take the time to discuss the illustration and name objects that appear in each. A good strategy is to write the naming word on a sticky note and place it in the book next to the object. Children can then revisit the book and use the sticky note as a reminder of the word. After another reading of the stories, compare and contrast the entire stories using a Venn diagram or other graphic organizer. If children struggle to remember events in the story, then it might be too soon to use this strategy.

Once children are familiar with the traditional story of *Goldilocks and the Three Bears*, introduce them to different versions and variants. *Goldilocks and the Three Dinosaurs* (2012) is retold by author and illustrator Mo Willems. After discussing the book cover, examine the endpapers that contain all sorts of possibilities for "Goldilocks and the Three . . ." stories. In Willems's retelling, Papa Dinosaur and Mama Dinosaur, and another dinosaur, who apparently is visiting from Norway, devise a plan using chocolate pudding to lure Goldilocks to their house. The Goldilocks in Willems's story "never listened to warnings about the dangers of barging into strange, enormous houses." She not only bursts into the dinosaur's house but proceeds to eat the three bowls of chocolate pudding despite each one being at a different temperature. Once stuffed full of pudding, Goldilocks looks for a place to take a nap and notices that all of the chairs and the beds are too tall or big. She realizes this is a dinosaur's house and quickly skedaddles. Compare this version with those by Marshall and the Buehners to determine the differences. Ask which story they liked better and why. What do they think about the moral of the story for Goldilocks and also for the dinosaurs?

Read other variants such as *Rubia and the Three Osos* (Elya, 2010) in which Rubia enters the Oso family's casita to dine on a nice bowl of *sopa* and rest on a *perfecta* little bed. Or Margie Palantini's humorous *Goldie and the Three Hares* (2011) in which Goldilocks falls down a rabbit hole after being chased by the three bears and hurting her foot. The Hare Family is happy to help nurse Goldie back to health but soon realizes that she is a very bad houseguest. In *Goldilocks and the Three Engineers* (Fliess, 2021) the yellow-haired heroine is an inventor who likes to create new gadgets. When "inventor's block" sets in, Goldilocks goes for a walk. Soon, three bear engineers enter the bungalow and tinker with the various contraptions, only to make them better. When Goldilocks returns, she is thrilled with the improved projects and invites the bears back in the spring (following hibernation) to "make the next big thing." These stories should be read, discussed, and compared following the reading of the traditional stories or later in the year. Comparing and contrasting builds on and strengthens skills in observing and these books encourage the development of both. They are also stories that easily lend themselves to dramatization.

Classifying

Some books such as *Sam Sorts* (Jocelyn, 2017) readily lend themselves to experiences in classification. Sam's things are in a heap and he needs to tidy up. As Sam sifts through the pile he finds a variety of things and begins to put them together according to different attributes. His categories include round things, pairs of items that rhyme, groups of things from nature, and even some that float or fly. Sam realizes some things can be classified in many ways. *Sort It Out* (Mariconda, 2008) features Packy the pack rat whose mother tells him to sort the things he has collected and put them away. Through rhyming text, Packy categorizes the items using different characteristics with the name of the category written on a card that is integrated into the colorful illustrations. Both of these books use ordinary items but show how they can be grouped into various categories. Using the items in the book or a collection of their own items, have children discuss attributes that could be used to classify the objects. After sorting, represent the results in table or graph form. The response to either story can utilize real-life analyses through skills related to observing, questioning, classifying, graphing, and interpreting data.

Other books have the potential to discuss and engage in classifying and sorting. *Pete the Cat and His Four Groovy Buttons* (Litwin, 2012) is perfect for preschoolers. Pete the Cat is wearing his favorite shirt with the four groovy buttons—each a different color. Does Pete cry when he loses his button? Goodness no, because "buttons come and buttons go." And of course, Pete keeps singing his song. This is a great book for sorting buttons as well as exploring math concepts. For kindergarten and primary grades, the classic beginning-to-read chapter book *Frog and Toad Are Friends* (Lobel, 1970) can serve a similar purpose. Frog and Toad have just returned home from a walk when Toad discovers he has lost a button off his jacket. He and Frog go back to all the places they have walked in an attempt to find it. Frog and several other animals find buttons, but none match the one Toad lost. They find a black one, but his was white. They find one with two holes, but his had four. Attribute by attribute, it is narrowed down to a white, four-holed, big, round, thick button. They cannot find it and an angry Toad returns home to find the button on the floor of his living room. Concerned about the trouble he has caused his friend, he sews on the button and also sews on all the other buttons they have found. The next day he gives his button-covered jacket to Frog.

After the teacher reads these stories, children can engage in the process of sorting. Since Pete the Cat lost buttons of various colors, preschoolers can sort buttons according to this attribute. Listeners of *Frog and Toad Are Friends* can determine what kind of button they would like to look for using the classifications Toad used or develop their own. Children could tell or write a story about their buttons. This is an enjoyable activity because it relates to the story and the teacher has selected a classification for each age level that is challenging, but not overwhelming. A variation of this activity, if the teacher doesn't have loose buttons to sort and count, would be for children to look at the buttons on their own clothing. A graph could be created showing the number of children who have red, blue, or white buttons along with a category for those children whose clothing have no buttons. A wonderful discussion could ensue about other ways to fasten clothes such as Velcro or snaps.

Children might be asked to classify some of the stories they have heard. If the categories are not given, children can begin to develop their own. They might divide stories into those they liked and those they did not like; they might divide stories into those that could happen and ones that are make-believe; or divide stories about animals and stories about people. The teacher guides the children to think about the content of the stories, and perhaps the format, and talks about how to find a variety of ways to classify them. When teaching first grade, my students would sort the books in the classroom library several times during the year. At the beginning of the year it was by color, then authors, and finally by types of books. This activity enabled them to discover the many books in the library and also to have responsibility for taking care of them.

Organizing

Another thinking skill is that of organizing. Young children can be helped to organize by learning to sequence events. Cumulative folktales, as well as many contemporary stories, are a rich source of material. Reconstructing the sequence of events in some tales, however, is a difficult task because knowing the order of events is a matter of straight recall. For example, *If You Give a Mouse a Cookie* (Numeroff, 1985) he will certainly need a glass of milk. You cannot expect him to drink the milk without a straw. And then he'll need a napkin. This cumulative tale builds from each object until it comes full circle. There is a cause-and-effect relationship related to the objects that make the organization of them necessary. Subsequent titles including *If You Give a Moose a Muffin* (1991), *If You Give a Pig a Pancake* (1998), and *If You Give a Dog a Donut* (2011) by Laura Joffe Numeroff and illustrator Felicia Bond also work well in organizing and sequencing a story.

Sometimes the pattern is that of chronological order. Jerry Pinkney's *The Little Red Hen* (2006) relates the classic story of a Little Red Hen who requests assistance from the cat, dog, rat, goat, and pig to help plant the seed, harvest the wheat, take it to the mill, and bake the bread. Each animal's reply is, "Not I." After doing all the work herself, the hen does not share the delicious bread with the animals but enjoys eating it with her baby chicks. In Pinkney's gloriously illustrated story, the animals' names appear in a color-coded font (red for the hen, brown for the dog, and so on) making it easy for young children to chime in for the repetitive phrase. *The Little Red Fort* (Maier, 2018) is a version of *The Little Red Hen* but this time Ruby finds some old boards and decides to build a fort. She invites her brothers Oscar Lee, Rodrigo, and José to help her but they just laugh and tell her that she doesn't know what she is doing. The boys change their tune once the fort is completed, but now it is only Ruby's. However, once they make a mailbox, plant some flowers, and paint the fort fire engine red, should Ruby invite them for a fort-warming party? In order for Ruby to build the fort she had to draw the plans, gather the supplies, cut the boards, and hammer the nails. And she receives assistance at each step from her mother and grandmother. The sequence in these two books reflects the way something is made. Children repeating the sequence can infer as well as recall what comes next.

Another technique to engage children in sequencing is to have them draw a picture of one thing that happened in the story. Working with three or four children, ask each to tell what is happening in his or her picture. Then ask them whose picture would come first in the story, next, and so on, until all are ordered. Work with small groups because the more pictures there are, the more complex the task becomes and children may tire of listening to numerous children describing their pictures.

Sequencing should allow children to be active participants, doing something that requires them to use the sequence, not just answering the question, "Then what happened?"

Applying

Books that describe "how to do it" can be used to give children the opportunity to apply what they are hearing or reading. The directions need to be clear for the intended age group and within their capabilities. Kate Messner follows up her *How to Read a Story* (2015) by chronicling the process of writing a story. There are ten steps to writing a story from searching for an idea to choosing a setting to developing a main character and finally sharing the story with others. Each step has some good suggestions for what to consider while writing a story. *How to Write a Story* (2020) also encourages creativity and imparts confidence to emerging writers. This is a good book to show that the writing process doesn't vary much whether you are a first-grader or a published children's author.

Eddie's Garden and How to Make Things Grow (Garland, 2009) follows a family's horticultural efforts to plant a vegetable garden. At the conclusion of the story, novice gardeners will find instructions for growing Eddie's plants, along with other pertinent information on soil, seeds, container gardening, and possible pests. Many early childhood classrooms plant seeds in small containers or in a school-wide garden. A teacher might read the directions and then work with the children, reading the directions again as the children complete each step.

Books can serve as models for children to dictate or write their own directions for doing or making something. Can they describe the procedure clearly enough for another child to follow the directions? A humorous example of writing directions for a unique task can be found in *How to Walk an Ant* (Derby, 2019). Amariya claims she is a skilled ant walker and offers her expertise in this clever nine-step guide. There are basic rules and helpful tips such as "Don't be antsy" and "Ants can smell fear with their ANTennae." This book would be useful and appreciated by first- through third-graders. Books that describe "how to" can assist students in following a process in order to achieve a desired goal, even if the task is one-of-a-kind.

Expanding the Ability to Reason Logically

For young children, basic experiences with logical thinking involve working with *if . . . then* propositions. If it rains, then we won't be able to go on the picnic. Certainly, much literature involves cause-and-effect relationships.

Letting children predict what will happen next in a story is one technique for encouraging them to think about causality and to determine when connections between events appear reasonable.

In Mark Hoffman's (2020) *Dirt Cheap*, Birdie wants to buy an XR1000 Super Extreme Soccer Ball. Since money doesn't grow on trees, or "anywhere for that matter," Birdie decides to sell dirt from her yard for twenty-five cents a bag. Soon she has raised enough money to purchase the ball, but her yard is completely demolished. What's a girl to do but start her own lawn-care service to raise money to buy, what else, dirt?

Another humorous cause-and-effect story is author and illustrator Adam Rex's (2020) *On Account of the Gum*. This laugh-out-loud tale begins by showing a young girl in bed blowing bubbles with her gum that soon rolls out of her mouth and into her hair. There are numerous attempts, informed by a variety of sources including websites, newspapers, and a well-meaning aunt, that only compound the problem. Soon the girl not only has gum in her hair but also butter, grass, noodles, a rabbit, and so much more. A couple of twists and turns as well as an unexpected ending show that one, or many, well-intended decisions can leave to a very unfortunate situation.

Encouraging Critical Thinking

The term *critical thinking* is used in this text to indicate children's thinking that involves making sense of information, inferring, analyzing, synthesizing, and comparing and contrasting. It is thinking that goes beyond the literal level. Strategies for encouraging children to think critically include:

- **Asking open-ended questions.** Literal questions are those where the answer is within the text whereas open-ended questions require children to pause and ponder. "What part of the story did you like? Why?" or "What do you think is happening?" or "What do you think [character name] will do next?"
- **Fostering curiosity.** Young children often ask "why" as they try to make sense of the world around them. Encourage children to explore, ask questions, and indulge in activities that will further their curiosity such as visits to the zoo, playing with blocks, exploring different art media, and of course, being exposed to a range of topics and stories found in books.
- **Evaluating information.** In sharing literature with children, particularly nonfiction, use strategies such as think-aloud to demonstrate your own thinking in evaluating whether the

information is true. For fiction stories, question if what a character is suggesting might be accurate or even feasible. Consider questions such as "Do you think the way they solved the problem in the story was a good solution?"

- **Promoting interests.** Share a variety of books with children by various authors and illustrators as well as different genres. Nonfiction and poetry (other than rhyming stories) are often not selected for reading aloud. Choose books about different places, people, and experiences. Possibly, a child will gain an interest in elephants, fire trucks, or even be intrigued by a specific book character or an author's books. Read widely to encourage and promote new and ongoing interests of children and promote critical thinking.

The research, book titles, and instructional strategies featured in this chapter foster critical thinking. As you read to and with children, devise questions that will develop higher-level thinking to engage children in processes such as interpretation (explaining cause-and-effect and drawing inferences), synthesis (combining pieces of information in a new way), and application (applying ideas from literature to new situations). Try to state your questions as concisely as possible so that young children don't lose the thread of meaning or answer one part before you finish the entire question. Pace yourself to wait for answers. If the question requires thought, then you must give children time to think. Silence makes some teachers and childcare providers nervous, so they answer the question themselves or ask another question to fill the space. Give children time to think! Also remember that not every book should be followed by questions. Discussion is only one means of exploring a book's ideas more fully. You need a balance between discussion, activities, and no follow-up at all—just sheer enjoyment.

Engaging in Problem-Solving

It's important that you help children to regularly define and solve their problems. How can Noah get a turn at the water center? What can Emma do to keep Liam from teasing her? What could the class make as gifts for their parents?

Literature presents ample opportunities for children to define and suggest possible solutions to the problems of book characters. Their solutions may not be ones chosen by the book characters but may offer an opportunity for additional conversation about problem-solving. It is important to help children realize there may be many solutions to a problem and that solutions are often evaluated according to their consequences. Some books present problems much like those children have themselves; others may be totally in the realm of fantasy.

A common dilemma for many children, particularly toddlers and preschoolers, is that of sharing. Familiar characters such as Anna Dewdney's Llama Llama provide children with ways to solve problems such as with *Llama Llama Time to Share* (2012). Nelly Gnu is visiting Llama Llama for a playdate and both struggle with sharing their toys. Ask children what they would do. Mo Willems's Gerald and Piggie are also well-loved characters that young children enjoy. *Should I Share My Ice Cream?* (Willems, 2011) is a question Gerald is pondering as he holds his "awesome, yummy, sweet, super, great, tasty, nice, cool ice cream." However, the ice cream is melting fast and Gerald's best friend, Piggie, isn't there to share it with him. What's an elephant to do? As with all Elephant and Piggie books, the solution to the problem is humorous and satisfying.

Viewing a problem through a "silly lens" can help make the point as in Laura Gehl's *One Big Pair of Underwear* (2014). Bears, yaks, goats, and cats just *hate* to share. There also never seems to be enough of anything for all the animals. The twisting, bouncy rhymes in this humorous story will provoke uncontrollable laughter as two bears contemplate sharing one pair of underwear. Sometimes humor reflects the absurdity of a situation that will have children pause to consider their own actions. Children can tell about a time they did or didn't share with a sibling, friend, or classmate. They also might want to share their reasons for why they didn't do so. Pose the question of how they would feel if someone didn't share with them or take turns at something they wanted to do.

Children can be asked to brainstorm ideas for ways they can share with others. In brainstorming, children try to think of as many ideas as they can, not stopping to evaluate any of them. The teacher lists their suggestions on the board or on chart paper. Once all the ideas are listed, the teacher leads a discussion to look at each suggestion and tell what might happen if it were done. As a group, the children decide on which solution they think has the most merit and discuss it further.

Because many stories involve some problem that must be solved, it is possible to stop in almost any book and ask children what the problem is and what solutions they might have for it. Doing this on a regular basis, however, is likely to lessen the enjoyment of the story. Select only one or two books on occasion that lend themselves to rich discussions about problem-solving. Look for ones where the problem is fairly clear.

Thinking of solutions to problems of book characters can be like a game. The idea is to present alternatives, not to guess what happened in the book.

For this reason, you might ask some of your problem-solving questions after a book has been completed. You can then discuss what a character might have done other than what he or she actually did do.

Box 6.2 Books About Problem-Solving

Don't Feed the Coos! (Jonathan Stutzman; ill. Heather Fox, 2020)
A House in the Woods (Inga Moore, 2011)
The Little Blue Bridge (Brenda Maier; ill. Sonia Sánchez, 2021)
Stuck (Oliver Jeffers, 2011)
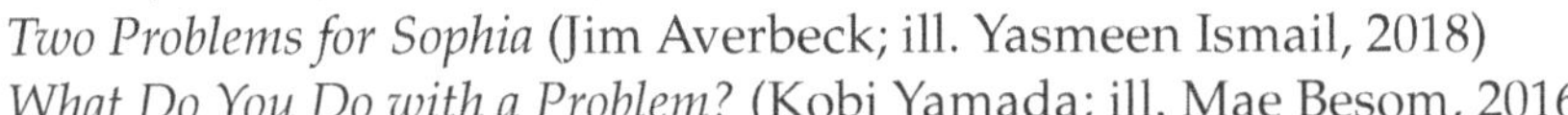
Two Problems for Sophia (Jim Averbeck; ill. Yasmeen Ismail, 2018)
What Do You Do with a Problem? (Kobi Yamada; ill. Mae Besom, 2016)

Nurturing Intellectual Development

Young children come to school with a wealth of information. They are attempting to organize that information, make sense of their world, and integrate their experiences. They are actively constructing concepts and engaging in the thought processes that are foundational in concept formation. Until they are six or seven, children tend to rely more on sensory data than on logic to reach conclusions regarding physical objects. They may also engage in reasoning by going from particular to particular without reference to the general, resulting in faulty conclusions.

Books offer opportunities for children to acquire and refine concepts. Often information that children could not discover on their own is presented in books. Other books, particularly concept books, are in themselves teaching aids because they organize information logically and present it with illustrations that add to children's understanding. Literature can both stimulate children to explore a topic and provide reinforcement for the knowledge they have acquired through direct experience.

Instructional Strategy from the Field: Partner Writing and Storytelling

Paige Robison teaches first grade at High Tech Elementary North County in San Marcos, California. Paige shares, "Writing at our school is usually centered around project-based learning, so students are engaged and motivated to create meaningful work for an authentic audience." She teaches several lessons to prompt the writing process using drawings that will enable children to tell their stories to a partner for feedback.

Lesson 1: Demonstrate to children how to use touch and tell where they will draw their story ideas to include a beginning, middle, and ending. When they are ready, they will touch each part of the paper and tell their story. Paige uses this framework:

1. Think of an IDEA
   a. A thing you do
   b. A thing that happened to you
2. PLAN
   a. Touch and tell
   b. Sketch across the pages
3. WRITE

Paige models how to think of an idea and then brainstorms ideas with students for their stories. Children then share their idea(s) with a partner.

Lesson 2: The focus of the second lesson is to expand on the story idea. Paige asks students to think about what they could add to their story.

She adds a fourth item to the framework:

4. REVISE
   a. Who? Where? When? What? How?

Paige returns to the story she is modeling for students and asks them to help her add to it using details that answer who, where, what, when, and how questions.

Students return to the story they began during Lesson 1 to see what they could add using who, where, when, what, and how. They work with their partner again who helps them add details.

Lesson 3: In this third lesson, students will practice storytelling with their partners. Paige talks about the different tools that writers use. One tool is to talk to other writers. Students once again work with their partners to plan their writing. There are several goals in this lesson for students: help each other plan their stories; use exact words in the story; try to tell the stories again with more details. Students return to the touch-and-tell strategy. Paige also provides the plan for storytelling with a partner:

1. One child tells their story.
2. The partner pictures the story, like a movie in their mind, and asks questions.
3. The first child tells the story again and adds more details to it.
4. The partners then switch and the other child tells a story and gets feedback.

Lesson 4: Students next share their writing with the class. The other students share what they noticed as the child was reading his/her story and suggest possible details to add.

Lesson 5: The last lesson is for students to tell their stories to their partners. Paige reminds them to remember to tell the beginning, middle, and end.

Paige sometimes will use Flipgrid to record students as they read their first drafts so other students can comment on the strengths of the story and suggest revisions.

Name:

Beginning

The Primary Pieces 2022

Name:

Middle

The Primary Pieces 2022

Name:

End

The Primary Pieces 2022

Name: Silas K

3

Beginning

one dpy a bee was

croling on my nek.

Name:

Middle

Professional References Cited

Anderson, J. L., Ellis, J. P., & Jones, A. M. (2014). Understanding early elementary children's conceptual knowledge of plant structure and function through drawings. *CBE Life Sciences Education, 13*(3), 375–386.

Barman, C. R., Stein, M., McNair, S., & Barman, N. (2006). Students' ideas about plants and plant growth. *American Biology Teacher*, 68, 73–79.

Bell, B. F. (1981). What is a plant? Some children's ideas. *New Zealand Science Teacher, 31,* 10–14.

Charlesworth, R. & Lind, K. K. (2010). *Math and science for young children* (6th ed.). Delmar Cengage Learning.

Essa, E. L. & Burnham, M. M. (2020). *Introduction to early childhood education*. Sage.

Gelman, S. A. (1996). Concepts and theories. In *Perceptual and cognitive development*. Academic Press.

Hohl, S. (November 23, 2021). Humorous Picture Books with Cindy Derby. https://www.stefaniehohl.com/new-blog/2021/11/22/i1kss2gzfd-7jo5u1l60oxb3t1gt75m

Huitt, W. & Hummel, J. (2003). Piaget's theory of cognitive development. *Educational Psychology Interactive*. Valdosta State University. [retrieved August 10, 2020 from http://chiron.valdosta.edu/whuitt/col/cogsys/piaget.html]

Lynch, S. A. & Warner, L. (2013). How adults foster young children's intellectual development. *Young Children*, *68*(2), 86–91.

McNair, S. & Stein, M. (2001). Drawing on their understanding: Using illustrations to involve deeper thinking about plants. Paper presented at the Association for the Education of Science Annual Meeting, January 18, 2001.

Papalia, D. & Martorell, G. (2021). *Experience human development* (14th ed.). McGraw-Hill.

Piaget, J. & Inhelder, B. (1969). *The psychology of the child*. Basic Books.

Vygotsky, L. (1978). *Mind in society: The development of higher psychological processes*. Harvard University Press.

Children's Literature Cited

Arrhenius, Ingela. P. (2019). *Where's the kangaroo?* Nosy Crow.

Arrhenius, Ingela P. (2021). *Where's the fire truck?* Nosy Crow.

Atinuke. (2019). *B is for baby*. Ill. Angela Brooksbank. Candlewick Press.

Buehner, Caralyn & Buehner, Mark. (2007). *Goldilocks and the three bears*. Penguin.

Collins, Ross. (2020). *This is a dog*. Nosy Crow.

Cordell, Matthew. (2017). *Wolf in the snow*. Feiwel & Friends.

Cordell, Matthew. (2019). *Explorers*. Feiwel & Friends.

Crews, Donald. (1978). *Freight train*. Greenwillow.

Derby, Cindy. (2019). *How to walk an ant*. Roaring Brook.

Derby, Cindy. (2022). *Blurp's book of manners*. Roaring Brook.

Dewdney, Anna. (2012). *Llama Llama time to share*. Viking Books for Young Readers

Elya, Susan Middleton. (2010). *Rubia and the three osos*. Ill. Melissa Sweet. Disney Hyperion.

Fliess, Sue. (2021). *Goldilocks and the three engineers*. Ill. Petros Bouloubasis. Albert Whitman & Co.

Garland, Sarah. (2009). *Eddie's garden and how to make things grow*. Frances Lincoln.

Gehl, Laura. (2014). *One big pair of underwear*. Beach Lane Books.

Harris, Chris. (2020). *The alphabet's alphabet*. Ill. Dan Santat. Little, Brown and Company.

Hesselberth, Joyce. (2016). *Shape shift*. Henry Holt.

Higgins, Carter. (2021). *Circle under berry*. Chronicle Books.

Hoffman, Mark. (2020). *Dirt cheap*. Knopf.

Jenkins, Steve & Page, Robin. (2017). *Who am I?: An animal guessing game*. Houghton Mifflin Harcourt.

Jenkins, Steve & Page, Robin. (2020). *What do you do if you work at the zoo?* Houghton Mifflin Harcourt.

Jocelyn, Marthe. (2017). *Sam sorts*. Tundra.

Lê, Minh. (2020). *Lift*. Ill. Dan Santat. Disney Hyperion.

Litwin, Eric. (2012). *Pete the Cat and his four groovy buttons*. Ill. James Dean. Harper.

Lobel, Anita. (2012/2022). *10 hungry rabbits*. Simon & Schuster.

Lobel, Anita. (2021). *Ducks on the road: A counting adventure*. Simon & Schuster.

Lobel, Arnold. (1970). *Frog and Toad are friends*. Harper & Row.

Lyon, George Ella. (2011). *All the water in the world*. Ill. Katherine Tillotson. Atheneum.

MacDonald, Suse. (2009). *Shape by shape*. Simon & Schuster.

Macorol, Catherine. (2022). *A is for axolotl*. Henry Holt.

Maier, Brenda. (2018). *The little red fort*. Ill. Sonia Sánchez. Scholastic Press.

Mariconda, Barbara. (2008). *Sort it out*. Ill. Sherry Rogers. Mount Pleasant, SC: Arbordale.

Marshall, James. (1988). *Goldilocks and the three bears*. Dial.

Messner, Kate. (2015). *How to read a story*. Ill. Mark Siegel. Chronicle Books.

Messner, Kate. (2020). *How to write a story*. Ill. Mark Siegel. Chronicle Books.

Numeroff, Laura. (1985). *If you give a mouse a cookie*. Ill. Felicia Bond. HarperCollins.

Numeroff, Laura. (1991). *If you give a moose a muffin*. Ill. Felicia Bond. HarperCollins.

Numeroff, Laura. (1998). *If you give a pig a pancake*. Ill. Felicia Bond. HarperCollins.

Numeroff, Laura. (2011). *If you give a dog a donut*. Ill. Felicia Bond. HarperCollins.

Palantini, Margie. (2011). *Goldie and the three hares*. Ill. Jack E. Davis. Katherine Tegen Books.

Pinkney, Jerry. (2006). *The little red hen*. Dial.

Portis, Antoinette. (2019). *Hey, water!* Holiday House.
Reinhart, Matthew. (2021). *Colors: My first pop-up!* Ill. Ekaterina Trukhan. Abrams Appleseed.
Rex, Adam. (2020). *On account of the gum*. Chronicle Books.
Rosen, Michael. (2009). *We're going on a bear hunt*. Ill. Helen Oxenbury. McElderry Books.
Rosenthal, Amy Krouse. (2009). *Duck! Rabbit!* Chronicle Books.
Schrey, Sophie. (2017). *Where's the penguin?* Ill. Chuck Whelon. Aladdin.
We're going on a bear hunt: My first 1 2 3. (2020). Candlewick Press.
We're going on a bear hunt: My first abc. (2020). Candlewick Press.
Wick, Walter. (1997). *A drop of water: A book of science and wonder*. Scholastic.
Willems, Mo. (2003). *Don't let the pigeon drive the bus!* Hyperion.
Willems, Mo. (2008). *The pigeon wants a puppy!* Hyperion.
Willems, Mo. (2011). *Should I share my ice cream?* Hyperion.
Willems, Mo. (2012). *Goldilocks and the three dinosaurs*. Balzer & Bray.
Willems, Mo. (2019). *The pigeon HAS to go to school!* Hyperion.
Willems, Mo. (2022). *The pigeon will ride the roller coaster!* Union Square Kids.

7

Supporting Children's Personality Development

> When I was little, I was really scared to jump off the diving board, even though I loved swimming and I loved the water. So as a creator for kids, I like to tell stories that kids can relate to. I figured a lot of kids would have a similar experience. But even if it's not an experience specifically with a diving board and a pool, everybody can relate to fear and overcoming it.
>
> (Gaia Cornwall, author, in Wasseluk, 2019)

Personality is the unique traits of a child that distinguishes them from others. Sometimes a child might be fearless in their actions or may need to overcome a fear such as Jabari in Gaia Cornwall's story *Jabari Jumps* (2017) about a young boy who perseveres to overcome a fear of diving. Often the stories authors tell are rooted in their own childhood such as Cornwall's fear of the diving board. Behavior and attitude are a part of personality development as is self-confidence and self-esteem which Cornwall explores in her second book, *Jabari Tries* (2020). Both of these books are highlighted later in this chapter. Literature such as Cornwall's books offers children the opportunity to explore characters' dispositions and temperaments, both positive and challenging, as they examine their own.

Personality Development in Young Children

Teacher, clinician, and theorist in psychoanalysis and human development Erik H. Erikson has been vastly influential regarding concepts of individual

DOI: 10.4324/9781003367635-7

identity, growth, and life cycle. He sought to explain personality growth by describing how humans respond to potential conflicts at specific periods in their lives. Erikson (1986) posits eight stages in a total life span, of which the first four are most applicable for young children.

In the first year of life, Erikson reports that it is critical for children to develop trust and mistrust. Trust develops when the primary caregiver responds warmly and lovingly to the child. During the ages of two and three, children struggle for autonomy. The conflict is between autonomy and doubt. Children want to explore, do things for themselves, and to be in control. Sometimes toddlers have difficulty sharing toys and often cannot remember rules. Children who have been encouraged by their parents to be independent at this age are more motivated to achieve when they begin school than are children who were not rewarded for independent behavior.

At ages four and five, children have a conflict between initiative, wanting to carry out activities on their own, and guilt over what they would like to do. For preschool and kindergarten teachers, this is when children can be encouraged to make choices and take action on their own.

From ages six to 11, children struggle with industry versus inferiority. Productivity becomes important. Children want to complete tasks, learn what is expected of them, and gain recognition for their efforts. These are crucial years in the development of self-concept and self-esteem.

Self-concept refers to individuals' ideas of their capabilities—what they see themselves as able to do. *Self-esteem* is the value individuals put on themselves or how worthy they feel. Self-concept and self-esteem are influenced strongly by how others react to and treat the individual. Children will think more highly of themselves when they know the important people in their lives value them. They become confident, leading them to attempt difficult tasks and anticipate success. Teachers and childcare professionals can aid the development of positive self-concepts in children by suggesting challenging yet attainable tasks. They can also show they value and support each child's efforts.

The development of self-concept begins early at home. So, too, does another learning based on children's interactions with parents. This is the process of identification where an individual accepts another's characteristics and beliefs as their own. For example, a boy may walk just like his father, or a girl may use her mother's mannerisms and voice inflection. This early identification with the parent of the same sex leads to adopting the sex roles considered appropriate in a particular culture. "Gender is one of the first social categories children become aware of and, in early childhood, is highly important to most children" (Haim & Lindner, 2013, p. 1). It is important to remember that identification is a lifelong process. As children encounter a larger social world, they begin identifying with models other than their parents. For example, teachers, friends, and characters from books, movies, and television may all be emulated. Thus, children acquire a complex system of beliefs and behaviors.

Children starting school are learning about themselves, their emotions, and their physical and social environments. One child may realize that his temper tantrum, which effectively provided attention at home, is ignored at school. Another child may find that many of her classmates, like her, fear the dark and being left alone. As children learn ways of expressing and managing their feelings, they realize what acceptable behavior in a particular situation is and what is not. In seeking to help children, the adult must provide experiences that enhance each child's self-concept, help them function as independently as possible, and assist them in dealing successfully with their emotions.

Involving Children in Making Choices

"Would you like to hear a story?" is often more of a rhetorical rather than a real question posed in a classroom or childcare center. You are not asking children for their preferences; you are telling them it is story time and the adult is going to read to them. Listen to your way of telling children about planned activities. If they have no choice, introduce the activity in a statement rather than a question form, such as, "Today, I will read a story about Elephant and Piggie," or, "Please get ready for story time. I think you'll be surprised how this story ends."

Presenting Options

Begin to think of ways children can be encouraged to make choices. If you present children with a choice, you must be willing to accept their decision. This means you should not offer objectionable options. As you share literature with children, there are many opportunities for them to make choices and ways for you to structure the choice-making so that all the alternatives are acceptable. Some are very simple ones. You may ask children which story or poem they would like to hear read or reread. Narrow the choices to two or three, and have all available. Poetry especially lends itself to this type of choice-making because poems become better liked as they become more familiar. In March, one preschool teacher constructed a poster board that featured different colored kites with poems about spring written on them. Children could select one of the kites, and the teacher would read the poem. After several days, the children knew which kite had the poem they particularly liked. Rereading poems helps children find poetry pleasurable and gives them a chance to choose.

Sometimes the choice will be one of sequence: What will be done first? Would they like to hear the story before or after snack time? Would they want to have art or story time first? These choices are group ones, where each child's opinion counts but are decided by what the majority prefers. Many others can be individual choices, where one child makes a choice, and the decision involves only the child's behavior.

One area for choice is whether the child wants to listen to a story. It may be in the form of announcing that all who are ready for a story should come to the story circle or go to the corner where an aide is sitting with the book to be read. One elementary school librarian reads to children before school each morning. Sometimes it is a picture book. Other times he spends a few weeks reading a short chapter book. Children need to arrive at school approximately half an hour early to hear the story. Parents are also invited to attend and listen. However, parents must understand it is the child's choice whether to come to school early and listen to the story. And because the schedule of books to be read is posted on the school's website each week, children can also choose which stories they want to hear. The choice is theirs each day. They do not need to make a long-term commitment even if a chapter book is read because the librarian provides a quick synopsis of the previous chapter each morning. In a classroom or childcare facility, children can choose to listen or not by having a listening center set up in the room. Those who want to hear a story or poem may go to the center; those who do not can engage in other quiet activities.

Encouraging Book Selection

Young children should have opportunities to engage in their own book selection. They can pick which book they would like to check out from the library to take to their room or perhaps from the classroom or center to their homes. Children then need to have time to look at their books. The length of this period may be determined by the child's age or the amount of interest shown in the chosen books.

As you encourage children to make book choices, ensure they have the information necessary to formulate satisfactory ones. If they are selecting a book from the library, do they know where the picture-book section is? Where can they find poetry? How do they get a librarian to assist them if they cannot find what they want? Do readers know to open the book and try reading a page or two to see how difficult it is or even if they like the book's story? Do emergent readers know to examine the illustrations to determine if it's a book they want to spend time exploring? For young children, the choices might be narrowed. As a school librarian, I would select books and set them up on tables so kindergarten and first-grade students were not overwhelmed with so many choices. Of course, children could also roam the bookshelves to see if a particular book caught their eye.

Once they have made their choices, encourage children to stay with the book long enough to give it a good try. Although it is unreasonable to force children to keep looking at books they are tired of, it is equally unproductive to allow children to change their choices capriciously. A part of learning to make choices is accepting responsibility for them. If children have made poor choices, this is the time to discuss the selection process they used and how it could be modified for better results.

Building Self-Concept

Literature can assist children in developing positive self-concepts through content and theme and response-based activities that may follow the sharing of a book. One aspect of self-concept is recognizing one's strengths and weaknesses.

Recognizing Capabilities

Literature for young children can emphasize the many capabilities they possess. In a charming picture book by children's musician Justin Roberts, Sally McCabe is *The Smallest Girl in the Smallest Grade* (2014). No one really noticed the young girl, but Sally was definitely paying "super extra special attention" to everything around her. She saw the abandoned kite in the tree, heard the howl of a hound dog, and spied the stray cats conducting a meeting in the church parking lot. Sally also noticed that Kevin McKuen was pushed off a slide, Tommy Torino was tripped in the hall, and there was an utterance of mean words on the playground. Finally, Sally was tired of seeing the cruel actions and hearing the mean words. So, in a loud voice with her finger in the air, the young girl exclaimed, "Stop hurting each other! This is enough!" There were a few giggles, but more importantly, Sally's classmates, the lunch lady, and even the principal joined Sally with their fingers raised high. Soon courtesy and kindness abounded. The smallest girl in the smallest grade transformed the world, or at least Sally's school.

Beginning with a wave to say hello, *Hands Can* (Hudson, 2003) shows the different things the hands of children can do—catching, throwing, clapping, and playing peek-a-boo. This book is perfect for toddlers and preschoolers because it has a rhyming text that directly ties to clear, colorful photographs. It is also available in hardcover, board-book, and e-book editions. Children listening to the story might take turns telling one thing they can do with their hands or perhaps demonstrate or pantomime the skill. They might play follow the leader using their hands to imitate each action. Both content and activities reinforce the concept that children are capable.

For toddlers who are in the process of being potty trained, *Potty* (Patricelli, 2010) may provide support and inspiration. A diaper-wearing toddler has to go potty and doesn't want to go in his diaper. He watches what the kitty and doggy do but realizes that isn't for him. After a few wiggles and sound effects, the child eventually sits on the potty and finds success. This board book presents the topic of potty training in a delightful and amusing manner.

Seeing Oneself Realistically

Stories can assist children in seeing themselves realistically with a focus on their strong points. In Alice B. McGinty's *Step by Step* (2021), a young boy is ready to start school but is a bit nervous. The boy's father reassures him that just like all the other things he has learned to do, such as walking, dressing, and making new friends, he will now learn to write, read, and count. This will happen step by step. The rhyming text and the repeating phrase "That's the way to get it done . . . one by one," will engage young children as various tasks in the story are accomplished. There is also a diverse cast of characters depicted in the pastel-colored illustrations.

Starting school is a common experience depicted in literature for young children. Even though they may reach school age, some children might think they are not quite ready for this new experience. Such is the circumstance in *Clover Kitty Goes to Kittygarten* (Salas, 2020). Clover is convinced she is not prepared for school. When Clover arrives at her classroom, the sensory-sensitive kitty feels the room is too loud, the lights are too bright, and everyone is too close to her. So, she decides to quit "kittygarden." Maybe Clover will reconsider after a classmate comes to check on her. Very few stories focus on children who are sensitive to stimuli. This book will undoubtedly prompt discussion with young children.

As children view and compare themselves in relation to others, both in characteristics and physical appearance, books can help them make realistic yet positive judgments. Dot is the littlest person in her multiracial family and in her class. Even though she is small, Dot can do all kinds of things because she's *Not Little* (Myers, 2021). Dot knows the square root of sixty-four is eight and that Jakarta is the capital of Indonesia. However, she is questioned when she wants to check out lengthy books from the library and is dismayed at the grocery store when asked if she wants a sticker because she's a "little girl." When the new kid, Sam, joins her class, Dot thinks he might be smaller than her. When Sam is bullied at lunch, Dot steps up and challenges the mean kid. While Dot may be tiny, she recognizes her ability to stand up to others and not be defined by her small stature. Create a chart by listing each child's name and have them share what he or she can do. As the school year progresses, continue to add to the list as new strengths and skills are identified.

Recognizing Growth and Change

Books can lead to another aspect of self-concept, the realization that one is continually growing and changing. Stories for young children often approach the topic of growing and developing through the eyes of an older sibling experiencing the arrival of a new family member. A boy realizes *It's Big Brother Time!* (Ahuja, 2021) when he needs to teach his baby brother the house rules, such as not playing with *his* toys or using *his* big boy blankie. While these are the boy's rules, the illustrations show the baby doing the opposite. By the story's end, the boy realizes his baby brother is destined to be his new best friend.

Little Miss, Big Sis (Rosenthal, 2015) uses bouncy, rhyming text as a young girl encounters her new baby sister, who seems to only sleep, fuss, eat, drool, and cry. Big sis comes up with a plan to help, and soon the two are inseparable. Even though baby sister is still annoying at times, the two are "forever connected." Peter H. Reynolds's cartoon-like, expressive illustrations will help budding big sisters and brothers discover the behavior, actions, and love a new baby will bring. Other books on the topic of a new baby in the family will assist siblings in understanding that changes will occur and that they are growing up and changing, too.

Children might articulate a list of skills they have acquired to demonstrate changes that aren't related solely to physical appearance but may include new abilities. They could create poems using the structure, "I used to __________," and with the next line being "But now I______________" (Koch, 2000). This results in a poem that tells about the changes in their lives. Children might tell stories about times when they learned to do something special: cross the street by themselves, ride a bicycle, or fix their cereal in the morning. They might even draw pictures showing what they hope to be able to do next year. The children's poems will relate to the good feelings of mastering new skills. Children will recognize that growth takes time; not all skills are acquired the moment one wants.

Becoming Confident

You can support children in seeing themselves as capable and having within themselves the resources to help meet challenges or unexpected demands. Many of the books you share with children will offer a story about a real or imagined character that succeeds in coping with a problem.

Overcoming fear and gaining confidence is something many children encounter just as author Gaia Cornwall shared in the quote at the beginning of this chapter. In *Jabari Jumps* (Cornwall, 2017), a young boy announces to his father, "I'm jumping off the diving board today!" After all, Jabari had finished his swimming lessons and passed his swim test, so now he was ready to jump. Once the father, son, and baby sister arrive at the pool, Jabari hesitates before climbing the very tall ladder. After much delay, Jabari decides that tomorrow might be a better day for diving. "It's okay to feel a little scared," his father reminds him. So Jabari takes a deep breath, ascends to the top of the ladder, curls his toe around the edge of the diving board—and jumps! "I'm a great jumper!" Jabari exclaims after the successful dive. In another story, *Jabari Tries* (Cornwall, 2020), frustration abounds as he attempts to make a flying machine. Once again, confidence overcomes self-doubt, and Jabari finds success.

In *When Sophie Thinks She Can't . . .* (Bang, 2018), Sophie believes she isn't smart after trying and trying to place tangrams into a perfect square. "I can't do ANYTHING!" she thinks. When her teacher assigns the task of building different rectangles using 12 small squares, Sophie knows she is doomed to fail. However, it appears the other children are struggling as well. The teacher tells them they may not have figured it out *yet* and to keep trying. Soon, the children develop multiple ways of creating rectangles. On the walk home, Sophie utters, "I'm getting smarter." An author's note talks about "fixed" and "growth" mindsets and how children may believe they can't do something but instead need to continue to grow by engaging in challenging tasks.

"You know, there's NOTHING I can't do when I believe in myself" begins the humorous story of *The Little Butterfly that Could* (Burach, 2021). A butterfly needs to migrate but has become separated from the group of butterflies. A whale befriends the befuddled butterfly and informs the insect that it must travel 200 miles to the migration point. "I'll never make it!" is the butterfly's response. However, with encouragement from the whale ("Believe you can"), and a lot of procrastination and doubt on the part of the butterfly, the journey finally begins. Two hundred miles later, the butterfly is reunited with the other butterflies, just in time to go dormant for the winter. There's a bit of science woven into this confidence-building story told through comic-style illustrations and hilarious speech bubbles.

Identifying with One's Heritage

Self-concept involves identification with one's heritage. There are books for young children that address this theme directly. There are times during the year when a focus is on heritage, such as Hispanic Heritage Month, Asian American and Pacific Islander Month, or Native American Heritage Month. Try not to isolate books about heritage and culture into a single month. Rather, infuse these books into the curriculum and select them as excellent options for reading aloud to young children throughout the year.

Fry Bread: A Native American Family Story, written by Kevin Noble Maillard and illustrated by Juana Martinez-Neal (2019), received the 2020 Robert F. Sibert Informational Book Award. Fry bread is not only food but also shape, sound, color, and flavor. It brings family and friends together for weekday suppers or festive holidays. The brief, yet detailed text relates the story and history of this indigenous staple. In addition, the author's note presents further details about fry bread's various aspects, making this an excellent picture book to share with preschoolers and primary-age students.

Alma Sofia Esperanza José Pura Candela has a very long name that just didn't seem to be a good fit. In *Alma and How She Got Her Name* (Martinez-Neal, 2018), the young girl hears the story of each family member whose name she has inherited and their extraordinary traits—ones that Alma possesses as well. Her father tells her that Alma was the name picked just for her so she can craft her own story that may be passed down to future generations. The graphite and colored pencil artwork is set against cream-colored backgrounds, making the blue and red details in the illustrations pop. There is a melding of past and present as Alma becomes enriched by learning her family's history and the significance of her name.

Author Mitali Perkins shares a story inspired by her childhood in *Home Is in Between* (2021). Shanti and her family have left the warm monsoon rains of India and immigrated to the United States. Soon, Shanti feels pulled in two different directions as she attempts to hold onto her heritage while trying to acclimate to a new culture. Trick-or-treating, ballet class, and books in English are unfamiliar, while funny stories in Bangla, dancing to Bollywood movies, and singing village songs as Ma plays the harmonium are what Shanti knows. Ultimately, Shanti discovers a balance between the two cultures that brings her peace. Observant children will spot the blue toy elephant that Shanti hugs in many scenes.

Shirley is spunky and full of big ideas for making her family's store profitable. In *Big Dreams, Small Fish* (Cohen, 2022), Shirley's parents' biggest problem is selling gefilte fish. When family members rush to the hospital because Aunt Ida is having a baby, Shirley, and store employee Mrs. Gottlieb, are left in charge. The store is soon bustling with customers, and Shirley has an idea—package the gefilte fish with each purchase as a "surprise." The only surprise Shirley's parents have when they return home is that the fish was given away instead of sold. However, the following morning customers are lined up to purchase this new delicacy. A glossary of Yiddish terms and an explanation and recipe for gefilte fish complete this enjoyable story about an enterprising young girl and a reminder that a new food might become a favorite dish.

Stories about characters of varying ethnic backgrounds are featured in this chapter and throughout the book. The suggested titles assist children in learning about others who are different from themselves, which is part of children's personality and social development. Therefore, teachers and child-care professionals should have a variety of cultures represented in the books they choose, no matter the ethnic makeup of their class. You will also want to be certain that you read books whose major characters represent the ethnic backgrounds of the children in your class.

Examining Gender Portrayal

Just as books present models for ethnic identification, so do they present models for gender identification. When reading books to children, be aware that you are showing them one perception of how the world is structured. For example, if you read only books that show female characters as passive and male characters as active, you are saying to them that this is the behavior expected of each gender.

Many books for children have broken away from gender-role stereotypes. They include more female characters who are active, assertive, and competent. Girls in some books are portrayed as risk-takers and successful in tasks previously represented by males. On the other hand, boys in stories are permitted to show tenderness and may cry. One second-grade girl pondered why it had been considered acceptable for girls to cry but not for boys to do so. Her solution was simple: Girls had more to cry about. Naturally, that triggered a lively discussion.

As you select books, eliminate those that present stereotyped characters. Stereotyping means that all individuals within a group are described as though they were alike: boys play baseball, and girls play with dolls. Books with stereotyped characters are not quality stories because the author has not developed the individuality necessary for good characterization. Thus, do not select these books on literary grounds.

A book's older copyright date does not mean that a stereotype exists. Some recent books present stereotyped characters, and many old favorites do not. One could hardly ask for a more dynamic and unique female character than *Madeline* in the books by Ludwig Bemelmans, the first of which was published in 1939. *William's Doll* by Charlotte Zolotow was published in 1972 and one of the first picture books to address gender stereotypes featuring a boy whose wish was for a doll. Many bibliographies of nonstereotyped books for children are provided by libraries and featured on numerous blogs and websites. Make sure you balance the types of characters in the total body of literature that you select. Just a reminder that even if another individual has recommended the book, it is always important that you pre-read it before sharing it with children.

Evaluating Nonconforming Gender Roles in Children's Books

Over the past few decades, picture books that tell stories about boys who dance, cook, and play with dolls have been published. There are also books where girls invent, build, and play with cars. Today, gender stereotypes are being challenged with an understanding that children need literature with non-traditional and non-sexist roles (Paris, 2011). Regrettably, picture books featuring characters who are gender nonconforming may be viewed as inappropriate for young children (Malcom & Sheahan, 2019). There needs to be an understanding by parents, teachers, and caregivers that nonconformity has nothing to do with sexual orientation or gender identity. Gender nonconformity in children's literature can assist young children in finding, accepting, and loving who they are without fear of prejudice; being a girl does not mean identifying with princesses and wearing pink, and boys can enjoy ballet lessons or wear a range of clothing.

Fred Gets Dressed (2021) was inspired by author Peter Brown's childhood. This charming and entertaining story depicts a young boy who loves to be naked. That is until he goes romping into his parents' closet and becomes inspired to try on their clothes. His father's shirt and tie don't feel comfortable, but his mother's blouse, scarf, and shoes are just perfect. What adds to the ensemble is a strand of pearls and a touch of lipstick—however, the application of it does go somewhat awry. When Fred's parents discover their newly outfitted son, they engage in a little wardrobe and makeup fun themselves.

Annie's Plaid Shirt by Stacy B. Davids (2015) depicts a young girl who loves wearing her plaid shirt to school, to parties—everywhere! So Annie thinks wearing her plaid shirt to Uncle Benny's wedding is perfectly acceptable. However, her mother has different ideas about what a girl should wear and the two go shopping for a frilly dress. When Annie's brother, Albert, questions why Annie has to wear a dress, his mother replies, "Little girls always wear dresses to weddings." Thanks to a caring and crafty brother, Annie is able to wear her plaid shirt as part of her wedding-worthy ensemble.

On Fridays, the whole school has an assembly where different children share their unique gifts, whether it's playing the tuba, doing magic tricks, or telling jokes. This week it's *John's Turn* (Barnett, 2022). John goes backstage and changes into a white leotard, black pants, and black slippers. When the curtain opens, John looks out at his classmates as his heart beats rapidly. Then the music begins to play, and John begins his ballet. Several pages show the sheer joy on John's face as he dances. When the music ends, John takes a bow and then hears the thunderous applause. The expressive art features confused looks on John's classmates' faces as the string music begins. Soon, the expressions turn to smiles and enjoyment as they watch John's talent and passion for dancing.

Rosie Revere, Engineer (Beaty, 2013) is an imaginative thinker whose inventions include hot dog dispensers, helium pants, and python-repelling cheese hats. After being laughed at for one of her creations, Rosie hides her tinkering under the bed. When great-great-aunt Rose (Rosie the Riveter) arrives, she encourages the budding engineer that a flop isn't anything to fear, but rather that is how you learn. A historical note shares information about Rosie the Riveter and her slogan, "We can do it!" The lively text and the colorful watercolor illustrations depict a young girl who is daring and imaginative—just like her aunt. *Izzy Gizmo* (Jones, 2017) is also about an aspiring inventor full of determination, ingenuity, and unique contraptions.

As you assess the role models in books that contribute to children's concept of their own sexuality and gender, plan to provide a variety of non-stereotypical characters such as those shared and allow discussion of roles. Literature offers a variety of characters and their actions that will broaden children's conceptions of themselves.

Box 7.1 Books Focused on Characters' Self-Esteem

I Am Every Good Thing (Derrick Barnes; ill. Gordon C. James, 2020)
If You Believe in Me (Rosemary Wells, 2022)
Sometimes, All I Need Is Me (Juliana Perdomo, 2022)
Stand Tall, Molly Lou Melon (Patty Lovell; ill. David Catrow, 2001)
Thelma the Unicorn (Aaron Blabey, 2015)
We Are Here (Tami Charles; ill. Bryan Collier, 2023)

Building Self-Esteem

Self-esteem is influenced strongly by the reaction of others to the individual. Children gain an impression of self-worth from their perception of the treatment the important people in their lives give them. Parents, teachers, caregivers, and classmates all contribute to the total picture. As a teacher or caregiver, you can influence this directly through your relations with the children and indirectly as you model behavior for children to use with others. You can also select curriculum materials and create activities that build self-esteem.

Using Content that Reaffirms Self-Worth

In exploring and reaffirming self-worth, children must understand that it comes from within. Grace Byers (2018) uses a lyrical text about loving who you are, respecting others, and being kind to one another in *I Am Enough*. This inspiring picture book presents diverse characters key to the young girl recognizing her self-worth. *I Am Me: A Book of Authenticity* (Verde, 2022) celebrates children being their true selves. This engaging picture book, illustrated by Peter H. Reynolds, reminds us that differences make life beautiful and that each of us matters, just as we are.

Board books by Jabari Asim, *Whose Knees Are These?* (2019a) and *Whose Toes Are Those?* (2019b), depict children of color and use a simple rhyme that assists in answering the book titles' questions. *Bright Brown Baby* (Pinkney, 2021) celebrates babies and includes five rhythmic poems perfect for sharing with newborns and toddlers. *I am Latino: The Beauty in Me* (Pinkney, 2007) contains buoyant text and joyful photographs that showcase traditional food, music, and more through the five senses using English and Spanish words and phrases. One of the critical components of sharing literature with children is that they can see themselves in the books they read. These diverse books all recognize and celebrate children while accentuating a sense of pride and self-worth.

In addition to diverse literature, there are stories that relate to feelings of self-worth that are applicable to many children. Max is lacking in self-confidence and supposedly in artistic ability when he proclaims, "I can't draw" (Martin, 2022). This conclusion is determined because Max's drawings look nothing like Eugene's (in fact, very few people would be able to match Eugene's drawings). In exchange for some of his cupcakes, Max reaches out to Eugene and asks for help learning how to draw. As Max and Eugene draw side by side, it is apparent the two differ in ability. Eugene suggests that Max copy his drawings, which solves one issue but then illuminates another—eliminating having fun. Finally, Max realizes he is an artist in his own way and exclaims, "I CAN DRAW!" Be sure to view the initial and final end pages for a tutorial on how to draw a cat. Through this process of self-doubt, Max finally understood that he is unique, and so is what he draws.

Who can resist a character who shouts, "I like myself" (Beaumont, 2004). The spunky girl is full of joy and loves everything about herself because "I'm ME!" Whether she had stinky toes, polka dot lips, or horns on her nose, she wouldn't care what others think of her. David Catrow's illustrations add to the quirkiness of the story. A book to pair with *I Like Myself!* is Kathi Appelt's *Incredible Me!* (2003). Stories where characters develop self-worth and those in which the characters exude it are both good to share with children.

Presenting Themes of Individuality

Children need to recognize and value their uniqueness. *Be Who You Are* (Parr, 2016) is the title and theme of this colorful book that advocates for individuality. Whether being silly or brave, sharing your feelings, or speaking your language, it's essential to be who you are. This book is perfect for toddlers and preschoolers, who will be encouraged to embrace all their unique qualities.

All children have a talent, whether it's physical such as singing, dancing, playing soccer, or walking the dog. Other talents often aren't quite as visible such as being friendly, treating others with kindness, or having a positive attitude. *Free to Be Elephant Me* by Giles Andreae (2021) begins with the young elephants trying to impress King Elephant Mighty with their talents, such as having a loud bellow or uprooting a tree. When it's Num-Num's turn, all attempts to show his abilities are laughed at by the King, and he is dubbed Elephant Nothing-at-All. The dejected elephant is devastated and searches for a new home. The animals who befriend him praise Num-Num for his attributes and encourage him to return and announce to the King his new name, Elephant Me! Sometimes it takes others to help children, and elephants, discover their personal talents.

One of the most beloved characters in children's books, and who definitely is her own pig, is Olivia. This high-spirited and quirky porcine questions why everyone wants to be a princess in Ian Falconer's *Olivia and the Fairy Princesses* (2012). At Pippa's birthday party, all attendees wore big, pink, ruffly skirts with sparkles. Olivia wore her French sailor shirt, a strand of pearls, and her gardening hat. And on Halloween, once again the girls were princesses while Olivia was a warthog. Oliva doesn't want to be like everyone else. After thinking about what she could be, a brilliant thought popped into her head. As with all of the Olivia books, there is a reference to a unique individual. This time, Olivia channels dancer and choreographer Martha Graham through a series of unique movements. Observant children will spy a photograph of the famous dancer and choreographer hanging above Olivia's bed.

All of these books, on different levels of difficulty, present a theme of the value of one's own decisions, special skills, and preferences. You can follow the reading of these books with activities that focus on your students' individuality. For example, have children make booklets about themselves, describing in words or pictures their special skills, what they might like to learn to do, what they enjoy, and what they dislike. Next, generate an "All About Me" box or bag. Each child can place four or five objects special to them or tell about something they like to do, places they have traveled, a photograph of a friend, family member, or pet, or a book they enjoy. This strategy works well for multilingual learners as they share something about themselves that others will connect with. Also, the teacher or parent can attach a sticky note to the items to further the learning of English and a sticky note in the child's language to assist others in learning new words as well. Finally, create a bulletin board containing giant puzzle pieces with each child's picture and sentence with the caption "We All Fit Together." Often, you can find a puzzle piece template on the internet or purchase an entire puzzle with blank pieces for a nominal cost.

Helping Children Understand and Express Their Emotions

Literature highlights the role of emotions in human lives. Books show what happens to a character, what a character does, and how that character feels. Recognizing the emotions being expressed is part of the reader's response to literature. The discussion of books significantly centers on characters' feelings towards one another and how their feelings influence their actions. Reading daily to children cannot help but aid their understanding of people and human emotions.

As you select books, it may be helpful for you to think of these four ways literature can contribute to young children's emotional growth. First, literature displays that many of the feelings children experience are also experienced by others, such as book characters, and are both normal and natural. Second, it explores feelings from several aspects, giving a fuller picture and providing the basis for naming those emotions. Third, literature, through the actions of various characters, shows options for dealing with particular emotions. And fourth, literature makes clear that one person experiences many emotions—sometimes conflicting.

Sad, Sad Bear (Gee, 2021) is a book that young children can relate to if their first time going to childcare or preschool made them sad. Mommy has to go to work, so Bear goes to Cub Care. He doesn't know anyone there at all, which makes him very, very sad. However, once Bear makes friends and begins to engage in all sorts of activities, such as building, cooking, and having a picnic, his sadness goes away and he can't wait to return to Cub Care tomorrow.

Molly Bang's *When Sophie Gets Angry—Really Really Angry* (1999) depicts Sophie's range of emotions through both text and illustration. Sophie's sister demands a turn at playing with the beloved stuffed gorilla, and her mother agrees. Sophie gets so angry that she wants to "smash the world to smithereens." Her anger is depicted through orange, red, and yellow illustrations. After Sophie calms down, her mood is shown in soothing tones of blue and green. Bang has created a story that will prompt children to discuss their emotions and also ways to resolve inner conflicts.

When reading books that depict characters' emotions, talk with children about what different colors represent. Red can mean anger but it can also show love. Blue is a calming color but can also be used to describe an emotion such as feeling blue. Young children can begin to learn how illustrators add meaning to the story through the colors they use.

Box 7.2 Books Focused on Characters' Emotional Response

Don't Worry, Murray (David Ezra Stein, 2022)
How to Help a Friend (Karl Newson; ill. Clara Anganuzzi, 2021)
Knuffle Bunny Free: An Unexpected Diversion (Mo Willems, 2010)
Louise the Big Cheese: Divine Diva (Elise Primavera; ill. Diane Goode, 2009)
Madeline Finn and the Therapy Dog (Lisa Papp, 2020)
Our Table (Peter H. Reynolds, 2021)

Discovering Others Share Similar Feelings

To show children that others have felt as they do, look for books that describe common childhood experiences. Books for toddlers and preschoolers often concentrate on a single emotion. They understand the distress felt by D.W. when she cannot find her blanket in *D.W.'s Lost Blankie* (Brown, 1998). Or they can share the nervous excitement of *The Night Before Preschool* (Wing, 2011) as a little girl anticipates the first day in a new school.

Children might relate to how Davy the sheep felt before his 12 brothers came along. *Another Brother* by Matthew Cordell (2012) shares Davy's feelings when he used to have time alone with his parents, who doted on him and gave him all the praise and attention he desired. Now his brothers follow him around and imitate his every move, prompting Davy just to want to be alone. When Davy realizes that being alone isn't quite what he remembered it to be, he discovers his brothers are now all doing their own thing—none of which Davy has any interest in doing. However, when another sibling arrives, Davy is thrilled to spend time with his new baby sister. After hearing this amusing story, children with younger siblings will want to share their feelings about a new baby in the house.

For some books, you can discuss with children times when they have felt the way the character does. At other times, you may want to focus entirely on the literature itself, drawing out how the character felt and how the author lets the reader know these feelings.

Examining the Emotions of a Single Book Character

Some of the books you read will show the many emotions of a single character. Preschoolers through primary-grade students enjoy reading about the antics of a rambunctious boy named David. David Shannon's semi-autobiographical picture books have become favorites because they present problems and emotions young children will find familiar. *No, David!* (1998) is a kid who breaks all of his mother's rules. He chews with his mouth open (and full of food), jumps on the furniture, and breaks his mother's vase. All this leads to his mother's constant cry, "No, David!" When *David Goes to School* (1999), he discovers his least favorite word, no, is spoken here also. No yelling, no pushing, no running in the halls. *David Gets in Trouble* (2002) is the series' third book, where the high-spirited boy always says, "It's not my fault! I didn't mean to! It was an accident." Whatever the situation, David has a good excuse for what has occurred. But David soon realizes that making excuses makes him feel bad, but saying he's sorry makes him feel better. In the most recent book, *Grow Up, David!* (2018), David is taunting his older brother by eating his Halloween candy, trailing him up the tree house, and making a mess in the bathroom. This time the repetitive phrase is, "You're too little!" Infants and toddlers can also meet David through board books with titles that include *David Smells!: A Diaper David Book* (2005a), *Oh, David!* (2005b), and *Oops!* (2005c).

Emergent readers enjoy the antics of Mo Willems's engaging characters, Elephant and Piggie. These best friends experience a range of emotions, such as sadness in *My Friend Is Sad* (2007a) and anxiousness regarding what to wear when Piggie shares, *I Am Invited to a Party* (2007b). Patience is demonstrated when Elephant realizes *Waiting Is Not Easy!* (2014), and they exhibit gratitude for their friends in *The Thank You Book* (2016).

A series of chapter books for second- and third-grade students features a lively character named Judy Moody, created by Megan McDonald. In the first *Judy Moody* (2000), third-grader Judy is in a bad mood on the first day of school until she gets an assignment to create a collage about herself. Next, *Judy Moody Gets Famous* (2001) when she realizes she could do something for others without seeking recognition. And finally, the plucky protagonist acquires a mood ring and tries to convince herself and her third-grade classmates that she can make predictions in *Judy Moody Predicts the Future* (2003). Recent books in the series include *Judy Moody Book Quiz Whiz* (2019) and *Judy Moody in a Monday Mood* (2021). In addition, Judy's brother Stink has his own series, including *Stink: The Incredible Shrinking Kid* (2013), *Stink and the Shark Sleepover* (2014), *Stink and the Hairy Scary Spider* (2020), and *Stink Superhero Superfan* (2023).

Following the reading of books such as these, plan ways for children to verbalize emotions, either their own or those of the book characters. They may add words to wordless picture books in dialogue or narrative form. They could dramatize a story, following the plot but providing dialogue, thus expressing feelings in their own words. Also, older children can role-play a situation. Look for times when children can use puppets or masks as they engage in dialogue. Children often speak more freely when they are speaking through an object such as a puppet.

Characters Who Overcome Fears

Typical childhood fears are the themes in some books and common occurrences in others. Characters may be frightened by animals or afraid of the dark. Sometimes children's fears are unfounded in reality, but at other times they are reflective of actual danger. In *Not Afraid of Dogs* (Pitzer, 2006), Daniel declares that he's not afraid of dogs; he just doesn't like them. When Aunt Rose goes on vacation, her dog Bandit comes to stay at Daniel's house resulting in the boy retreating to the safety of his bedroom. Daniel soon realizes that even dogs can be afraid, and he becomes the one to comfort Bandit during a thunderstorm. Children talking about their fears and those of characters in the books are gathering information that will help them determine which fears help provide an awareness of dangerous situations and which inhibit them in areas where the potential danger is minimal. In facing fears, they are taking the first step in overcoming them.

Literature can help children cope with fears of the known and unknown by providing knowledge about everyday objects, events, and new experiences they are about to undertake. *Saturday Is Swimming Day* (Yum, 2018), and a young girl always seems to wake up with a stomach ache. Once she arrives at the pool, the girl slowly changes into her strawberry-patterned swimsuit and joins the other children. The swimming instructor, Mary, tells the girl that it's okay to sit by the edge if she doesn't want to get in the water. The following Saturday, the girl once again has a stomach ache. Mary encourages her to practice kicks in the pool while she holds her. With continued encouragement, the girl gains confidence each week, and the stomach ache seems to go away. Many children will relate to the fear felt by the girl as they share stories about overcoming their own fears, possibly as they learned how to swim.

Young children are often afraid of separation. For decades, children and parents alike have found comfort in the suggestion of sharing a special "secret" by reading Audrey Penn's *The Kissing Hand* (1993). Many children suffered from separation anxiety following the pandemic when their parents began returning to work. *Wherever You'll Be* (Guttman, 2021) follows a working mother and her child throughout the day while they are apart. Whether at work or school, they find comfort in thinking of each other all through the day. This quiet story celebrates the connection between parent and child that transcends location and is another type of "secret" children can share with their parents.

Children between ages five and nine are in a period of realizing that death, the ultimate separation, is permanent. Books about the passing of a pet or grandparent will give them an idea of how others feel when a death occurs. Just as adults have varied beliefs about death, a range of opinions is also presented in literature. Children have a greater chance of coping if adults are honest with them, admitting that this final separation resulting from death is painful.

Over a year's time, you could read several books in which a death occurs, each giving new information about characters' responses to it. In the Caldecott Honor book *The Rough Patch* (Lies, 2018), Evan and his dog do everything together. Their favorite place is Evan's extraordinary garden, where plants and vegetables flourish. But when Evan loses his best friend, his garden is no longer a happy place. This heart-tugging story is multilayered and told through text and illustrations. Jane Yolen's (2011) *The Day Tiger Rose Said Goodbye* deals with the difficult topic of coping with the loss of a cat. Always be mindful of students' situations and sensitivity before reading any story about coping with death. Sometimes sharing a story about the death of a pet soon after a child has experienced this loss is not the right time.

The passing of a grandparent can also be difficult for young children. In *Grandpa's Stories* (Coelho, 2019), a girl and her grandfather explore the budding plants in springtime and engage in imaginary play with toy race cars in the summer. When autumn comes, her grandpa makes a notebook with handmade paper bound with ruby Indian-leather string so the girl can write and draw all her dreams. In the winter, her grandpa tells about the Indian sweets and homemade toys he had as a child. When the girl's grandpa dies, she discovers a new notebook where she writes and draws all of her favorite memories of the time the two spent together. This lovely book celebrates the relationship between grandparent and grandchild while accentuating that cherished memories can live on through stories.

To encourage children to talk about their fears and to see ways they might lessen them, read several books that present fears children commonly have. Some children may volunteer to talk about their fears; others may tell about them when asked. You will learn about areas where you may be able to help, and children may show empathy and offer valuable advice to one another.

Recognizing One's Values

Values are the belief system one holds about what is important. Children learn values from the people who are central to their lives. Parents are of primary importance for toddlers and preschool children; for the school-age child, teachers, peers, and parents have an influence. Children in school are exposed to more than one set of values and can think about them in terms other than Mommy is right, or Mommy is wrong.

In its exploration of actions and motivations for such, literature presents a panorama of value systems. Books presenting conflicts clearly lend themselves to discussions and activities by which children can judge their beliefs. C.J. wonders why he has to go with his Nana on the bus to a neighborhood with "crumbling sidewalks and broken-down doors, graffiti-tagged windows and boarded-up stores." It's the *Last Stop on Market Street* (de la Peña, 2015) where C.J. and Nana will soon serve food in an urban soup kitchen. At first, C.J. resents having to visit the rundown part of the town while his friends are having fun. However, the many diverse characters he meets on the bus and at the soup kitchen, along with the words of wisdom spoken by Nana, helps C.J. realize "sometimes when you are surrounded by dirt . . . you're a better witness for what's beautiful." You can ask children, "How did C.J.'s attitude change from the beginning of the story to the end? Have you ever been asked to do something you didn't want to do but you felt better after doing it?" Children can share their responses through art, writing, or oral activities. This is one step in discovering what they value, how consistently they initially perceive people or surroundings, and how they feel about it after knowing more.

Other times, you can emphasize the reasons for holding a particular value and the consequences of acting on it. In the classic book *Frederick* (Lionni, 1967), a group of mice is preparing for winter. All but Frederick are gathering and storing corn, nuts, and wheat. Frederick sits alone and explains that he is collecting sun rays, colors, and words for cold winter days. When winter arrives, the mice eat through their store of supplies. Then they call upon Frederick, who alleviates their discomfort by reciting a poem that makes them feel the sun and see the colors of the summer. They also share their remaining food with the whimsical mouse.

Ask children to write down whether Frederick should have been permitted to share the mice's food because he did not gather any of it. Having them write yes or no on paper forces them to decide for themselves and not be swayed by what a friend says or what the majority seems to feel. Those who said yes and those who said no can be grouped. Each group is to list all their reasons for feeling as they do. They could also be asked to select what the group thinks is the best reason.

Preschool, as well as primary-grade children, can identify the values a book character holds if they are asked what is important to that character. *The Empty Pot* by Demi (1990) focuses on a boy's honesty. When a Chinese emperor proclaims that his successor will be the child who grows the most beautiful flowers from the seeds they are given, Ping is overjoyed. The young boy loves flowers, and anything he plants bursts into bloom. But the seeds are not growing despite months of loving care. Even though Ping has an empty pot, he still appears before the emperor, who chooses the boy as his successor. It is revealed the seeds the children were given had been cooked and could not have possibly yielded the beautiful blossoms brought forth. The engaging text is coupled with equally stunning illustrations that will prompt discussion about the story and how it is told visually. Asking children if it is permissible to be dishonest in order to receive an honor or award will offer a lively conversation.

In these examples, children are not told what to believe but asked only to think about their beliefs. You will find literature often revolves around questions of values. The strategy of having students take a stand, think through their reasons for it, listen to the reasoning of those who differ, and discuss the consequences of acting on various value systems applies to many books. It opens the way for children to consider other positions and perhaps make more knowledgeable and informed choices.

Emotions, values, and feelings about self are all a part of personality. Erikson seeks to explain personality growth by describing how humans respond to conflicts at specific periods of their lives. The way adults and peers respond to them is central to how children resolve such conflicts and to the development of self-esteem and a positive self-concept. Literature can assist in this regard.

Instructional Strategy from the Field: Transitional Readers and Series Books

Series books such as Junie B. Jones, Magic Tree House, Percy Jackson and the Olympians, or Harry Potter have long been a staple in readers' lives. Children are drawn to series books because they offer stories that are humorous and sometimes poignant, feature common experiences that relate to children's lives, contain short chapters, focus more on plot and action than description, and invite readers to solve problems with the character(s).

Children in primary grades are making the transition to chapter books. To assist readers in selecting books that are appropriate to read independently, it's helpful to begin with what students have already been successful with and assist them in locating books that align with these reading preferences. "If you liked ____, you might like _____."

When Marie LeJeune was conducting research in a second-grade classroom, she conducted whole-class and individual conferring "interviews" about favorite books. Marie and the teacher kept running notes on what books might appeal to certain children. This enabled them to say to a student, "This book made me think of you." Marie knew that transitional readers liked "books which had reoccurring plots, continuing characters, familiar plot structures, text features, and appealing writing styles."

> I knew that in order to support students in being able to sustain comprehension, they needed to read text that was challenging, but not beyond their range of comprehension. We conducted mini-lessons on previewing books, making predictions, and inferring. One of the mini-lessons was to view the table of contents for students to predict, preview, and infer based on the chapter titles. After the mini-lesson, we set out book baskets containing a variety of transitional books that were grouped by genre, theme, author, characters, mysteries, adventures, friendship, graphic novel format, and others. Several different chapter book series were also book talked. We knew that series books were ones that several students were already reading. We conducted a second mini-lesson called Trying Something New. The following sentence stems helped to focus the lesson and the conversation about trying a new book:
>
> - If I try a new book . . .
> - When I tried a new book . . .
> - I got started reading my favorite series because . . .
>
> Some of the responses include, "I learned to like a new author," "I learned about a new format," and "I fell in love with a new character."

Sabina chose to read a book in the Lotus Lane series. This series has easy-to-read text, engaging characters, fast-paced plots, and illustrations on every page. One of the pages in the book shows where each of the four characters lives on Lotus Lane. Sabina drew a picture of her house and the one next door in response to the book. She also created a calendar similar to the one in the books showing different activities for each day. Sabina then wrote suggestions about things you can do when you are bored that could also be items on the calendar.

Series books are often some of the first sources of inspiration for student writers. They learn familiar patterns and features of their favorite series and mimic them in their writing. Students also understand important features of the narrative that often influence their writing as well.

11-2-17

Hi my name is Sohi[illegible]
I am waiting for us
to get t the market
thing 1 to do when
your bord. Read. Thing
2 wright. Thing 3 do
joks with your self.
Thing 4 talk to your
self. Thing 5 ask your
mom for a maker to
draw. Thing 6 look

ut the window. Thing 7
to do when your bord
make up your own
game. Thing 8 do
tricks with your 2
finggers. Thing 9 do
figger pupets with your
fingers. Thing 10
make anamals with your
hands. Thing 11 ask
your mom if you can

Professional References Cited

Erikson, E. (1986). *Childhood and society* (35th anniversary ed.). Norton.

Haim, M. L. & Lindner, N. C. (2013). Gender self-socialization in early childhood. *Encyclopedia on Early Childhood Development*. https://www.child-encyclopedia.com/pdf/expert/gender-early-socialization/according-experts/gender-self-socialization-early-childhood

Koch, K. (2000). *Wishes, lies, and dreams*. Perennial.

Malcom, N. L. & Sheahan, N. (2019). From *William's doll* to *Jacob's new dress*: The depiction of gender nonconforming boys in children's picture books from 1972 to 2014. *Journal of Homosexuality*, *66*(7), 914–936.

Paris, L. (2011). Happily ever after: Free to be . . . you and me, second-wave feminism, and 1970s American children's culture. In J. L. Mickenberg & L. Vallone (Eds.), *Oxford handbook of children's literature* (pp. 519–538). Oxford University Press.
Wasseluk, M. (April 30, 2019). Why this story? Interview with Gaia Cornwall. https://firstbook.org/blog/2019/04/30/q-and-a-with-gaia-cornwall-author-of-jabari-jumps/

Children's Literature Cited

Ahuja, Nandini. (2021). *It's big brother time!* Ill. Catalina Echeverri. Harper.
Andreae, Giles. (2021). *Free to be elephant me*. Ill. Guy Parker-Rees. Orchard Books.
Appelt, Kathi. (2003). *Incredible me!* Ill. G. Brian Karas. HarperCollins.
Asim, Jabari. (2019a). *Whose knees are these?* Ill. LeUyen Pham. LB Kids.
Asim, Jabari. (2019b). *Whose toes are those?* Ill. LeUyen Pham. LB Kids.
Bang, Molly. (1999). *When Sophie gets angry—really really angry*. Scholastic.
Bang, Molly. (2018). *When Sophie thinks she can't . . .* The Blue Sky Press/Scholastic.
Barnett, Mac. (2022). *John's turn*. Ill. Kate Berube. Candlewick Press.
Beaty, Andrea. (2013). *Rosie Revere, engineer*. Ill. David Roberts. Abrams.
Beaumont, Karen. (2004). *I like myself!* Ill. David Catrow. Clarion Books.
Bemelmans, Ludwig. (1939). *Madeline*. Viking.
Brown, Marc. (1998). *D.W.'s lost blankie*. Little, Brown and Company.
Brown, Peter. (2021). *Fred gets dressed*. Little, Brown and Company.
Burach, Ross. (2021). *The little butterfuly that could*. Scholastic.
Byers, Grace. (2018). *I am enough*. Ill. Keturah A. Bobo. Balzer & Bray.
Coelho, Joseph. (2019). *Grandpa's stories*. Ill. Allison Colpoys. Abrams Books for Young Readers.
Cohen, Paula. (2022). *Big dreams, small fish*. Levine Querido.
Cordell, Matthew. (2012). *Another brother*. Roaring Brook Press.
Cornwall, Gaia. (2017). *Jabari jumps*. Candlewick Press.
Cornwall, Gaia. (2020). *Jabari tries*. Candlewick Press.
Davids, Stacy B. (2015). *Annie's plaid shirt*. Ill. Rachael Balsaitis. Upswing Press.
de la Peña, Matt. (2015). *Last stop on Market Street*. Ill. Christian Robinson. Putnam.
Demi. (1990). *The empty pot*. Henry Holt.
Falconer, Ian. (2012). *Olivia and the fairy princesses*. Atheneum.
Gee, Kimberly. (2021). *Sad, sad bear*. Beach Lane.

Guttman, Arielle Prince. (2021). *Wherever you'll be*. Ill. Geneviéve Godbout. Flamingo Books.
Hudson, Cheryl Willis. (2003). *Hands can*. Photographs by John-Francis Bourke. Candlewick Press.
Jones, Pip. (2017). *Izzy Gizmo*. Ill. Sara Ogilvie. Peachtree.
Lies, Brian. (2018). *The rough patch*. Greenwillow Books.
Lionni, Leo. (1967). *Frederick*. Pantheon.
Maillard, Kevin Noble. (2019). *Fry bread: A Native American family story*. Ill. Juana Martinez-Neal. Roaring Brook Press.
Martin, Stephen W. (2022). *I can't draw*. Ill. Brian Biggs. Margaret K. McElderry Books.
Martinez-Neal, Juana. (2018). *Alma and how she got her name*. Candlewick Press.
McDonald, Megan. (2000). *Judy Moody*. Candlewick Press.
McDonald, Megan. (2001). *Judy Moody gets famous*. Candlewick Press.
McDonald, Megan. (2003). *Judy Moody predicts the future*. Candlewick Press.
McDonald, Megan. (2019). *Judy Moody book quiz whiz*. Candlewick Press.
McDonald, Megan. (2021). *Judy Moody in a Monday mood*. Candlewick Press.
McDonald, Megan. (2013). *Stink: The incredible shrinking kid*. Candlewick Press.
McDonald, Megan. (2014). *Stink and the shark sleepover*. Candlewick Press.
McDonald, Megan. (2020). *Stink and the hairy scary spider*. Candlewick Press.
McDonald, Megan. (2023). *Stink superhero superfan*. Candlewick Press.
McGinty, Alice B. (2021). *Step by step*. Ill. Diane Goode. Simon & Schuster.
Myers, Maya. (2021). *Not little*. Ill. Hyewon Yum. Neal Porter Books/Holiday House.
Parr, Todd. (2016). *Be who you are*. Little, Brown and Company.
Patricelli, Leslie. (2010). *Potty*. Candlewick Press.
Penn, Audrey. (1993). *The kissing hand*. Child & Family Press.
Perkins, Mitali. (2021). *Home is in between*. Ill. Lavanya Naidu. Farrar Straus & Giroux.
Pinkney, Andrea Davis. (2021). *Bright brown baby*. Ill. Brian Pinkney. Orchard Books.
Pinkney, Sandra. (2007). *I am Latino: The beauty in me*. Photos. Myles Pinkney. Little, Brown and Company.
Pitzer, Susanna. (2006). *Not afraid of dogs*. Ill. Larry Day. Walker.
Roberts, Justin. (2014). *The smallest girl in the smallest grade*. Ill. Christian Robinson. Putnam.
Rosenthal, Amy Krouse. (2015). *Little miss, big sis*. Ill. Peter H. Reynolds. Harper.
Salas, Laura Purdie. (2020). *Clover Kitty goes to kittygarden*. Ill. Hiroe Nakata. Two Lions.
Shannon, David. (1998). *No, David!* Scholastic.
Shannon, David. (1999). *David goes to school*. Scholastic.

Shannon, David. (2002). *David gets in trouble*. Scholastic.
Shannon, David. (2005a). *David smells!: A diaper David book*. Scholastic.
Shannon, David. (2005b). *Oh, David!* Scholastic.
Shannon, David. (2005c). *Oops!* Scholastic.
Shannon, David. (2018). *Grow up, David!* Scholastic.
Verde, Susan. (2022). *I am me: A book of authenticity*. Ill. Peter H. Reynolds. Abrams.
Willems, Mo. (2007a). *My friend is sad*. Hyperion.
Willems, Mo. (2007b). *I am invited to a party!* Hyperion.
Willems, Mo. (2014). *Waiting is not easy!* Hyperion.
Willems, Mo. (2016). *The thank you book*. Hyperion.
Wing, Natasha. (2011). *The night before preschool*. Ill. Amy Wummer. Grosset & Dunlap.
Yolen, Jane. (2011). *The day Tiger Rose said goodbye*. Ill. Jim LaMarche. Random House.
Yum, Hyewon. (2018). *Saturday is swimming day*. Candlewick Press.
Zolotow, Charlotte. (1972). *William's doll*. Harper & Row.

8

Fostering Social-Emotional and Moral Development

> Be confident. Stand up for yourself. Be energetic. Be peaceful. Be the best that you can be.
>
> Just be who you are!
>
> (*Be Who You Are* by Todd Parr, 2016)

Children's social and emotional well-being during their early years helps to shape who they are, who they become, and their understanding of the world. Author and illustrator Todd Parr has written several books including *It's Okay to Make Mistakes* (2014), *The Don't Worry Book* (2019), and *Be Who You Are* (2016) that empower children through powerful text and positive images. Children's literature can play a role to support social and moral development and fortunately, books such as Parr's are being read and discussed with young children.

Children who are emotionally healthy often maintain positive relationships with adults and peers (Trawick-Smith & Dziurgot, 2011). Parents, childcare providers, and early childhood educators assist children in learning how to establish these positive and constructive relationships with others. They also support children's "forming of friendships and provide opportunities for children to play and work together" (Copple & Bredekamp, 2009, p. 150).

The models of behavior that children see are a powerful force in their learning. According to social learning theorists, children observe how behaviors are performed and in what situations. If they see a teacher treating children courteously and kindly, they are likely to adopt this behavior toward

DOI: 10.4324/9781003367635-8

one another. They are also influenced by the rewards that follow behaviors, both when the reinforcement comes directly to them and when they observe it being given to someone else. For instance, when one child is praised for completing a task, both that child and the observers learn that completing tasks is a behavior that will be rewarded. Likewise, negative reinforcement identifies behavior to be avoided. Much social learning involves determining when and where behaviors will likely be condoned and learning the behaviors themselves.

Some behaviors are culturally defined. Children are reared in a cultural context that shows them aspects of social relationships, and they may take these unwritten rules for granted. Children learn when it is appropriate to touch, when not; if one looks directly at an authority figure or keeps one's eyes downcast; whether one competes or cooperates. Then, when encountering others whose expectations and constraints differ, they may be shocked and uncomfortable. Although teachers and childcare providers cannot know the norms and expectations of all the cultures represented in their group of children, they can work toward understanding and respect for differing backgrounds and model this for children.

Friendships are paramount for children for several reasons. First, they provide opportunities for children to learn and practice social skills. Adults often interpret a child's unclear request or stop the conflict the minute it begins. But children engage with one another as equals, which requires that communication be clear to be effective and that techniques of handling conflicts or making requests be learned. Second, friendships give children a context in which they can compare themselves. Who is the taller of the two? Who can run faster? This social comparison helps children develop a valid sense of their own identity. Finally, friendships foster a feeling of group belonging, a security different from that achieved within the family. However, friendships may have undesirable as well as desirable effects. They may cause jealousy, rejection of others, or antisocial behavior, as well as security, self-acceptance, and trust. Friendships are not the same as popularity. A person can get along with others and have status in a peer group yet not be able to form caring and reciprocal relationships.

The capacity for friendship generally has more significance for long-term development than popularity. However, prosocial children are generally perceived positively and tend to be popular with their peers. Children often want to be friends with prosocial children more than aggressive children. Prosocial children usually have positive peer relationships that may result in friendships (Findlay et al., 2006)

As children mature, their concept of friendship changes. The two-year-old will likely describe a friend in terms of physical attributes by saying,

"Kelly is the same size as me." Children at this age infer friendship based on helping and sharing (Afshordi & Liberman, 2021). For preschoolers, friendship is about having fun together, and they favor other children who like to do the same things. Children around this age have a limited capability to see different perspectives and assume other children think the same way they do. Around the ages of five to seven, children are concerned about fairness and reciprocity—if they do something nice for a friend, they expect the same in return. Children also become judgmental of themselves and others and assume they aren't liked because of something they are wearing or what they brought for lunch. By age eight or nine, children describe the traits they like or dislike and start to see friendship as a relationship that lasts over time.

Children likely develop part of their concept of friendship from observing adult friendships. It appears, however, that the major portion of their understanding comes from their encounters with others and how they integrate what they have learned. Thus, children need to experience working with each other in large and small groups. However, adults must recognize that children vary in their social needs and styles and must respect these differences.

Moral Development

Moral as well as social development is related to intellectual development. Jean Piaget and Lawrence Kohlberg saw the growth of moral reasoning as developing in stages that coincide with those of cognitive growth. Piaget (1955/1935) describes two broad phases of moral development. In the first stage, children have difficulty seeing situations from another's point of view and perceive acts as either totally right or wrong. They tend to judge an act based on consequences and not on intention. The child who broke the cookie jar into many pieces trying to dry it is guiltier than the child who only cracked the jar while trying to sneak a cookie. They follow the rules set down by adults, not because they believe in the need for a particular rule, but because the adult who gives it wields authority.

In the second stage, children are more likely to be able to see another's point of view. They are not absolute in their judgments and will assess acts more by intentions than consequences. They also begin to favor less punishment for wrongdoers. Piaget sees this shift in stages as occurring when the child is around eight or nine years old.

Kohlberg (1981) based his studies on Piaget's model of moral development. He describes six stages of development, each keyed to the individual's sense of justice and the reasoning used to solve moral dilemmas. Children age four to 10 reason at the first two stages, at the pre-conventional level. In stage 1, punishment and obedience orientation, they obey rules to avoid punishment. In stage 2, instrumental purpose and exchange, they conform to rules out of self-interest and do things for others to get something in return. As they mature, they pass through further stages. Stage 3 is doing what "good boys" and "good girls" do, and stage 4 is respecting the laws to maintain society. Finally, in the last two stages, personally developed moral principles take precedence over concern with authority. Kohlberg believed that most Americans operate at about stage 4.

Children develop their ability in moral reasoning through consideration of ethical problems and contact with the moral sense of others. Reasoning just one stage above their own is more meaningful to them than reasoning that is several stages higher. The stage at which children and adults reason about moral questions is not always a predictor of their actual behavior in a situation involving a moral question.

Although moral reasoning and social learning theories have different key elements, they are not contradictory when applied to young children. Children reasoning at Kohlberg's stage 1, behaving in a particular way to avoid punishment, will significantly be influenced by rewards and punishments, the behavior they see modeled, and the consequences it brings.

Theories help guide young children's moral development. Piaget and Kohlberg illustrate the need for children to discuss the reasons behind moral decisions and help teachers understand the kinds of reasoning common among young children. Social learning theories remind teachers of the importance of the models of the behavior they present through their actions and vicarious sources introduced into children's learning environments.

Envisioning the Potential of Literature

Literature provides a rich source of data from which children can begin to gain information, make inferences, and check the validity of inferences they have made. As stories unfold, characters reveal more of their feelings and reasons for acting as they do. Children can make hypotheses at several points in a story and, as the story progresses, see if their hypotheses are accurate. The situation is non-threatening—there is no penalty if their predictions do not happen in the story. Children explore whether there was ample evidence to support their guesses or whether they missed some important clues to the character's feelings.

Interpreting Nonverbal Language in Illustrations

The illustrations in books give children experience in reading and interpreting body language and facial expressions. Because these illustrations are static, catching a moment in time allows children to study them and talk about their specific aspects. *Making Faces: A First Book of Emotions* (2017) is a board book that introduces five essential expressions: happy, sad, angry, surprised, and silly. Each expression is paired with a large image of a baby's face. The next page shows a group of babies where the child can pick out the baby that displays the expression from the previous page. You can invite young children to imitate the emotion shown as well.

A little girl and her family adopt an adorable tiny puppy in Karl Newsom Edwards's *I Got a New Friend* (2017). This sweet picture book is perfect for preschoolers and will give them lots to interpret regarding the facial expressions of both girl and puppy. The cheery, first-person text explains that her new puppy friend likes to play outside, is a sloppy eater, and needs "lots of hugs, kisses, and even more kisses." There is brief text on each page, while copious white space makes the cartoon-like illustrations of the two new friends appealing.

Carmela Full of Wishes by Matt de la Peña (2018) provides lyrical, stirring text to accompany the evocative artwork of Christian Robinson. When Carmela wakes up on her birthday, her wish has already come true—she's finally old enough to join her big brother as he completes family errands. They go to numerous places as the jingling of Carmela's bracelets increasingly annoys her brother. When Carmela finds a lone dandelion growing on the pavement, she holds onto it until she can blow on the fuzzy white bulb to make a wish. As Carmela's day comes to a close, she realizes that sometimes things don't always work out the way she had hoped, but often they become even better!

Wordless picture books are excellent sources of material in which body language and facial expressions are emphasized. This is especially true with Chris Raschka's *A Ball for Daisy* (2011). Daisy loves her red ball. The adorable pooch plays with it constantly, that is, until another dog accidentally deflates it. Daisy is devastated! However, happiness returns when Daisy is given a new blue ball. The variety of emotions provides an opportunity for young children to draw inferences. This expressive book will appeal to toddlers and preschoolers because of the loveable dog and the connection and sense of loss in losing a favorite toy. The simple storyline will also enable children to narrate the events occurring in each watercolor vignette. This book also appeals to multilingual learners because of the dependence on the illustrations to tell the story.

Wordless picture books vary in difficulty, just as other picture books do. *Every Little Kindness* by Marta Bartolj (2021) highlights the universal theme of being kind to others, but the storyline requires more attention to follow the progression of events. A young woman tacks up posters in hopes of finding her lost dog. Her simple act of kindness in giving an apple to a street performer sparks another then another act of kindness. In the course of a single day, each considerate action transforms a diverse neighborhood into a caring community. A pop of red in the otherwise black-and-white illustrations signals the object or person that becomes the focus of a kind act, such as gifting a crying girl a red balloon, sharing a red umbrella during a thunderstorm, or bringing a bouquet of red flowers to a friend. As the characters' actions weave together, the young woman receives a phone call and is soon reunited with her dog. Through facial expressions and body language, a range of emotions is shared, from initial feelings of despair to looks of sheer joy.

Books with text may have illustrations that are as explicit in conveying characters' actions and feelings as those in wordless picture books. Children do not have to make the interpretations themselves but should be given the opportunity to discuss the pictures. Asking children about a character based on initial illustrations assists them in observing a change that may occur in the story along with the character's mood or tone.

When looking at the cover of *A Dog Wearing Shoes* (Ko, 2015), children can discuss how the dog feels standing near a fire hydrant with cars whizzing by. In the opening pages, the dog wearing yellow shoes is now sitting in the middle of traffic. Mini's mother screeches to a stop and jumps out to retrieve the dog. The vignettes on these pages display a range of emotions by the dog and the people. Even though Mini's mother points out that the dog is wearing yellow shoes and probably has an owner, the young girl is determined to keep him. Mini is delighted that she and the dog attract a crowd who exclaim that the dog is adorable. After performing various tricks for the group, Mini removes the dog's collar and throws a stick for it to fetch. But the dog runs away instead. Feeling distraught, Mini and her mom visit the animal shelter the next day and locate the missing dog. Mini now realizes that she needs to find the dog's real family. Emotions abound as owner and dog are reunited. So, the next day, Mini and her mom revisit the animal shelter, and the girl finds her forever dog. The black-and-white illustrations include splashes of color, including the yellow shoes on the dog and the newly purchased red leash. Stories about dogs will always prompt children to want to share their own dog stories. Ask them to place their hand on their heart if they have a pet at home. Then have them turn and tell the child next to them about their pet or the pet they would like to own. This way, you can honor children's desire to tell their stories in a structure where everyone can participate.

When interpreting nonverbal language in illustrations, it's important to slow down while reading the story so children can view the illustrations.

Another option would be to project them onto a wall or screen using a doc camera. In some instances, you may want to ask children to interpret some of the illustrations and make predictions about what may happen next as you read a story. At other times, you may want to complete an entire story before engaging children in discussion. You can decide how to approach the story by remembering that enjoyment and comprehension are the central purposes of your reading. If interrupting the narrative would ruin the story, wait until it is completed before talking about the illustrations. But if the children seem confused or if discussion during the story heightens interest, then pause at appropriate times and encourage conversation.

Look for illustrators who are particularly adept at showing facial expressions and body language. Marla Frazee, Eric Rohmann, Sophie Blackall, Bryan Collier, Raul Colón, and Emily Gravett are just a few whose work almost always captures easily recognizable emotions in physical expressions.

Relating Voice Inflection to Meaning

Children gain experience in relating voice inflection to meaning and the feelings of the speaker. The facets of language linguists have identified are *pitch*, the high and low tones; *stress*, the emphasis with which a particular word or syllable is said; and *juncture*, the pause between syllables, words, or sentences. Variations in these tell the listener whether the sentence is a question or a statement, whether the phrase is "ice cream" or "I scream," and whether the speaker is being sincere or sarcastic.

Children do not need to know the terms or how to isolate pitch, stress, and juncture. However, they need to hear expressive speech to begin generalizing for themselves about the speaker's meaning. You can provide many examples through your skillful reading. In order to do so, it is vital that you pre-read a book you want to share with children. That way, you know when to pause, when to make your voice louder, or when to emphasize certain words or phrases.

Some books naturally lend themselves to understanding how the words or phrases should be read due to the size of the font. *Oh, No!* by Candace Fleming (2012) begins with a little frog falling into a very big hole. Unfortunately, the hole is located where a tiger is sleeping. Since the frog is too little to jump out, he calls for help. One by one, animals come to assist, but they fall into the hole, too. Oh, no! The commotion wakes the tiger, and he spies the animals trapped in the hole. As the tiger leaps into the hole and hopefully retrieves his perceived dinner, an elephant comes along and rescues the animals—all except one, of course. Now there's only one animal stuck in the hole—the tiger. The jaunty text is perfect for reading aloud. Sounds like "Ribbit-oops!" and "Pippa-eeek!" are written in larger font, so it's clear they need to be spoken louder and emphasized. "Oh, no" is written in various font sizes, which offers a clue as to how they should be read. Eric Rohmann's woodcut illustrations showcase the animals' feelings before, during, and after their experience of falling, struggling to help others, and rejoicing at being rescued.

When a book such as *Oh, No!* has a large font featuring a repetitive phrase, children can join in when the words appear. This way, they can begin practicing their own inflection as to how the phrase should be read. This works best after reading the story once and then returning to discuss how authors assist readers in knowing what a character is feeling and the expression needed when reading.

Extending Beyond the Literal Interpretation of the Narrative

Children can be given the opportunity to analyze when the narrative can be accepted at face value and when a meaning other than a literal interpretation of the words is intended. No character uses persuasive language more than the short-tempered Pigeon in Mo Willems's delightful picture book series appropriate for all children. Whether the pigeon is attempting to drive a bus, even though the driver has emphatically stated *Don't Let the Pigeon Drive the Bus* (2003), or having the tables turned on him by a wide-eyed ducking in *The Pigeon Finds a Hot Dog!* (2004), or insisting it is his childhood dream to own a pet in *The Pigeon Wants a Puppy* (2008), or hearing the feathered fowl loudly object when he discovers *The Pigeon HAS to Go to School* (2019), toddlers, preschoolers, and primary-grade children alike find much to discuss regarding the Pigeon's emotional quandaries.

This Is Not My Hat (Klassen, 2012) is a Caldecott Medal recipient that begins with a self-confident fish who has pilfered a blue bowler from a much larger sleeping fish. The smaller fish immediately confesses he has stolen the hat and offers details of when the theft occurred. The narrative states, "he probably won't notice that it's gone," which shows the large fish looking upward and noticing the hat is missing. The small fish then assuredly says, "he won't know where I am going," yet it appears the large fish is in hot pursuit. The small fish is also confident no one will inform the large fish where he can be found. This also is shown not to be true in the illustrations. The small fish swims into his hiding place, but then we see the large fish go into the plants and emerge with the hat firmly placed on his head. The text offers a narrative of what the fish believes, while the illustrations provide a completely different scenario. Several of Klassen's stories have a somewhat ambiguous ending that promotes speculation as well as affirmative responses as to what has happened to the unaware thief.

Following a Sequence of Action

The meaning behind some narratives is related to an entire sequence of action. Only if the readers know what happened earlier can they interpret the actions or behaviors of various characters accurately. Understanding a sequence of actions enables children to retell story events in the order they occurred. These stories also offer opportunities to improve predicting because children become more skilled in recognizing plot structures and that stories have a beginning, middle, and end.

In the 2011 Caldecott Medal winner, *A Sick Day for Amos McGee* (Stead, 2010), zookeeper Amos always makes time during his day to play chess with the elephant, run races with the tortoise (who consistently wins), sit quietly with the shy penguin, lend a handkerchief to the rhinoceros with a runny nose, and read stories to the owl who is afraid of the dark. When Amos becomes sick with a cold and decides to stay home, his animal friends begin to worry and are soon boarding a bus to go to Amos's house to cheer him up. Once there, the animals now perform the same comforting and enjoyable activities for Amos that he did for them at the zoo. Even aspects such as Amos's bus ride each morning are mirrored in the activities the animals execute. Children must be aware of the reciprocal actions to understand and enjoy the story's nuances fully.

Bikes for Sale (Higgins, 2019) begins with parallel stories about two characters who might be destined to be friends. Maurice sells lemonade from a cart attached to his yellow bike. Lotta's red bike has a basket where she puts the sticks she has collected and then gives them away. Both ride their bikes in the park, but they never meet until a stick becomes entangled in Maurice's spokes, propelling him into a tree, while Lotta's bike skids on some lemon rinds, which causes her to crash as well. Now neither bike is operable. Fortunately, Sid finds both bikes and fashions them into a tandem ride for the new owners, Maurice and Lotta. Textual and visual clues provide a sense the two characters are both riding in the park and the two will meet. More subtle indicators are that Chipmunk Maurice has vivid, red fur while Porcupine Lotta is a pale yellow, similar to lemonade. A map of the park is featured on the end pages so children can track where each has traversed.

Following the sequence of action is also helpful for making inferences about characters' feelings and intentions. Young children develop an understanding of action and reaction in human relationships when they see an entire drama played out in book form. Amos cares for the animals, so they reciprocate in nursing him back to health. Maurice and Lotta have not only acquired a new bike that allows them to continue selling lemonade and collecting sticks, but they have also gained a new friend.

Observing Patterns of Behavior

Besides understanding a sequence of actions, some children are beginning to learn their actions influence the actions of others, as in the story of Amos McGee. To illustrate, when one child grabs a toy or book another child wants, the second child will often grab it back, and an oral or physical argument might ensue. The opposite can also occur when a child shares a snack and the other child reciprocates by sharing some of their own.

Children vary in their comprehension of the total situation in which action occurs. To help them see specific behaviors in a broader context, share books in which the action–reaction pattern is reasonably clear, and use these books as the basis for dramatization. There is a definitive action–reaction scenario in *We Don't Eat Our Classmates* by Ryan T. Higgins (2018). Penelope the dinosaur is very excited about the first day of school. She has a new backpack, and her dad has packed 300 tuna sandwiches and one apple juice for her lunch. When Penelope arrives at school, she is surprised that her classmates are children. So, she eats them because children are delicious. Her teacher, Mrs. Noodleman, tells her to spit them out. Unfortunately, now all the children are not only covered in slime but they are afraid of Penelope. When the class pet, Walter the Goldfish, chomps Penelope's finger as she attempts to befriend him, she realizes what it's like to be someone's snack. From that moment on, Penelope doesn't eat any more of her classmates, and soon she has made new friends.

Another book that provides an action–reaction plot is *Lacey Walker, Nonstop Talker* (Jones, 2012). Lacey Walker is quite the talker. In fact, she never stops talking. She talks while she's eating, she talks during class, and she talks while her brother is trying to watch a monster movie. When Lacey wakes up one day and realizes she has lost her voice, she mopes through breakfast and most of the day. However, now that she has stopped talking, Lacey appreciates her friend Nadine's sense of humor, grasps why her brother loves monster movies, and earns a gold star at school for finishing all her work. Once her voice returns, Lacey still talks, but she now understands the value of listening.

Box 8.1 Books that Present a Moral Dilemma

A Bike Like Sergio's (Maribeth Boelts; ill. Noah Z. Jones, 2016)
Can I Play Too? (Mo Willems, 2010)
Cheese Belongs to You! (Alexis Deacon; ill. Viviane Schwarz, 2013)
Do Unto Otters: A Book About Manners (Laurie Keller, 2007)
I Really Want the Cake (Simon Philip; ill. Lucia Gaggiotti, 2020)
Lilly's Purple Plastic Purse (Kevin Henkes, 2006)

Empathizing with a Book Character

As children learn to "read" another's feelings, they become more sensitive to those emotions. You can ask children to empathize with a character by having them think about how they would feel if something similar happened to them. In *Madeline Finn and the Library Dog* (Papp, 2016), the other children in her class earn gold stars for being good readers. Madeline Finn never earns a gold star because she does *not* like to read—or rather, she is challenged by reading and is afraid of making a mistake when she doesn't know or understand words. Fortunately, Madeline meets Bonnie, a library dog. When Madeline reads out loud to Bonnie, she doesn't get embarrassed. Actually, reading becomes a lot more fun because Bonnie is a good listener. Children who struggle with reading will empathize with Madeline. They also might find a solution for gaining confidence with their reading. There are numerous programs in schools, public libraries, and animal shelters where children can read to a patient and supportive canine.

Children, especially toddlers, and preschoolers, who experienced trepidation in starting school will empathize with Bear in *So Big!* (Wohnoutka, 2019). Bear is big enough to dress and pour his cereal for breakfast. On this first day of school, he feels very confident walking to the bus stop. When the bus arrives, Bear is feeling a little less big. The size of the school bus is so big, as are the other passengers, such as the elephant and giraffe. When he reaches the school, which is *so big*, Bear is overwhelmed and begins to cry. However, he's not the only one. Squirrel has an equal reaction. So the two walk into school and their classroom together, where it feels just right. The text is limited to the words "so big," but the illustrations depict the range of emotions for both Bear and Squirrel. Children will undoubtedly want to share their first day of school experiences, whether confident or fearful.

For some discussions, you might want to return to several different places in a book and ask children how they think the character may have felt at that time and why they think so. Depending on the story, you may want to do this as you read. For example, ask children what they see on the cover of *Madeline Finn and the Library Dog*. After reading the first two pages that depict a scowl on Madeline's face as she sits with her arms crossed and books strewn across the floor, pause to ask how she is feeling and what might be the problem. Brainstorm with children the different reasons why Madeline may not like to read. There are other points in the story to stop and discuss Madeline's emotions, such as when Madeline does not receive a star on her paper or the expression on her face when she sees a room in the library filled with dogs and children.

The bear in *So Big!* displays several emotions beginning on the cover. Discuss with children how Bear is feeling. A strategy for the second reading of this story might be to have children watch the illustrations to see when Bear's expression changes each time during the remainder of the story and why. Use sticky notes to write the words "happy," "surprised," and "sad" to describe Bear's emotions, and place each note on the corresponding page. This way, children can revisit the book independently or in small groups and retell the story using the descriptive words that have been generated. Literature offers an excellent opportunity for children to empathize with a book character and to view characters within stories, empathizing with one another.

Fostering Children's Ability from the Viewpoint of Others

When children recognize that not everyone thinks as they do, they are ready to see from the viewpoint of another. The books and activities that help give children experience recognizing how others feel provide a base for developing skills in taking various perspectives. First, children can talk about how the character felt or how they would feel under the same circumstances. Next, they can take the role of a character reacting as that character would, saying what that character thinks, and doing what they believe that character would do in a new situation.

Sharing Books that Present Several Viewpoints

You can help children recognize other viewpoints by reading them several books in which different points of view are clearly illustrated.

Days Like This by Oriane Smith (2022) begins with the poem's full text on the first page. Once the page is turned, one poetic line stated at a time is presented and repeated on the facing page. The illustrations display the same setting but from two contrasting viewpoints—a child and a squirrel. The artwork by Alice Gravier is stunning and thought-provoking, as children can ponder how the same moments can be viewed so differently. Slow down and savor this book as it will prompt a lot of ideas and opinions by children. Also, remove the book jacket to view a different illustration and viewpoint on the book's casing.

Children should be familiar with the traditional tale of *The Three Little Pigs* to understand the story's humor and the different perspective the wolf provides in *The True Story of the Three Little Pigs* (Scieszka, 1989). The wolf claims he was only trying to borrow a cup of sugar from his neighbor, the pig, when he sneezed and unfortunately blew the pig's house down. The Big Bad Wolf asserts that it was all a misunderstanding, and now he's trying to set the record straight. A book to pair with Scieszka's version is *Tell the Truth B. B. Wolf* (Sierra, 2010), who relates his transgressions with various fairy-tale characters. Other books offer the traditional telling of a fairy tale that can be coupled with a version from another character's viewpoint.

The Day the Crayons Quit by Drew Daywalt (2013) is told from the viewpoints of overworked and overused crayons. When Duncan opens his box of crayons, he finds complaint letters from the crayons—red states it is the most used crayon and is tired of working, even on holidays; blue needs a break from coloring all those bodies of water; and black crayon is tired of outlining and feels he could contribute more. What can Duncan do to appease the crayons? *The Day the Crayons Quit* lends itself to talking about the feelings and points of view of others. Children can use the book's format and write or dictate a letter response from Duncan to the crayons. A new story could be created about an everyday object that decided to quit, such as a bicycle or soccer ball. Literature offers viewpoints of characters and also models for writing.

Providing Models of Prosocial Behavior

Literature portraying characters engaged in social behavior shows children a way of acting and the ingredients necessary for prosocial behavior. That is, a character can recognize that another needs help, feels confident they can provide that help, and sees the risk as not too great to get involved. Therefore, when you share stories that include prosocial behavior, such as helping, sharing, cooperating, and comforting, you might call attention to these aspects individually and also look at the action as a whole.

Reading Books that Demonstrate Prosocial Behavior

A Small Kindness (McAnulty, 2021) follows a diverse group of children on their first day of school. The initial page is in sepia tones as children line up with their new teacher. One girl, Alice, is in full color and is shown helping Lucas put his backpack on a shelf on the next page. As Lucas waves hello to Jasmine, he is now depicted in full color. As each child's act of kindness is passed on to another student, the pages are filled with vivid hues while demonstrating one small action can make a difference in another child's life and sometimes attitude. The simple acts are also ones that any child can accomplish.

Acceptance, kindness, and inclusion can be demonstrated by real and inanimate characters. *The Big Umbrella* (Bates, 2018) sits by the front door on a rainy day but is quickly whisked away by a child. The big umbrella likes to help and spreads its arms wide. When others are caught in the rain, no matter how tall, hairy, or plaid an individual (or animal) might be, there is enough space for everyone. The umbrella is used as a metaphor to demonstrate that everyone is welcome and there is always room.

Prosocial behavior does not need to be confined to school or the neighborhood but can be expanded globally. *Boxes for Katje* (2003) is based on an incident from author Candace Fleming's mother's life. Set during World War II, the people of Olst in Holland are having difficulty getting necessities such as soap, socks, and warm clothing. When a box arrives from Rosie in Indiana, Katje is thrilled with its contents. She even shares the chocolate bar with her mother and the postman. After Katje writes a thank you note to her new friend in America, another box arrives bearing more gifts. This continues over several months, with the boxes becoming more plentiful in supplies and numbers. The townspeople of Olst are so thankful for the many gifts being sent to them that they find a way to reciprocate in an extraordinary way. The idea that one person can make a difference is a strong theme in this book.

Planning Prosocial Behavior

Consider grouping books that show social behavior so children can make generalizations. One grouping would be reading books where a character becomes a bully. The rhyming text and engaging illustrations in *Llama Llama and the Bully Goat* (Dewdney, 2013) make this a perfect book for preschoolers. Gilroy Goat is equally mean to his peers, whether in the classroom or on the playground. Llama Llama does not want a bully goat for a friend. *Stick and Stone* (Ferry, 2015) become friends when Stick rescues Stone from a prickly situation, and later Stone is able to repay the kindness. Bullying can take many forms, including intentionally ignoring others or excluding them from games or even birthday parties. Brian is *The Invisible Boy* (Ludwig, 2013), who is never chosen for a kickball team, sits alone at lunch, and listens to the fun everyone had at a birthday party he wasn't invited to attend. When new kid Justin joins the class, Brian is the first to reach out. Finally, *I Walk with Vanessa: A Story About a Simple Act of Kindness* (Kerascoët, 2018) is a wordless picture book depicting a young girl who is bullied on her way to school until another girl decides to take a stand.

After reading two or three books about bullies and bullying, have children think of someone who wasn't nice to them. Then have them list all the good things they could say and do for that person to help them be kinder to others. Next, have the children think about a time when they were not kind to another person. What could they have done differently then and now? Sharing books that provide realistic situations for children enables them to see themselves and others in the story and generates discussion and problem-solving strategies.

A book character is just one model among many to which children are exposed. Some books that you present will show behavior that you would not choose to have children emulate. Often the problem to be solved in the book results from the behavior of one of the characters, which may not reflect values you condone. However, you would not want to select only those books in which characters exhibit prosocial behavior. This would eliminate excellent literature that may portray humans in some of their very human but not-so-lovable thoughts and actions. You would be exercising a kind of censorship, a screening of literature based on the values presented. Rather than eliminating those books, add them to the collection of books that show children engaged in prosocial behavior. Help children see that they can aid others in a given situation and that there are internal rewards for such behavior.

Box 8.2 Story Retelling Frame

Somebody (character)
Wanted (what did the character want?)
But (what was the problem?)
So (how did the character solve the problem?)
Finally (what happened next?)
In the end (how did the story end?)

Encouraging Children to Judge the Appropriateness of Particular Behaviors

Learning when a behavior is appropriate requires generalizing about types of situations and types of behaviors. A social encounter is not likely to be repeated in exact form. However, children can be assisted in generalizing the appropriateness of behaviors by seeing examples of behaviors and their consequences. Some instances will come from direct observation or participation, but others will come from vicarious experiences such as literature.

Preschoolers and primary-grade children will enjoy reading the antics in *No, David!* (Shannon, 1998). David wreaks havoc in every room of the house. He reaches too far for the cookie jar, tracks in too much dirt, bangs too loudly on the pans, and plays with his food at dinner. The text consists mainly of "No, David" or variations of that statement. When a broken chair leads to a time-out and a tear runs down his cheek, a motherly hug makes it clear that David is still loved. Share with children the author's note that explains this is a semiautobiographical tale. Children will recognize that even authors were not always well behaved when they were young.

The Sour Grape (2022) is the sixth book in the "Food Group" series written by Jory John and illustrated by Pete Oswald. Grape likes to hold a grudge which makes him a sour grape. If someone upsets or insults him, he'll never forget what they have done. When nobody showed up after Grape rigorously and vigorously planned a birthday party complete with a Ferris wheel, a magician, and even a fireworks display, Grape went from a sweet grape to a bitter grape, to a snappy grape, to finally becoming a sour grape. He was grumpy and mean to everyone. One day, Sour Grape hurried to meet his friend Lenny (a lemon who was just as sour) and arrives three hours late after having a flat tire on his bike, missing the bus, and then getting off at the wrong stop. Lenny was furious. Grape finally realized he needed to change his behavior. He also saw that he had written the wrong date on his party invitations which explains why no one showed up. Grape understood that being kind, considerate, forgiving, and grateful can actually be pretty sweet. Other books in this series also offer opportunities to discuss particular behaviors.

Children who hear a story and know the full context of a situation can be asked to judge a character's behavior, noting the circumstances that may have influenced it and the punishment that may follow. As children become accustomed to viewing single incidents within broader contexts and are able to predict the reactions of others, they will be able to assess more accurately the behaviors that are most likely appropriate in any given situation.

Helping Children Learn About and Value Diversity

Children's literature scholar Rudine Sims Bishop has addressed a need for children to see themselves in the books they read and learn about others. She has stated:

> Books are sometimes windows, offering views of worlds that may be real or imagined, familiar or strange. These windows are also sliding glass doors and readers have only to walk through in imagination to become part of whatever world has been created and recreated by the author. When lighting conditions are just right, however, a window can also be a mirror. Literature transforms human experience and reflects it back to us, and in that reflection, we can see our own lives and experiences as part of the larger human experience. Reading, then, becomes a means of self-affirmation, and readers often seek their mirrors in books.
>
> (Bishop, 1990, p. ix)

Basic to being open to others is feeling good about oneself. Thus, many of the activities designed to enhance the self-concept of young children aid in their acceptance of others. As they explore what they can do, they see also what their classmates can do; as they tell what they like, they hear what their classmates like. They are beginning to see the diversity within their own small group and to value both themselves and their friends.

Selecting Literature that Values Diversity

Literature can focus on how individuals vary and emphasize the value of this variance. Rashin has just moved to Brooklyn from Iran, and she can't wait to get some *Saffron Ice Cream* (Kheiriyeh, 2018) at the beach. As her family travels by subway, Rashin remembers what it was like to go to the beach in Iran. There, her father drove his old car as they listened to Persian music on the radio. Rashin also took her best friend, Azadeh, along where they might share a kebab, swim on the female's side of the segregated beach, and indulge in saffron ice cream. When Rashin and her family get off the Q train at Ocean Parkway and walk to Coney Island, she sees families of all colors, hears the vibrating music, and observes that both men and women share the beach. Unfortunately, the ice-cream vendor does not have saffron ice cream, resulting in Rashin discovering a new flavor, chocolate crunch.

The theme of valuing others differently from oneself or the norm appears in literature at all levels. *Where Are You From?* (Méndez, 2019) is a question a young brown-skinned girl is constantly asked. She responds, "I'm from here, from today, same as everyone else." However, her answer is not accepted. "No, where are you *really* from?" When she poses the question to Abuelo, he tells her that she comes from the pampas, the gaucho, mountains, blue oceans, and grandmothers waiting for their grandchildren. When she continues to ask the question, he finally points to his heart and says, "You're from here." The simple yet evocative language will validate many young children's experiences and may generate conversations about race and racial aggression.

Mei, meaning "beautiful" in Chinese, is the daughter of Chinese immigrants to the United States. While sometimes people may call her different or even exclude her, Mei's parents want her to know there is power in being different. "You are strength. You are power." Mei's parents also want her to know and say, "I am golden" (Chen, 2022). Her eyes, her hair, and her skin are like a lotus flower blooming in the darkest water. Mei's cultural heritage is special, and many great Asian Americans have come before her. Author Eva Chen is the daughter of Chinese immigrants, and *I Am Golden* is a tribute to her parents and a wish for children to love themselves and the unique beauty of their family history.

Diverse books have been woven throughout this text but are highlighted in this section because diversity is a part of social and moral development. Sharing books with differing characters allows children to view themselves and others in books that become mirrors, windows, and sliding glass doors.

Focusing on Similarities

It's important to acknowledge and celebrate differences. It's also important for children to experience books in which there are similarities among people who may differ from them but share common experiences, emotions, and needs.

In the Caldecott Honor book *Me & Mama* (Cabrera, 2020), a young Black girl enjoys a rainy day alone with her mother. Each moment is special whether it is the oatmeal breakfast they share, the choice of barrettes that match Mama's fuchsia dress, or the delight of jumping in rain puddles—splash! The love between mother and daughter is evident in the illustrations rendered in a muted color palette. Children can talk about their outings with a parent and what they like best to do.

Some children may relate to Daisy Ramona as she zooms around the neighborhood because *My Papi Has a Motorcycle* (Quintero, 2019). Daisy's face radiates joy as she and her papi snap on their helmets and ride through the streets on his electric blue motorcycle. Set in Corona, California, the two roar past Abuelita's church, Joy's Market, where Mami buys gummy bears, and murals that tell the history of citrus groves and the immigrants who worked them. They wave as they cruise by Abuelito and Abuelita's yellow house surrounded by lemon trees. Daisy absorbs her beloved hometown's sights, sounds, smells, and delights in the time spent with Papi. In an author's note, Quintero shares her childhood memories of riding with her papi on the back of a motorcycle. The illustrations by Zeke Peña capture the enjoyment, and the love shared between child and parent while incorporating various Spanish phrases. *Me & Mama* and *My Papi Has a Motorcycle* exude the happiness children feel in sharing experiences with a parent.

Facilitating Group Activities

Children develop social skills only in a context where they have the opportunity to practice them. Childcare centers, preschools, and elementary schools are natural places for this to occur. When planning the presentation of literature and related activities, capitalize on opportunities to help children be a part of the group where all are working together, especially if an attitude of cooperation permeates the endeavor. An activity may be simply listening to a story, being quiet so others can hear, or laughing at humorous passages. It might be a group response to the literature: participating as the book is read a second time, singing the words to the song illustrated as a picture book, engaging in choral speaking, or doing fingerplays. Children enjoy activities such as these more fully when each child feels secure in their own group membership.

When planning ways of extending books, develop activities that require children to work together. For preschoolers working side by side but not *with* one another, suggest projects where they must share materials or space. For instance, they may make a collage after listening to *My Heart is Like a Zoo*

(Hall, 2010). This brightly colored book, with simple rhymes about emotions, features a variety of zoo animals that will delight young children. Each animal is constructed primarily of heart shapes. Provide children with cut-out hearts in a variety of sizes and colors. Have them create animals that their heart is like using the book as inspiration. Cut the hearts out of construction paper, fabric, wallpaper, wrapping paper, or other materials. Place these in a central location accessible to small groups of children. Children are then grouped around the materials, thus encouraging conversation as they work. They can comment about each other's cut-outs or tell others about their collages. Children become engaged in social interaction because of how the activity is structured. Other activities that promote the development of social skills are those that require joint planning. Creative dramatics, puppetry, writing group stories, dancing with partners, and making murals all need children to participate and listen to the ideas of others to be successful.

Stimulating Children to Explore Moral Problems and Ethical Questions

Whether you plan to or not, you will likely read stories to children that represent various levels of moral reasoning on the part of the characters. In Kohlberg's stage 1, moral reasoning is based on the concept of punishment. The child believes that if the consequence of an action is punishment, then the action is wrong. Todd Parr's (2014) *It's Okay to Make Mistakes* addresses the idea that everyone makes mistakes and you can learn from them. "It's okay if you spill your milk. You can always clean it up" tells children that spilling milk is an accidental action but that it does occur, and the response should be cleaning it up rather than punishment. Of course, children should understand there is a difference between an intentional action and an accidental one. Spilling milk is generally an accident while hitting someone in anger is intentional. For example, text in Parr's book says, "It's okay to get upset. Your friends are there to cheer you on," showing that looking to friends for support is better than reacting in anger. *It's Okay to Make Mistakes* is a good picture book to share with toddlers and preschoolers that will elicit a lively discussion about actions and punishment.

The character in *How to Heal a Broken Wing* (Graham, 2008) reasons at Kohlberg's stage 2, instrumental purpose and exchange. In this stage, personal reward determines ethical decisions. In the busy city, no one saw the bird hit the glass and fall softly to the sidewalk. Everyone walks by except for Will, who sees that the bird has a broken wing. Will and his mother scoop up the bird and take it home, hoping the wing will mend. In this story, Will expressed a different view than others who were hurrying down the street.

He chose to stop and made a personal decision to rescue the helpless bird. In turn, he gets the satisfaction of seeing the bird take off in flight once healed.

Moral reasoning at stage 3 is widely represented in book characters' decisions. This stage is often called the "good boy–good girl" orientation, in which the interpersonal relationship of moral development focuses on living up to social expectations and roles. There is an emphasis on conforming, being "nice," and considering how choices influence relationships. *A Boy Like You* (Murphy, 2019) celebrates boys contributing positively to the world around them. Whether it's playing hard at a sport, baking a cake, conducting science experiments, or just being curious, the most important thing is for the boy to express himself in healthy ways, especially as he continues growing up. The boy receives advice to listen to people's stories, walk with his head up, and leave every place and person better than he found them. It's also okay to cry, which is a sign of strength. The illustrations by Kayla Harren portray a diverse array of boys. A book note states, "In an age when boys are expected to fit into a particular mold, this book celebrates all the wonderful ways to be a boy." As society changes and evolves, so must the perceptions of social expectations and roles.

Children grow in their ability to reason about moral questions as they hear the reasoning of others. In general, they understand the reasoning at their own stage, the stages below theirs, and one stage above. Hearing various stages of rationale expressed by book characters and classmates expands reasoning powers and is instrumental in children's movement from one stage to another.

Engaging Children in the Reasoning Process

No other literature poses problems or presents a moral dilemma more than fairy tales and folktales. These stories are based on an oral tradition from hundreds of years earlier and intended to teach young children a lesson. Therefore, reading various fairy tales engages children in discussing the characters' behavior and action while thinking about what they would do in a similar situation.

Consider sharing several variations of a traditional story, such as *The Little Red Hen* which has been described in a previous chapter. First, read a traditional version, such as one retold and illustrated by author and illustrator Jerry Pinkney (2006). In this classic folktale, a chicken requests assistance from a variety of animals who decline to help her grow and harvest wheat, which she then uses to bake bread. Of course, the animals want to help the Little Red Hen eat the bread, but she shares it with her chicks instead. After reading this beautifully illustrated version, ask, "Why don't you think the animals would help the Little Red Hen grow and harvest the wheat? Should the Little Red Hen share the bread with the other animals? What will the animals do next time the Little Red Hen asks for their help?" Byron Barton's colorful version of *The Little Red Hen* (1994) is perfect for toddlers and preschoolers and comes in an assortment of formats, including as a big book.

Next, share several variations of the story. Brenda Maier's *The Little Red Fort* (2018) uses the same story structure, but this time, a young girl, Ruby, decides to build a fort. She asks her three brothers to help her draw the plans, gather the supplies, cut the boards, and hammer the nails. Instead of helping Ruby, they laugh at her. When her fort is completed, Ruby asks, "Who wants to play in my fort?" All three brothers exclaimed enthusiastically, "I'll play!" Ruby decides she will play in the fort by herself. Meanwhile, her brothers get to work making a mailbox, planting some flowers, and painting the fort a fire-engine red. When Ruby fixes some delicious food for her fort-warming party, her brothers are invited. This variation presents a girl as the builder with assistance from her mother and grandmother in cutting and hammering.

Another variation children enjoy is *The Little Red Hen (Makes a Pizza)* by Philemon Sturges (1999). The Little Red Hen cannot get help from the duck, the dog, or the cat, so she kneads the dough, cuts and chops vegetables (and a few other ingredients), and bakes an enormous pizza. The clever ending will surprise young children. *Mañana, Iguana* by Ann Whitford Paul (2004) contains a Latin beat and an uplifting storyline. Iguana wants to throw a fiesta and asks for assistance from her friends Conejo (rabbit), Tortuga (turtle), and Culebra (snake), but all declined to help her. Their response, "Mañana, Iguana." So the Iguana does all the work herself and refuses to allow her friends to attend the party . . . or does she?

In addition to asking the suggested questions posed after reading Jerry Pinkney's version of *The Little Red Hen* that can be adapted to fit the other versions and variants, you might create a chart to compare and contrast the stories. For example, a column could be created indicating the animals or individuals for each version and variant, the tasks that needed to be completed, and whether the characters redeemed themselves. Add a column to list the main character's decisions and the responses from those that were asked to help. Vote whether they agreed or disagreed with the choices.

Reading several books concerning an issue provides added dimensions. Children begin to look at situations where the answer to what is right requires them to weigh possible actions themselves and use their reasoning power. The purpose is not to recommend specific actions but to encourage children to reason about moral questions.

Instructional Strategy from the Field: Literature Circle Discussions

Literature circles are small groups of students who gather together to discuss a book in depth. Literature circles provide natural ways for readers to apply the skills and strategies acquired through the read-aloud and learned from shared, guided, and independent reading (Johnson & Giorgis, 2007). Discussing a book with the structure of a literature circle benefits all students regardless of age or ability because it supports and encourages readers to "discuss insights, raise questions, cite related experiences, and wonder or puzzle over situations prompted by what they read" (p. 99).

Literature circles are fairly common in upper elementary grades. The structure for these discussions usually involves assigning students roles such as discussion director, fact finder, literary luminary, or character critic. While children in primary grades can eventually assume roles such as these, it is important to first provide them with the skills needed to be successful in discussing a story.

The read-aloud is the optimal anchor and inspiration not only for what is taught but also for generating discussions. The book selected needs to be worthy of discussion. The read-aloud also offers an opportunity to practice listening skills such as being quiet when another student is talking, not interrupting, and taking turns. When initially launching literature discussions, read aloud a book for children to discuss. This way, all children can have access to the story and participate in the discussion.

To acquaint students with the story, first conduct a picture walk so predictions or questions can be generated based on what is observed in the illustrations. Ask, "What did you see? What are you wondering? What are you feeling?" with their response beginning with, "I see . . ., I wonder . . ., or I feel . . ." This provides students practice in responding to questions and to think deeply about the story other than saying, "I like . . ."

Next, read the first page of the picture book to establish a purpose, generate questions, and discern the kinds of support children might need in listening to and later responding to the story. Pause after a few pages and ask, "What are your questions?" or "What are your connections." Demonstrating the think-aloud strategy during the read-aloud assists children in seeing what active readers do.

After practicing how to discuss a book, students are now ready for literature circles. In this first-grade classroom, students had chosen an illustrator to study in small groups. Each illustrator selected had a unique style of art so students could engage in discussing the story and the illustrations. One of the groups was exploring the books of Lois Ehlert. Ehlert's colorful collage illustrations invited discussion while the range of stories enabled emergent and proficient readers to be in the same group. Each child had a response journal to share with the group and to facilitate the discussion.

Over the rest of the school year, the children continued to engage in literature discussions either based on the read-aloud or in small groups after reading a book independently or with a buddy. Students' comments continually extended beyond literal comprehension to making connections and engaging in meaningful discussions.

Illustrator Literature Circles

Name of Illustrator Lois Ehlert

Title of Books	Author	Illustrator
COLOR ZOO	Lois Ehlert	

Sketch a favorite piece of your Illustrator's work for the cover.

Professional References Cited

Afshordi, N. & Liberman, Z. (2021). Keeping friends in mind: Development of friendship concept in early childhood. *Social Development*, *30*(2), 331–342.

Bishop, R. S. (1990). Mirrors, windows, and sliding glass doors. *Perspectives*, *1*(3), ix–xi.

Copple, C. E. & Bredekamp, S. (Eds.). (2009). *Developmentally appropriate practice in early childhood programs serving children from birth through age 8* (3rd ed.). National Association for the Education of Young Children.
Findlay, L. C., Girardi, A., & Coplan, R. J. (2006). Links between empathy, social behavior, and social understanding in early childhood. *Early Childhood Research Quarterly, 21*, 347–359.
Johnson, N. J. & Giorgis, C. (2007). *The wonder of it all: When literature and literacy intersect.* Heinemann.
Kohlberg, L. (1981). *The philosophy of moral development.* Vol. 1. Harper.
Piaget, J. (1955/1935). *The moral judgment of the child.* Macmillan.
Trawick-Smith, J. & Dziurgot, T. (2011). "Good-fit" teacher–child play interactions and the subsequent autonomous play of preschool children. *Early Childhood Research Quarterly, 26*, 111–123.

Children's Literature Cited

Bartolj, Marta. (2021). *Every little kindness.* Chronicle Books.
Barton, Byron. (1994). *The little red hen.* Greenwillow Books.
Bates, Amy June. (2018). *The big umbrella.* Simon & Schuster.
Cabrera, Cozbi A. (2020). *Me & mMama.* Simon & Schuster.
Chen, Eva. (2022). *I am golden.* Ill. Sophie Diao. Feiwel and Friends.
Daywalt, Drew. (2013). *The day the crayons quit.* Ill. Oliver Jeffers. Philomel Books.
de la Peña, Matt. (2018). *Carmela full of wishes.* Ill. Christian Robinson. G. P. Putnam's Sons.
Dewdney, Anna. (2013). *Llama Llama and the bully goat.* Viking.
Edwards, Karl Newsom. (2017). *I got a new friend.* Knopf.
Ferry, Beth. (2015). *Stick and stone.* Ill. Tom Lichtenheld. Houghton Mifflin Harcourt.
Fleming, Candace. (2003). *Boxes for Katje.* Ill. Stacy Dressen-McQueen. Farrar, Straus & Giroux.
Fleming, Candace. (2012). *Oh, no!* Ill. Eric Rohmann. Schwartz & Wade.
Graham, Bob. (2008). *How to heal a broken wing.* Candlewick Press.
Hall, Michael. (2010). *My heart is like a zoo.* Greenwillow.
Higgins, Carter. (2019). *Bikes for sale.* Ill. Zachariah OHora. Chronicle Books.
Higgins, Ryan T. (2018). *We don't eat our classmates.* Disney Hyperion.
John, Jory. (2022). *The sour grape.* Ill. Pete Oswald. Harper.
Jones, Christianne. (2012). *Lacey Walker, nonstop talker.* Ill. Richard Watson. Picture Window Books.
Kerascoët. (2018). *I walk with Vanessa: A story about a simple act of kindness.* Schwartz & Wade.
Kheiriyeh, Rashin. (2018). *Saffron ice cream.* Arthur A. Levine Books/Scholastic.

Klassen, Jon. (2012). *This is not my hat*. Candlewick Press.
Ko, Sangmi. (2015). *A dog wearing shoes*. Schwartz & Wade.
Ludwig, Trudy. (2013). *The invisible boy*. Ill. Patrice Barton. Knopf.
Maier, Brenda. (2018). *The little red fort*. Ill. Sonia Sánchez. Scholastic.
Making faces: A first book of emotions. (2017). Abrams Appleseed.
McAnulty, Stacy. (2021). *A small kindness*. Ill. Wendy Leach. Running Press Kids.
Méndez, Yamile Saied. (2019). *Where are you from?* Ill. Jaime Kim. Harper.
Murphy, Frank. (2019). *A boy like you*. Ill. Kayla Harren. Sleeping Bear Press.
Papp, Lisa. (2016). *Madeline Finn and the library dog*. Peachtree Press.
Parr, Todd. (2014). *It's okay to make mistakes*. Little, Brown and Company.
Parr, Todd. (2016). *Be who you are*. Little, Brown and Company.
Parr, Todd. (2019). *The don't worry book*. Little, Brown and Company.
Paul, Ann Whitford. (2004). *Mañana, Iguana*. Ill. Ethan Long. Holiday House.
Pinkney, Jerry. (2006). *The little red hen*. Dial.
Quintero, Isabel. (2019). *My papi has a motorcycle*. Ill. Zeke Peña. Kokila.
Raschka, Chris. (2011). *A ball for Daisy*. Random House.
Scieszka, Jon. (1989). *The true story of the three little pigs*. Ill. Lane Smith. Harcourt Houghton Mifflin.
Shannon, David. (1998). *No, David!* Scholastic.
Sierra, Judy. (2010). *Tell the truth, B. B. Wolf*. Ill. J. Otto Seibold. Knopf.
Smith, Oriane. (2022). *Days like this*. Ill. Alice Gravier. Milky Way Picture Book.
Stead, Philip C. (2010). *A sick day for Amos McGee*. Ill. Erin E. Stead. Roaring Brook Press.
Sturges, Philemon. (1999). *The little red hen (makes a pizza)*. Ill. Amy Walrod. Dutton Books for Young Readers.
Willems, Mo. (2003). *Don't let the pigeon drive the bus*. Hyperion.
Willems, Mo. (2004). *The pigeon finds a hot dog!* Hyperion.
Willems, Mo. (2008). *The pigeon wants a puppy*. Hyperion.
Willems, Mo. (2019). *The pigeon HAS to go to school*. Hyperion.
Wohnoutka, Mike. (2019). *So big!* Bloomsbury Children's Books.

9

Generating Children's Aesthetic and Creative Development

> If your child likes to write or draw, make sure that he/she always has paper available. Encourage children to experiment when it comes to art, and remind them to have fun and not be concerned with creating a masterpiece. If, as adults, we value art and books, our children will, too.
>
> (Kevin Henkes, author-illustrator, 2020)

Every child has creative potential. "The ability to be creative, to create something from personal feelings and experiences, can reflect and nurture children's emotional health. The experiences children have during their first years of life can significantly enhance the development of their creativity" (https://www.pbs.org). Children should have opportunities to express themselves through creative play or creative activity to try out new ideas, experiment with different materials, engage in problem-solving, gain an appreciation of the arts, and develop their imagination. Through a focus on aesthetic and creative development, early childhood education also promotes and enhances intellectual, language, personality, and social-emotional growth and development.

Kevin Henkes, whose books are highlighted in Chapter 4 for the suggested author-illustrator study, not only supports the nurturing of the aesthetic and creative ability of young children but writes and illustrates books that engage them as listeners and readers. Encouraging children and offering them the time, space, and materials to explore their creativity often fosters critical thinking and problem-solving abilities as well.

DOI: 10.4324/9781003367635-9

Aesthetic and Creative Development in Young Children

Aesthetic development denotes a person's increasing sensitivity to and appreciation of beauty in art and nature. Creative activity relates to visual arts, music, dance, and drama, providing the base for children's aesthetic development. Creativity itself has been defined as "a way of thinking or acting or making something that is original for the individual and valued by that person or others" (Kemple & Nissenberg, 2000, p. 67). View creativity as the ultimate outlet of self-expression in which children can express themselves freely and openly. The arts offer children ways to express their thoughts and feelings that might not have been understood through words alone.

Many researchers today advocate a multiple-literacies perspective that asserts "printed forms of academic or standard literacy are just one form of communicating meaning" (Collins & Griess, 2011, p. 14). Collins and Griess contend visual, physical, kinesthetic, and musical should also be considered literacy practices. Multiple literacies support children's communication as they practice and reinforce academic English, practice and reinforce informal and home language skills, build receptive language skills, develop social skills, and learn content vocabulary (p. 18). As a teacher, you judge whether there is enough freedom in an activity to meet various needs or whether you must make adjustments so that all can participate.

Childcare providers and teachers should work to help children enjoy participating in the arts, use their imaginations and creative potential, and progress toward more complexity in aesthetic values. A successful arts program gradually introduces new forms of art to children, expanding their skills of both expression and impression. This allows children to accommodate new information and gain control over new techniques. It also encourages children to expand their creative potential.

Creative Potential of Young Children

Fleith (2000) points out that a misconception about young children's inability to think productively has led to an "overemphasis upon recall and reproduction to the neglect of problem-solving, creative thinking, and decision-making in the early years" (p. 149). Sousa et al. (2004) agree and state that creativity is a cognitive activity that results in a new or novel way of viewing a problem or situation. It is a process in which learners first become aware of personal gaps in knowledge, problems, or disharmonies and then set about resolving any inconsistencies. Children look for new relationships among existing information. They make, test, modify, and perfect hypotheses and communicate their results to others. Many researchers agree that creative learning can occur in any subject area.

In the arts, three-year-old Maddy exhibits creative learning as she attempts to make a snake from modeling clay, only to have it separate into segments as she rolls it out. Maddy has encountered a problem. The teacher helps not by telling her what to do or doing it for her, but by asking questions that stimulates Maddy's thinking. Where is it breaking? Why do you suppose that's the place it breaks? What could you do differently? Maddy then hypothesizes that keeping the clay thicker, not rolling it so rapidly, using both hands to roll, or moving her hands along the snake as she works might help. She tries these ideas and reports to the teacher when the snake is finished.

Creativity involves divergent thinking, fluency in producing ideas, flexibility, originality, and elaboration. Teachers and childcare providers can encourage creative thinking by establishing an atmosphere of acceptance in the classroom and by asking questions and structuring activities that permit a variety of responses. Creativity is viewed as a process as well as a product and a quality that all people have to some degree. As you plan activities in the arts, provide opportunities for children to use creative thinking. This will enable you to foster their aesthetic and creative development and capabilities in the arts.

Development in Art

A sequence of development in art is relatively predictable. However, as with other developmental sequences, the age levels corresponding with each stage are approximations. Most children begin scribbling at about two years of age, although some may start a few months earlier. Toddlers will experiment with making straight lines, arcs, and dots (Casbergue & Strickland, 2016). Around age three, children often want to make a line look a certain way or possibly represent a specific object. By age four, most children can create shapes that are round or rectangular. Size relationships are more likely to be determined by the order in which children create each object and the medium they use than by any attempt for accurate representation. Children may also exaggerate size to show what is important to them. Color is not chosen for accuracy but may be determined by preference or simply by what is available for use.

Around age four-and-a-half years or five, children begin developing their ideas for drawings or paintings before starting the work. Children may look to adults for guidance and use their own previous work or that of peers as models. They may practice a skill to gain mastery over it, sometimes repeating a picture or sculpture. Generally, children at this age are able to tell about their work and may include more detail if they are encouraged to reenact an experience or discuss a theme.

Children start developing more complexity in their work in the early elementary grades. In pictures, they frequently place all figures along a baseline, but by the end of third grade, they begin using overlapping shapes to show distance. Children become aware of relative size, being dissatisfied now if their flowers are as tall as their houses. The stereotyped notion of proper colors—green leaves, brown tree trunks—is often used, although children will respond to structured observations and opportunities to mix colors. They enjoy art activities based on imaginative themes (Brewer, 2006).

Teachers and childcare providers can assist children in developing artistic ability in several ways. They can provide a variety of media and give children ample time to experiment. Children need to see how paint runs together before they can begin to master its use. They can try several ways to put legs on their clay figures or use the sides and points of their crayons to produce various coloring techniques.

Adults can give suggestions that encourage children to solve their own problems. This means refusing to draw the dog for the child who complains of being unable to do it. Instead, ask what elements make up the dog or what is special about the dog that the child might want to emphasize.

As children show their work, teachers and childcare providers can comment objectively on what has been done, such as, "You used thick, straight lines and then wavy ones" or "You've mixed several colors together to make a new shade." Use vocabulary when talking about art so children can learn colors, types of lines, or names of shapes. Be sure children recognize that their art should look different from their peers. You can share art created by adults with children, such as various paintings that include a piece of fruit or a landscape. Seeing different styles of art reinforces the idea that one style is not better than another and introduces children to the art they might not see otherwise. Professional art can be used to discuss the process employed but should not be a model for children to copy. An excellent resource to view a variety of iconic artworks can be found in Sabrina Hahn's *ABCs of Art* (2019). This book will spark children's creativity as they view artwork by Edward Degas, Katsushika Hokusai, Mary Cassatt, and Vincent van Gogh. The oversized board-book format allows children to view details in the paintings, while the plastic-coated pages can be wiped clean easily in case artistic inspiration gets messy.

Introducing Art Elements

Art and text in picture books work in concert to create meaning (Giorgis, 2015), where both have been created with a conscious aesthetic intention

(Arizpe & Styles, 2003). Children's book illustrators use the elements of art in various ways to set mood or tone, provide a sense of movement, or convey a feeling of loneliness. Illustrations in picture books extend and enhance rather than merely accompany the text. As children begin to read the illustrations in picture books, "they often see details not mentioned in the written text, which in turn enriches their understanding of the story" (Aghalarov, 2011, p. 32). Gaining knowledge about the various art elements offers the opportunity to talk with children about the creative process used by illustrators while also heightening the visual interpretation of the story. Here are a few art elements that can be introduced to children in the context of sharing picture books.

Lines can be thin, thick, wavy, curvy, straight, jagged, or diagonal. Lines assist in moving readers' eyes across the page. They also create movement, such as the rain falling in Kevin Henkes's *A House* (2021). This is a simple yet excellent book to share with young children about the use of lines. There are horizontal lines that provide stability for the house, jagged lines that offer a glimpse at the sun and stars, and wavy lines that depict the snow piling up on the rooftop and on the ground. Henkes also uses lines to frame the image of the house. *TouchThinkLearn: Wiggles* (Zucchelli-Romer, 2018) offers a tactile experience in exploring lines. This colorful board book contains lines that are straight, spiral, zigzag, and form circles. Very young children can place their fingers on each page's recessed tracks and dots and engage in the book's suggested activities.

Colors portray mood, emotions, settings, characters, and concepts. Books might be colorful or rendered in black and white. Laura Vaccaro Seeger's trilogy of books featuring green, blue, and red provide not only the mood and tone of a story using color but also present new vocabulary. In *Green* (2012), various hues and textures of green accompany text featuring "lush green forests, juicy freshly cut limes" and the pea-green color of certain vegetables. *Blue* (2018) depicts the bond between child and dog through shades of blue, whether it's the blue pastel baby's blanket, stormy blue weather, or feeling chilly blue in the winter. *Blue* also explores the emotion of loss. Dark red, light red, lost red, and bright red are part of exploring anger, fear, hostility, and love in *Red* (2021). A little fox becomes separated from his family and searches for a way home. All three books incorporate die-cuts which provide glimpses of color on the next page.

Perspective provides another layer of meaning or interpretation of the story. Sometimes it's a bird's-eye view by looking down on a scene or a worm's-eye view gazing upward. Chris Van Allsburg's *Two Bad Ants* (1988) and *Hey, Little Ant* by Phillip M. Hoose (1998) present the visual perspective of small creatures. Brendan Wenzel's *They All Saw a Cat* (2016) celebrates perspective along with observation, curiosity, and imagination as various creatures view the cat quite differently. These books provide a visual and character perspective throughout the story.

Space is an overlooked element in the telling of a story. One of the best examples of using space is Maurice Sendak's *Where the Wild Things Are* (1963). As the forest grows in Max's room, the white space surrounding the illustrations and text becomes smaller and smaller. This eventually leads to several double-page spreads featuring the wild rumpus. *Leonardo the Terrible Monster* by Mo Willems (2005) really isn't so terrible except that he is terribly lonely. Willems shows Leonardo in the corner of a double-page spread encased in tons of white space. This is in opposition to Tony, the monster, who has 1,642 teeth, or Eleanor, whose purple pedicure and hairy legs are the only things that can fit on the page. Space can effectively depict a character's emotions, whether sad or lonely, overbearing or booming.

Texture invites children in for a closer look, especially when an object appears to be rough or smooth, hard or soft. Collage is the media Micha Archer employs in *Wonder Walkers* (Archer, 2021) as two children ask imaginative questions as they explore the wonder of the world outside. Children will want to reach out and touch the images to feel the texture. Eric Carle's (1984) *The Very Busy Spider* actually contains a textured spider web in the hardcover version that offers a multisensory experience.

When children are given the language of illustration, they not only begin to describe what they see using the terminology, but they also start to understand how line, color, space, perspective, and texture serve a role in telling a story.

Observing Design Elements in Picture Books

In *Reading Picture Books with Children* (2015), Megan Dowd Lambert advocates a Whole Book Approach to sharing picture books. This approach emphasizes the picture book's illustration, design, and production elements as an art form (p. xxi). Just as art elements play a crucial role in storytelling, so does design. It's important to slow down and savor every aspect of a picture book as well as board books. Here are a few design elements to observe and examine with young children:

Size and orientation. Board books are usually smaller so toddlers, who are the intended audience, can hold them comfortably. Picture books are sometimes square but are generally horizontal (landscape) or vertical (portrait). *Madeline* by Ludwig Bemelmans (1939) is vertical and larger than most picture books. The size enables children to view the expansive "twelve little girls in two straight lines" who live in an old house in Paris covered with vines. The book's height also accommodates the Eiffel Tower that looms in the background. The horizontal orientation of Jerry Pinkney's *The Tortoise &*

the Hare (2013) vividly displays the sprawling desert landscape where Hare is literally leaping off the page. Pinkney also uses panels to illustrate the two competitors at various times during the race. This nearly wordless picture book prompts readers to slow their pace as they relish the art.

Book jacket and casing. We often judge a book by its cover. When perusing the shelves of a bookstore or library, children and adults will select a book because it is eye-catching. The cover illustration is an invitation to read the book. For picture books, the cover shouldn't be cluttered but rather intriguing enough to warrant opening the book. Caldecott Medal illustrator Jon Klassen's "hat" trilogy simply features a picture of the main protagonists on the book jacket. Whether it is the bear in search of his missing hat in *I Want My Hat Back* (2011) or the hat-wearing fish in *This Is Not My Hat* (2012), or the two turtles who are featured on the book jacket of the third book in another hat-related caper, *We Found a Hat* (2016). Art elements, as discussed previously, are in play when book selections are made. Illustrators who demonstrate this awareness include Eric Carle, Tomie de Paola, Bryan Collier, Michaela Goade, Denise Fleming, Christian Robinson, Eric Rohmann, and Marla Frazee, to mention a few.

Sometimes when removing the book jacket, there is what I term "a treasure" or surprise. The book casing might reveal the same illustration as the cover or a completely different one. This only holds true for hardcover books that include a book jacket. One illustrator who never disappoints in adding another storytelling element on the book casing is Matthew Cordell. His Caldecott Medal-winning *Wolf in the Snow* (2017) displays a young girl, her family, and their cherished dog in small vignettes on the front book casing, while on the back are images of the wolf pup and its family. None of these illustrations are included in the story but definitely add another element. Cordell added a "treasure" in his recent books as well, including *Every Dog in the Neighborhood* (Stead, 2022) and *Evergreen* (2023).

End pages. When opening a hardcover book, the end pages are the first and last you see. Think of them as curtains that open and close on a performance or play (Trelease & Giorgis, 2019). Unfortunately, when adults begin reading a book, they immediately go to the title page or first page with text and overlook the end pages entirely. *Brown Bear Brown Bear, What Do You See?* written by Bill Martin Jr. and illustrated by Eric Carle (1983) shows the bands of color that represent the colors of the animals in the story in the order they appear. While this isn't crucial to the storytelling, it adds an element that children often see and may use to remember the animals' sequence.

Other times, the end pages are a solid color that has significance to the story. In the previously mentioned *Wonder Walkers* (Archer, 2021), the initial end pages are a pleasant light green as the children begin their nature walk, while the concluding end pages are the same blue-green as the night sky as their walk comes to an end. The end pages in *My Red Hat* (Stubbs, 2020) are red, which corresponds directly to the story.

Hey Bruce!: An Interactive Book (Higgins, 2022) uses end pages to introduce the story as mice Rupert, Thistle, and Nibbs discuss the attributes of an interactive book. In the story, the grumpy bear Bruce attempts to nap. Meanwhile, the mice are struggling to wake Bruce up and enlist the help of the reader to tap the page, rock the book, and tilt it sideways. Unfortunately, this all occurs with disastrous results. After numerous unsuccessful attempts, the end pages show the mess created by "helping" Bruce and the question, "Are you asleep yet, Bruce?" These pages are as pivotal to the story as those that begin after the title page.

Front matter. Similar to end pages, the front matter is often skipped in viewing a story as being introduced on the title page and starting with the first full page of text. If you don't view the initial illustration in *Bully* (Seeger, 2013) before the title page, you miss a vital part of the story. The first illustration shows a big gray bull yelling, "GO AWAY!" to the little brown bull. This sets up the story as the smaller bull feels rejected, which leads him to bully others.

Following the lavender end pages in *Special Delivery* (Stead, 2015), a boy is shown on the first page yelling, "Hey, Sadie!" The next page depicts the boy running after Sadie, saying, "Wait up!" Sadie appears to be holding onto a string attached to an elephant's tail on the next page. These initial pages set the stage for this story about Sadie, who is trying to mail an elephant to her Great-Aunt Josephine. When mailing the massive creature isn't an option, Sadie seeks alternatives like borrowing an airplane, which unfortunately crashes. After numerous attempts, Sadie and the elephant finally arrive at Aunt J.'s. Observant children will spy several visual clues and creatures within the illustrations as the story progresses.

Front matter is a device used in nonfiction by author Candace Fleming. The text for *The Tide Pool Waits* (2022) begins after the end pages and says, "The waves . . . CR-A-A-A-A-SH in. And then . . . cr-e-e-e-e-p out." Three pages of initial text immediately set the tone and establish the setting. After the title page, the informational text is coupled with illustrations of the creatures who are revealed as the tide goes out. There is also back matter that tells more about the various creatures and locations where tide pools can be explored.

Typography. Typography refers to the arrangement and design of words on a page. The size, color, slant, framing, and weight of the font can impact the interpretation of the story and how the words are read. *I Don't Want to Be Quiet!* (Anderson, 2020) a young girl exclaims, much to the dismay of her mother and teacher. What the girl loves best is chatting, laughing, and clapping at school and stomping, drumming, and humming at home. At the library, she loudly proclaims, "This place is too QUIET! This place is the WORSE!" Others disagree, which embarrasses the girl enough that she grabs a book and begins reading. She discovers that being quiet is much better than she imagined. Throughout the book, typography is used to emphasize the many sounds initially preferred by the young girl.

Typography also plays a role in how the font appears in speech bubbles. Speech bubbles are a graphic convention and a design element to represent the thoughts or speech of a character. A grandmother lives in a small house with her very, very big family that includes multiple grandchildren. In Vera Brosgol's *Leave Me Alone!* (2016), the old woman reaches the end of her rope, packs up her things, and shouts, "LEAVE ME ALONE!" She repeats this phrase several times as she desperately seeks a quiet place. Unlike the young girl in the previous story, the grandmother realizes that being alone might be a little too quiet. Both of these books use typography to express the feelings and emotions of the characters. The typography is very effective in helping children understand how to say these words—loudly!

It's important to pay attention to typography, especially in books for whom young children are the intended audience. If the text in a beginning reader is written in script or font where it isn't clear what the letters are, then that book might not be the best choice. However, an adult can read the text and point out to children that sometimes font can differ depending on the story and the purpose of how the letters are written.

These design elements add another layer of enjoyment and meaning to the story. Sometimes repeated readings of the same book illuminate features that might have initially been overlooked. Children are much more observant and will probably identify art or design elements before an adult reader.

Examining Art in Picture Books

Children often encounter art for the first time in the context of picture-book illustrations (Yohlin, 2012, p. 261). Children may not initially realize the picture book they are seeing or holding is an art object (Marantz, 1977). Some of the most imaginative and stunning art created today is by children's book illustrators.

Presenting Art as Personal Expression

One way to show art as personal expression is to share books that demonstrate the concept directly. *Hey Wall: A Story of Art and Community* (Verde, 2018) tells about a wall that is a city block big but has been neglected and is now just ugly concrete. That is until a boy decides to gather pencils, paints, dreams, imagination, and memories along with family, friends, and neighbors to make the wall beautiful. Not only is the wall transformed, but it also tells the story of the neighborhood. Author Susan Verde and illustrator John Parra share notes about how street art has influenced them as children and adults.

Art & Max by David Wiesner (2010) may take repeated readings to fully appreciate the exploration of art media, style, and friendship. Art & Max are two lizards that have a somewhat feisty friendship. Art(hur) is an accomplished artist, and Max also wants to paint but lacks ideas. So, Art suggests, "Well . . . you could paint me." Max takes the suggestion literally and soon has doused Art with paint. Outraged, Art's armor begins to shatter, and the vivid acrylics are now dusty pastels that Max attempts to blow away. One solution leads to the next problem, and Art is soon reduced to an outline that ultimately unravels. This is a clever and inventive picture book where each page should be savored and discussed. A good question bubbling up from the book is: what is art?

Another book that raises and examines this same question is *Outside Art* (Kloepper, 2021). Pine Marten is curious about watching the human indoors doing all sorts of peculiar things. When the human begins putting "colors on a board using a furry stick," Pine Marten is even more confused. A chickadee says the human is making art. However, neither Pine Marten nor any of the other animals in the forest question, "What is art?" They all define it based on their own needs, whether gathering food, seeking shelter, or even playing. Soon the animals realize they can make their own marks in the snow with their hooves, wings, and scratches. This beautifully illustrated book will assist children in considering how the world around them is art.

At times, a book can address several different themes. This is the case with *Bob the Artist* (Deuchars, 2016), who discovers he has a talent for art while gaining self-acceptance and admiration from others. Bob, the bird, has very long, skinny legs that other animals feel compelled to ridicule. Bob attempts to alter his appearance through strenuous exercise, excessive eating, and wardrobe adjustments, but he is still teased. Feeling dejected, Bob wanders into an art museum where inspiration strikes. Bob begins to paint his own beak, and each day the design honors a different artist, such as Matisse, Jackson Pollock, and others. The bullies are now very impressed with Bob's beak, and he is very happy with himself. This book speaks to artistic expression along with kindness and inclusivity. *Bob the Artist* also offers an opportunity to explore artistic masters.

Stories about visiting museums can help bring that experience to children. When Simon and his parents visit an art museum, the young boy quickly becomes bored. He would rather visit the museum cafe than spend time in the enormous gallery upstairs. In *Simon at the Art Museum* (Soontornvat, 2020), people become Simon's fascination, rather than the art. As he observes how art makes people react, whether smiling, squinting, or sometimes even arguing, Simon realizes the art museum is a pretty unbelievable place. *Anna at the Art Museum* (Hutchins & Herbert, 2018) also features a young child who hasn't quite learned the rules of behavior when visiting a museum. While her mother slowly views each item of art, Anna decides to roar at the painting of a lion, climb on a colorful sculpture, and munch on her snack while sitting on the gallery floor. After she spies a half-open door, the museum attendant allows her inside, where a painting that looks just like Anna is being restored. Suddenly, Anna makes a connection to art. An explanation of the art shown in the story is in the back matter.

Children can be prompted to expand their notion of what a museum is and even create their own, which is the premise of *The Museum of Everything* (Perkins, 2021). What are the things that cause you to pause, appreciate, contemplate, and enjoy that would belong in your own Museum of Everything? What are the things seen in the outside world that could become both real and imaginary exhibits? Overall, this would be a unique museum filled with all kinds of things that catch your attention and make you wonder. *The Museum of Everything* requires abstract thinking and would work best with primary-grade students. However, expanding the idea of museums as well as art make this a worthwhile book to explore with children.

Box 9.1 Books About Artists

The Artist Who Painted a Blue Horse (Eric Carle, 2011)
A Boy Named Isamu: A Story of Isamu Noguchi (James Yang, 2021)
Henri's Scissors (Jeanette Winter, 2013)
My Name is Georgia (Jeanette Winter, 1998)
The Noisy Paint Box: The Colors and Sounds of Kandinsky's Abstract Art (Barb Rosenstock; ill. Mary Grandpré, 2014)
A Splash of Red: The Life and Art of Horace Pippin (Jen Bryant; ill. Melissa Sweet, 2013)

Offering Children Experience with a Variety of Art Media

Closely examining the media used in picture-book illustrations can focus children's attention on the visual vocabulary and range of expression that artists employ to tell a story. This examination also increases children's enjoyment and understanding of the challenges of artistic expression. Children familiar with a variety of media can choose the one that will best express their ideas. Their selection will also be geared toward what they enjoy or feel most successful in using. As children experiment with different media, they need time to use each repeatedly to gain mastery and explore variations for its use.

Experimenting with Media Used by Illustrators

Providing opportunities for children to experiment with art materials does not mean the teacher never gives assistance. One child may need help learning how to hold scissors. Another may benefit from the teacher's suggestion to arrange pieces of a collage before the child begins pasting them onto the paper. Help is given in technique, but the work is not done for the child.

One way picture books can stimulate children to explore various media is for adults to call attention to the medium used by the illustrator and have materials available for any child who would like to try using them. Some of the more common media used in illustration are materials generally available in classrooms.

Collage is a technique of composing art by gluing various materials like fabric, paper, photographs, and other items onto a backing, often creating a three-dimensional effect. Melissa Sweet's *Balloons over Broadway: The True Story of the Puppeteer of the Macy's Parade* (2011) is about puppeteer Tony Sarg, whose imagination created the first balloons for the annual parade. Ezra Jack Keats's classic, *The Snowy Day* (1962) features a little boy named Peter who puts on his snowsuit, steps out of his house, and explores the wonders of snow on a cozy winter day. Children enjoy touching the pages of this endearing story in an attempt to feel the texture of Keats's illustrations.

Pencil drawings used in illustrations may utilize graphite or colored pencils. Artists use the pencil's fine point for drawing lines and details and the side for broad strokes. *Jumanji* by Chris Van Allsburg (1981), a story about a game that has come to life, was created using graphite pencil, while *Ask Me* by Bernard Waber (2015) is illustrated by Suzy Lee using colored pencils. *Ask Me* tells the story of a daughter with unlimited questions and a father who patiently and lovingly answers them.

Watercolors are finely ground pigments of colors mixed with water. They are usually transparent and allow light to reflect from the surface of the paper. Kevin Henkes used colored pencils and watercolors for the paintings in *A House* (2021). Matt Phelan's expressive watercolor illustrations set the mood and tone for Aimee Reid's biographical picture book *You Are My Friend: The Story of Mister Rogers and His Neighborhood* (2019).

Oil pastels resemble sticks of chalk but are oil-based, less powdery, and more difficult to blend. Showing books that use oil pastels will inspire children to use chalk. Using only two words per page, *Blue Sky* by Audrey Wood (2012) uses oil pastels to show a family at the beach on a sunny day, the electricity of a thunderstorm sky, and the magic of a rainbow. Chris Van Allsburg's classic story *The Polar Express* (1985) is also rendered in oil pastels.

Digital art is created on computers using software and scanners. The art for *What Are You?* (2022) was created digitally by Mike Curato, while the text by Christian Trimmer touches on themes such as identity, families, and stereotypes. Jan Thomas's *The Chicken Who Couldn't* (2020) is digitally illustrated in a cartoon style in which a chicken, after several mishaps, adopts the mantra, "I am a strong and powerful and nice-looking chicken."

After children have an opportunity to examine the media used in picture books, encourage them to experiment. Be sure this isn't an isolated activity but an ongoing exploration and discussion about the art in picture books. If you are unsure of the media, it is generally indicated on the copyright page in a picture book.

Development in Music

In music and movement, as in art, some abilities and responses are governed by the children's physical and motor development. Young children sing between middle C and G or A, the middle range of a piano. Gradually, they add a tone or two below C, and by age eight they will have added a tone or two above G. From the initial stages of not matching melodic tones at all, children move to a juncture where they engage in directional singing. They approximate the tones, moving in the direction of the melody. Then, with practice, they become more accurate in singing tunes within a range of four or five notes.

Children respond to music from a very early age and seem to respond most markedly to music with a strong rhythm or melody. Babies have a wonderful sense of rhythm and will bounce to the beat. They respond to slow, long narrative songs that help them relax into sleepiness (Honig, 2004). Toddlers will sing along with their favorite tunes and enjoy moving their bodies gracefully and dreamily to slow music. Children can respond to music at ages three and four through walking, running, clapping, and other physical movements. At first, they may repeat the same motion throughout the rhythmic experience, but gradually they will begin to experiment. Children, ages four and five, are developing in coordination and can add hopping and skipping to their repertoire of movement. They enjoy using rhythm instruments such as triangles, bells, blocks, and rhythm sticks. As children mature and engage in musical experiences, they move more accurately with the rhythm and develop more self-control in using rhythm instruments. With instructions that help them explore body movements, they use space, time, and weight variations in their response to music and in dramatizations. Teachers and childcare providers help children gain these concepts by engaging them in directed movement activities. For example, to explore space, instruct children to find an area where they will not touch anyone else when arms are outstretched. Then, have them use as little space as possible and then as much as possible. Adding the element of time, they can move slowly, using all their space; move rapidly, using the lower half of their space; or be a frightened mouse or angry bear moving in their space.

Many teaching strategies that support development in art also apply to development in music and movement. Just as children need time to experiment with various media, they also need time to experiment with singing, instruments, and movement. Children need an area where they can use rhythm instruments and tone bars in an unstructured setting, listen to the sounds, try different rhythms or melodies, or sing. Some teachers provide a designated area to use when other "sound-producing" activities are in progress. Others have distinct rooms for musical experimentation. There also should be times when children use rhythm instruments in a group response to music or literature.

Children should have the opportunity to sing often, both for enjoyment and to learn to reproduce a melody. Songs to be taught should be within the vocal range of the children. The most easily learned songs repeat melodic lines or refrains. Teachers can help children recognize the directionality of the music and introduce the concept of musical notation by moving their hands to indicate the movement of the melody or by showing the movement with lines on the whiteboard. Duration of notes can be shown by hand movements or written symbols, with long motions or lines indicating notes to be held and short motions or lines indicating eighth or quarter notes.

Childcare providers and teachers can give children the vocabulary to talk about music and movement just as they can with art. They may comment objectively on children's responses: "You are marching in a steady rhythm," or "The tones you are using all have a high pitch." They may also use the vocabulary as they share adult music. Many vocabulary words are appropriate for use in several of the arts; therefore, as children hear them used in more than one context, they gain a clearer conception of the meaning of the terms.

Integrating experiences with music in the early childhood classroom supports multilingual learners by providing children with structured and open-ended musical activities, creating an atmosphere of mutual trust and respect, and encouraging music appreciation and language development as they engage in singing (Pacquette & Rieg, 2008).

Teachers, parents, and caregivers of young children can engage them in activities that foster their aesthetic and creative development and build self-confidence in expression and impression. The satisfaction that children experience as they participate in these types of activities is a reward for the teacher as well as the child.

Box 9.2 Books About Music

About a Song (Guilherme Karsten, 2021)
Ada's Violin: The Story of the Recycled Orchestra of Paraguay (Susan Hood; ill. Sally Wern Comport, 2016)
Because (Mo Willems; ill. Amber Ren, 2019)
Here We Come! (Janna Matthies; ill. Christine Davenier, 2022)
Lupe Lopez, Rock Star Rules! (E. E. Charlton-Trujillo & Pat Zielow Miller; ill. Joe Cepeda, 2022)
Violet's Music (Angela Johnson; ill. Laura Huliska-Beith, 2004)

Offering Children a Variety of Musical Experiences

Literature can give added dimension to children's musical experiences in the early years, contributing to their participation in singing, listening, using rhythm instruments, and movement. Many songs commonly taught to and enjoyed by young children are available in picture-book format, on the internet, and through various apps.

Sharing Picture Books of Illustrated Songs

In selecting board books or picture books of songs that you plan to teach to children, use the same criteria you would use for choosing other songs. Look for tunes within the range of the children's voices, have some repetition of words or melody, and do not have large melodic intervals. Nursery rhymes are often illustrated, such as Yu-hsuan Huang's Sing Along with Me! board-book versions of *Hickory Dickory Dock* (2019) and *Baa Baa Black Sheep* (2022). These books, along with Huang's *This Is the Way We Go to School* (2018), have sliders, just perfect for tiny fingers, that move items in the illustrations. Each board book has a free instrumental and vocal version of the nursery rhyme. Simply scan the QR code for little ones to listen and sing along!

Some books beg to be sung. *There's a Hole in the Log on the Bottom of the Lake* (Long, 2018) is one of them. As this cumulative tale and song progress, one more element is added about the log, the frog, the fly, the gnat, and a wayward hair. There's also a fish on the bottom of the lake, who with a "chomp, snap, gulp!" swallows all the inhabitants on the log. The music and the verses are included in the book for this lively song. A second reading will offer the opportunity to read the ongoing side comments by snail and turtle, which adds to the fun.

If You're a Monster and You Know It (Emberley & Emberley, 2010) utilizes the melody "If You're Happy and You Know It," and features wacky and colorful monsters who invite children to twitch their tail, wiggle their warts, and give a roar! This book illustrates a visual interpretation of the song and provides a variation of the famous tune.

Classic songs are increasingly being featured in picture-book format. *Peace Train* (2021), based on the song by Cat Stevens and illustrated by Peter H. Reynolds, conveys the message of peace in the world. Bob Thiele's popular song has been beautifully illustrated by Tim Hopgood in *What a Wonderful World* (2014). Generally, you can find these songs on the internet to play for children. At times, the music and lyrics are included in the back of the book. Sharing these books provides an opportunity to point out to children that the book tells you what notes to play and sing. Present the song as a whole, not line by line. It is often helpful to show the direction of the notes with your hand or by drawing lines on the whiteboard. Besides introducing notation, hand movements or lines are drawn to help children visualize the direction of the melody.

After you have taught the song, sing it with the children as you show the illustrations in the book. Children will see the words to the song on each page as they sing and will understand they are singing about the pictures. Suppose more than one book is shared about a song, such as illustrator Ashley Bryant's version of *What a Wonderful World* (1995), which features diverse characters and vibrant colors. In that case, children will see that artists can interpret a song differently. This might prompt them to want to illustrate songs themselves.

Using Rhythm Instruments with Literature

Rhythm instruments can be used in conjunction with literature. Children add rhythmic accompaniments to nursery rhymes with a strong beat and steady rhythm, such as "Hickory Dickory Dock." Children might also use instruments to capture the rhythm of *We're Going on a Bear Hunt* (Rosen, 2009) as they "splash, splosh, and swish swish" through all the things they must go through on their walk.

Stories that have a cadence or rhythm are those that work best with instruments. For example, after reading aloud *Smashy Town* (Zimmerman

& Clemesha, 2020), revisit the story and have children pay attention to the words written in large colorful letters on numerous pages, such as "Rumble, rumble, rumble" or "Smash, smash, smash." What instrument would work well to make those sounds? The repetitive words "Go!" and "No!" could also be assigned to an instrument. Using a book that highlights repetitive words will assist children in knowing what sounds will be made and what instruments used at that portion of the story.

Wheels by Sally Sutton (2020) lends itself to using instruments for making sounds of different vehicles that go whizzing by. What instrument works best for a motorbike or fire truck? What about a taxi? There is also repetitive phrasing where instruments could be used instead. It's important to read aloud the book a few times to give children a sense of rhythm and then assign or discuss the instruments to be used.

Explore other books, such as stories in rhyme, featured in this and other chapters to find ones that will be enhanced by children generating sounds. Sounds may correspond to a particular character, accompany a repetitive phrase, augment words that should be said loudly or softly, or signal the type of movement a particular animal makes. Again, the key is to allow children's imagination to generate these sounds rather than telling them which rhythm instrument to use.

Moving in Response to Literature

Movement is a natural response to music, poetry, and prose that has a solid rhythmic beat. Two- and three-year-olds, still responding to their own rhythms, might move to stories or songs by adding motions rather than keeping time. *Barnyard Dance!* by Sandra Boynton (1993/2014) has long been a favorite for getting children up and moving. Stomp your feet and clap your hands. Soon children will be bowing, twirling, bouncing, strutting, and spinning as they create the dance along with the barnyard animals. *Can You Make a Scary Face?* (Thomas, 2009) will have toddlers and preschoolers jumping, wiggling, and laughing as they react to a bossy, toothy ladybug. "STAND UP! No, I changed my mind. SIT DOWN! No. STAND UP!" The ladybug even says to pretend there is a tiny bug on your nose and wiggle it off. This lively book encourages movement and imagination.

Yoga is becoming more popular for engaging young children in movement and mindfulness. *You Are a Lion!: And Other Fun Yoga Poses* (Yoo, 2012) provides simple instructions and bright, clear illustrations. Children are asked to pretend they are an animal and flutter like a butterfly, hiss like a snake, roar like a lion, and more. Yoga promotes flexibility and is also suitable for incorporating other types of movement. *Breathe Like a Bear: 30 Mindful Moments for Kids to Feel Calm and Focused Anytime, Anywhere* (Willey, 2017) offers mindfulness exercises for children to manage their bodies, breath, and emotions. These simple, short breathing practices and movements can be performed anytime and anywhere.

Select books where children can generate movement in response to the story. *A Frog in the Bog* (Wilson, 2003) serves as a counting book where children can imagine just how a frog would eat a variety of swamp delicacies. As he eats a tick off a stick, two fleas in the reed, and three flies buzzing in the skies, children can create a movement for how these creatures might be gobbled up. How would you eat that tick off a stick? How can you devour a fly buzzing in the sky? There's also an alligator lurking nearby, watching as the frog becomes bigger and bigger due to what he has eaten. Pair this book with a version of "There Was an Old Lady Who Swallowed a Fly" to prompt other mouth-watering movements.

Revisit the books you have read that could stimulate children to create movement, with or without music. As you share literature with children, make notes about the musical possibilities of stories and poems, including options for singing, listening, rhythmic response, and movement.

Box 9.3 Books About Dance and Movement

Boys Dance (John Robert Allman; ill. Luciano Lozano, 2020)
Glad, Glad Bear! (Kimberly Gee, 2020)
I Will Dance (Nancy Bo Flood; ill. Julianna Swaney, 2020)
Ready for the Spotlight! (Jaime Kim, 2022)
When Langston Dances (Kaija Langley; ill. Keith Mallett, 2021)

Stimulating Creativity in Art, Music, and Movement

Suppose creativity involves the ability to restructure information in new ways, to see inconsistencies or gaps in knowledge, and to generate and test hypotheses to fill these gaps, to be open and flexible, and to be able to elaborate on ideas. In that case, certain teaching approaches and materials are more likely than others to foster such behavior. Three that apply to literature as a stimulus for creativity in the arts are the use of questions and activities that lead to divergent responses, the use of books that are inventive, and the practice of encouraging children to give more than one response.

Evoking Divergent Responses

When you suggest activities to expand on literature or pose questions about literature structure, these may lead to numerous different responses on the part of children. For example, questions that ask, "What would happen if . . .?" or "Tell us one thing you would do if . . ." or "What else could this character have done . . .?" can be answered in a variety of ways. There is no one correct answer, although you need to ask children to support their ideas.

Activities, too, should have more than one acceptable response. Several children may demonstrate their answers about how a giraffe could dance before and then after hearing *Giraffes Can't Dance* (Andreae, 2001). Gerald is a giraffe who simply can't dance. Try as he may, his long, spindly legs buckle whenever he starts to boogie. Every year he dreads going to the Great Jungle Dance until one night he finds his own special music. Children's answers will reflect their thinking and may draw on the book's perspective that sometimes you just need a different type of music. The object is to develop a unique idea, not to remember an answer from a book.

If you are engaging children in movement, allow them to choose motions themselves or expand the motions exhibited in the book. In *I Got the Rhythm* (Schofield-Morrison, 2014), a young girl and her mother embark on a walk to the park. Music is everywhere, from street performers to butterflies to ice-cream sellers. The girl blinks, sniffs, claps, snaps, shakes, and stomps to the various rhythms. This rollicking read-aloud will invite children to boogie to the beat of the book and their own movements. While it shows the girl blinking or snapping, children will create their own motions. Your reading of the text gives a structure to their responses, but you do not tell them how to move.

The criterion of providing for divergent responses can be applied to any activity designed to extend a child's understanding of a book or poem. This does not mean an excuse for a child to do whatever they please, disrupting everyone else. It does mean your acceptance of their ideas, even if they are not ideas you had thought of or expected. When using rhythm instruments to accompany books, children can decide which instruments give the sounds they think fit, how to put together the sounds, when they should be loud or soft, and how fast to play them. It is their interpretation that is important, their feel for the book, and the mood of the "rumpus" that is the story's climax. Allowing children to continue to play the instruments when the group is beginning a new activity or to damage the instruments from misusing them is neither developing their creativity nor helping them to accept responsibility.

Presenting Books that are Inventive

Select books in which the authors and illustrators have been inventive themselves, and use these to suggest inventiveness on the children's part. *Press*

Here (Tullet, 2011) is a highly interactive book that delights toddlers and preschoolers and offers another perspective of what a book can do. Each page of this engaging book instructs the reader to press the dots, shake the pages, tilt the book, and then see what happens. This unique picture book presents the concept of cause and effect in an imaginative way. Other similar books by Tullet include *Mix It Up!* (2014), *Let's Play!* (2016), and *Say Zoop!: A Book of Sound* (2017). Because of the interactive nature of these books, it is best to share them one-on-one with a child or with small groups.

Books with endings that make the reader wonder are also inventive. *I Want My Hat Back* (Klassen, 2011) features a bear searching for his missing hat. The book is presented in dialogue with the bear's statements in black font and the response from the animals he queries in a variety of colors. Younger children may wonder why the rabbit is missing at the conclusion of the story, while older children will understand that the rabbit is no longer with us.

Endlessly Ever After by Laurel Snyder (2022), illustrated by Dan Santat, is essentially a choose-your-own-adventure picture book that provides hilarious twists on classic fairy tales, including The Three Little Pigs, Hansel and Gretel, Snow White and the Seven Dwarfs, and more. Children can decide where the story goes next by turning to a specific page. These are not linear storylines, but the story still proceeds from beginning to middle to end. Children familiar with traditional fairy tales and who also like a challenging book will enjoy the twists and turns that they decide will happen. This picture book is over 85 pages, so it will probably work best with primary-grade children. However, the inventive nature of storytelling will certainly find its way into the stories of young writers.

Finally, encourage children to give several responses. Honor those responses that believe the rabbit is only missing in *I Want My Hat Back* or how the story is constructed in *Endlessly Ever After*. Changing ideas, adding new elements, and being flexible in approach encourages children to use their creative abilities as they read, think, and write.

Instructional Strategy from the Field: Integrating Science with Art

April Robert owns a nature-based microschool, Little Leaders Academy, in St. Louis, Missouri. The students at her school engage in process art. She describes the activity below in this way:

> Science and art are a process! Scientists take the time to create theories and do their research to discover facts. This Electric Starry Night Canvas offers children the opportunity to see how art is a process by having the space to freely design and not copy any artistic style.
>
> Why process art? It's through this process that children truly learn. Maria Montessori believed children reach their potential when they have space and freedom to express themselves and this includes artistic expression. Process art benefits a child by strengthening their fine-motor skills, developing their spatial intelligence and cognitive thinking, and supporting the ability to think creatively.

The book *Vincent Can't Sleep* written by Barb Rosenstock and illustrated by Mary GrandPré about Vincent van Gogh provided the inspiration for the starry night paintings. In conjunction with reading the book, children also studied the solar system and talked about galaxies, planets, and stars.

CANVAS

Box 9.4 Books that Blend Science with Art

Goodbye Winter, Hello Spring (Kenard Pak, 2020)
Have You Ever Seen a Flower? (Shawn Harris, 2021)
I Wonder (Kari Anne Holt; ill. Kenard Pak, 2019)
Outside In (Deborah Underwood; ill. Cindy Derby, 2020)
We Are Water Protectors (Carole Lindstrom; ill. Michaela Goade, 2020)
Wonder Walkers (Micha Archer, 2021)

Professional References Cited

Aghalarov, S. (2011). Reading and creating with art: Picture books in the art classroom. *WOW Stories, 4*(1), 32–39.

Arizpe, E. & Styles, M. (2003). *Children reading pictures: Interpreting visual texts.* RoutledgeFalmer.

Brewer, J. (2006). *Introduction to early childhood education* (6th ed.). Allyn & Bacon.

Casbergue, R. M. & Strickland, D. S. (2016). *Reading and writing in preschool: Teaching the essentials.* Guilford.

Collins, K. M. & Griess, C. J. (2011). Supporting the many ways that children communicate. *Young Children, 66*(2), 13–18.

Creativity and Play: Fostering Creativity. https://www.pbs.org/wholechild/providers/play.html

Fleith, D. (2000). Teacher and student perceptions of creativity in the classroom environment. *Roeper Review, 22*(3), 148–153.

Giorgis, C. (2015). Illustrations in picture books: The art of reading images. In D. A. Wooten & B. E. Cullinan (Eds.), *Children's literature in the reading program: Engaging young readers in the 21st century* (4th ed., pp. 76–82). International Literacy Association.

Henkes, K. (2020). A Q&A with Kevin Henkes. https://kevinhenkes.com/about/a-qa-with-kevin-henkes/

Honig, A. (2004). Communicating with babies through music. *Scholastic Early Childhood Today, 18*(5), 24–26.

Kemple, K. M. & Nissenberg, S. A. (2000). Nurturing creativity in early childhood education: Families are a part of it. *Early Childhood Education, 28*(1), 67–71.

Lambert, M. D. (2015). *Reading picture books with children.* Charlesbridge.

Marantz, K. (1977). The picture book as art object: A call for balanced reviewing. *Wilson Library Bulletin, 52,* 148–151.

Pacquette, K. R. & Rieg, S. A. (2008). Using music to support the literacy development of young English language learners. *Early Childhood Education, 36*(3), 227–232.
Sousa, R., MacLin, K. M., & Maclin, O. H. (2004). *Cognitive psychology* (7th ed.). Macmillan.
Trelease, J. & Giorgis, C. (2019). *Jim Trelease's read-aloud handbook* (8th ed.). Penguin.
Yohlin, Elizabeth. (2012). Picture in pictures: Art history and art museums in children's picture books. *Children's Literature in Education*, 43, 260–272.

Children's Literature Cited

Anderson, Laura Ellen. (2020). *I don't want to be QUIET!* Philomel Books.
Andreae, Giles. (2001). *Giraffes can't dance*. Ill. Guy Parker-Rees. Orchard Books.
Archer, Micha. (2021). *Wonder walkers*. Nancy Paulsen Books.
Bemelmans, Ludwig. (1939). *Madeline*. Viking.
Boynton, Sandra. (1993/2014). *Barnyard dance!* Boynton Bookworks.
Brosgol, Vera. (2016). *LEAVE ME ALONE!* Roaring Brook Press.
Carle, Eric. (1984). *The very busy spider*. Philomel Books.
Cordell, Matthew. (2017). *Wolf in the snow*. Feiwel and Friends.
Cordell, Matthew. (2023). *Evergreen*. Feiwel and Friends.
Deuchars, Marion. (2016). *Bob the artist*. Laurence King.
Emberley, Rebecca & Emberley, Ed. (2010). *If you're a monster and you know it*. Orchard Books.
Fleming, Candace. (2022). *The tide pool waits*. Ill. Amy Hevron. Holiday House.
Hahn, Sabrina. (2019). *ABCs of art*. Sky Pony Press.
Henkes, Kevin. (2021). *A house*. Greenwillow.
Higgins, Ryan T. (2022). *Hey Bruce!: An interactive book*. Disney Hyperion.
Hoose, Phillip M. (1998). *Hey, little ant*. Ill. Debbie Tilley. Tricycle Press.
Huang, Yu-hsuan. (2018). *Sing along with me! This is the way we go to school*. Nosy Crow.
Huang, Yu-hsuan. (2019). *Sing along with me! Hickory dickory dock*. Nosy Crow.
Huang, Yu-hsuan. (2022). *Sing along with me! Baa baa black sheep*. Nosy Crow.
Hutchins, Hazel & Herbert, Gail. (2018). *Anna at the art museum*. Ill. Lil Crump. Annick Press.
Keats, Ezra Jack. (1962). *The snowy day*. Viking Press.
Klassen, Jon. (2011). *I want my hat back*. Candlewick Press.
Klassen, Jon. (2012). *This is not my hat*. Candlewick Press.
Klassen, Jon. (2016). *We found a hat*. Candlewick Press.

Kloepper, Madeline. (2021). *Outside art*. Tundra Books.
Long, Loren. (2018). *There's a hole in the log on the bottom of the lake*. Philomel Books.
Martin, Bill Jr. (1983). *Brown bear brown bear, what do you see?* Ill. Eric Carle. Holt.
Perkins, Lynne Rae. (2021). *The museum of everything*. Greenwillow Books.
Pinkney, Jerry. (2013). *The tortoise & the hare*. Little, Brown and Company.
Reid, Aimee. (2019). *You are my friend: The story of Mister Rogers and his neighborhood*. Ill. Matt Phelan. Abrams Books for Young Readers.
Rosen, Michael. (2009). *We're going on a bear hunt*. Ill. Helen Oxenbury. McElderry Books.
Rosenstock, Barbara. (2017). *Vincent can't sleep: Van Gogh paints the night sky*. Ill. Mary GrandPré. Alfred A. Knopf.
Schofield-Morrison, Connie. (2014). *I got the rhythm*. Ill. Frank Morrison. Bloomsbury.
Seeger, Laura Vaccaro. (2012). *Green*. Roaring Brook Press.
Seeger, Laura Vaccaro. (2013). *Bully*. Roaring Brook Press.
Seeger, Laura Vaccaro. (2018). *Blue*. Roaring Brook Press.
Seeger, Laura Vaccaro. (2021). *Red*. Holiday House.
Sendak, Maurice. (1963). *Where the wild things are*. Harper.
Snyder, Laurel. (2022). *Endlessly ever after: Pick your path to countless fairy tale endings!* Ill. Dan Santat. Chronicle Books.
Soontornvat, Christina. (2020). *Simon at the art museum*. Ill. Christine Davenier. Atheneum Books for Young Readers.
Stead, Philip C. (2015). *Special delivery*. Ill. Matthew Cordell. Roaring Brook Press.
Stead, Philip C. (2022). *Every dog in the neighborhood*. Ill. Matthew Cordell. Holiday House.
Stevens, Cat. (2021). *Peace train*. Ill. Peter H. Reynolds. Harper.
Stubbs, Rachel. (2020). *My red hat*. Candlewick Press.
Sutton, Sally. (2020). *Wheels*. Ill. Brian Lovelock. Candlewick Press.
Sweet, Melissa. (2011). *Balloons over Broadway: The true story of the puppeteer of Macy's parade*. Clarion Books.
Thiele, Bob. (1995). *What a wonderful world*. Ill. Ashley Bryant. Atheneum Books for Young Readers.
Thiele, Bob. (2014). *What a wonderful world*. Ill. Tim Hopgood. Henry Holt.
Thomas, Jan. (2009). *Can you make a scary face?* Beach Lane/Simon & Schuster.
Thomas, Jan. (2020). *The chicken who couldn't*. Beach Lane/Simon & Schuster.
Trimmer, Christian. (2022). *What are you?* Ill. Mike Curato. Roaring Brook Press.

Tullet, Hervé. (2011). *Press here*. Chronicle books.
Tullet, Hervé. (2014). *Mix it up!* Chronicle books.
Tullet, Hervé. (2016). *Let's play!* Chronicle books.
Tullet, Hervé. (2017). *Say zoop!: A book of sound*. Chronicle books.
Van Allsburg, Chris. (1981). *Jumanji*. Houghton Mifflin.
Van Allsburg, Chris. (1985). *The Polar Express*. Houghton Mifflin.
Van Allsburg, Chris. (1988). *Two bad ants*. Clarion Books.
Verde, Susan. (2018). *Hey wall: A story of art and community*. Ill. John Parra. Simon & Schuster.
Waber, Bernard. (2015). *Ask me*. Ill. Suzy Lee. Houghton Mifflin Harcourt.
Wenzel, Brendan. (2016). *They all saw a cat*. Chronicle Books.
Wiesner, David. (2010). *Art & Max*. Clarion Books.
Willems, Mo. (2005). *Leonardo the terrible monster*. Hyperion Books for Children.
Willey, Kira. (2017). *Breathe like a bear: 30 mindful moments for kids to feel calm and focused anytime, anywhere*. Ill. Anni Betts. Rodale Kids.
Wilson, Karma. (2003). *A frog in the bog*. Ill. Joan Rankin. Margaret E. McElderry Books.
Wood, Audrey. (2012). *Blue sky*. Blue Sky Press/Scholastic.
Yoo, Taeeun. (2012). *You are a lion!: And other fun yoga poses*. Nancy Paulsen Books.
Zimmerman, Andrea & Clemesha, David. (2020). *Smashy Town*. Ill. Dan Yaccarino. Harper.
Zucchelli-Romer, Claire. (2018). *TouchThinkLearn: Wiggles*. Chronicle Books.

10

Planning and Implementing Your Literature-Rich Curriculum

> We believe our classrooms are filled with wonder not only because of the presence of literature but also by the presence of our students.
>
> (Nancy J. Johnson & Cyndi Giorgis, 2007, p. 167)

How do we measure curiosity? Evaluate awe? Cultivate wonder? Foster inspiration? It may be in the way toddlers are touching the pages of a book to feel the perceived texture of the illustrations. Or observing a small group of preschoolers as they lean forward to catch every word you read from a story that has captured their attention. Or listening to first-graders as they discuss whether characters acted in a compassionate manner toward each other. As you begin to plan the literature program for toddlers, preschoolers, or primary-grade children, consider the selection criteria discussed in Chapter 2 and strategies for sharing literature as presented in Chapter 3. Choose books for their literary value and the quality of text and illustrations. Then think about how the literature itself, or the extensions of it, supports the goals of early childhood education and your curriculum in particular. Next, consider how you would partner with literature, as demonstrated in Chapter 4, and the needs and interests of the children. Also, be cognizant of multilingual learners and those challenged by reading as you consider implementing your literature-rich program.

To determine the ways you might share literature with children, you may want to begin with one book. One book often has many possibilities, as evidenced by the cornerstone text highlighted in Chapter 4. Here are some

DOI: 10.4324/9781003367635-10

examples that address the developmental goals described in earlier chapters in this textbook.

A Book for Toddlers and Preschoolers

Nursery rhymes have been a part of children's literary heritage for decades and even centuries. Learning nursery rhymes provides the opportunity to improve cognitive, language, and social development. They also support aesthetic and creative development as young children interpret and dramatize the rhymes they hear. By speaking nursery rhymes, young children develop mouth and tongue muscles and increase memory and recall skills. Hearing nursery enables children to learn how the sounds are put together to make words and then sentences. There is also a rhythm to nursery rhymes which enhances listening and speaking.

One of the most beloved and appealing nursery rhymes is *Three Little Kittens* (2010) which has been beautifully retold by Jerry Pinkney, the Caldecott Medal-winning illustrator of *The Lion & the Mouse* (2009): "Three little kittens, / They got new mittens /And they began to cheer." This traditional rhyme begins with three adorable kittens peering out on the book jacket, which also contains the title featured in raised teal-colored lettering. The front end pages show the felines looking at the window, longing to go outside. When turning to the title pages, readers see the kittens' gloomy faces plastered against the window, watching the flittering scarf- and hat-wearing birds outside. Once the nursery rhyme text begins, children have already been introduced to these cherubic kitties and their patient, knitting mother through Pinkney's expressive watercolor illustrations. The rhyme itself is well paced and has words such as "meow" and "purr" presented in a colorful font that invites children's interaction with the text. As the rhyme unfolds, the naughty kittens proceed to acquire, lose, and find their mittens while also getting them dirty, having them washed, and scurrying outside to play again. Pinkney's palette of warm autumn colors is perfect against the kittens' colorful mittens. *Three Little Kittens* is both a textual and visual delight and begs to be revisited again and again. Following are some examples of how this book can be used to support the goals of early childhood education. These goals have been explored in-depth in Chapters 5–9, focusing on language, intellectual, personality, social and moral, and aesthetic and creative development. The stated goals below are those found in their respective chapters. This final chapter provides an overview of how these goals are integrated into the literature program through the sharing of *Three Little Kittens*.

Language Development

Goal: "Children will enjoy the creative and aesthetic use of language." The rhyming text, simple story structure, and patterned language make this a nursery rhyme that young children will enjoy hearing over and over. They should have the opportunity to listen to it more than once, either through its selection by them as an "old favorite," through an aide or other adult sharing it with small groups, or by listening to an audio version as they turn the pages of the book. Young children will also begin hearing rhyming words throughout *Three Little Kittens*. A fun activity can be found at https://growingbookbybook.com/the-three-little-kittens-rhyming/ where paper mittens are cut out, stickers are attached of different items that rhyme, and then children match the mittens with the same sticker.

Goal: "Children will become skilled listeners." Adults can enhance children's attentive listening by having them say the words they know as the book is being read. A special feature of Pinkney's version is the words "meow" and "purr," which are creatively displayed using a color-coded script that provides a cue for toddlers and preschoolers to chant along. The short, simple sentences are easily remembered, while the rhythmic properties are entertaining. Alliteration is also abundant throughout *Three Little Kittens*. The more the rhyme is read to children, the more familiar they will become with the phrasing until, eventually, these are memorized and spoken independently.

Nursery rhymes provide numerous opportunities for dramatization. Prior to inviting children to act out the scenes, read aloud the rhyme using a range of vocal inflections. Have children repeat lines and phrases so they can recognize the pattern and flow of the rhymes and feel them rolling off of their tongues. This is particularly helpful to multilingual learners to assist them in becoming familiar with nursery rhymes in English and in building word families around rhyming words.

Intellectual Development

Goal: "Children will become skilled in a variety of thinking processes." This book encourages observation, particularly about the facial expressions of the kittens. Ask children how the kittens are feeling in each situation, such as when they are given the mittens and allowed to go out and play, when they lose their mittens, and then when they find them once again. Also, point out the expression on the face of the mother cat. How does she feel about the antics of her young, feisty felines? Children can predict what might happen at each stage of the rhyme as it progresses to the satisfying and circular story ending.

The children also might demonstrate their grasp of the sequence of the story—and thus gain experience in organizing—by telling or helping to tell the nursery rhyme using felt-board figures. Cut out pictures of the mother cat, her three kittens, and their mittens, then back them using felt, Velcro, or magnetic strips. Let the children select which one will be needed next as you tell the story, or let them arrange the pieces and tell the story themselves. This activity assists in the development of hand–eye coordination and spatial placement.

Goal: "Children will engage successfully in problem-solving." You might ask children, "What should the kittens do when they lose their mittens? How should they go about finding them? Is the punishment of 'You shall have no pie!' appropriate for losing mittens? What should the kittens do so they don't lose their mittens again?"

Personality Development

Goal: "Children will weigh the evidence and make appropriate choices." After reading the rhyme, you might suggest that the children decide what activity they would like to do in relation to the book. It might be a group decision between activities such as making felt-board characters or puppets in order to retell the rhyme. They may make individual decisions, with some choosing to make pictures using watercolor paints, the media that Pinkney used for his illustrations. Finally, children might decide whether they want to work by themselves or with others on the project.

Social and Moral Development

Goal: "Children will view a situation from more than one perspective." If children are dramatizing the story or retelling it with puppets or felt-board characters, they should have the opportunity to play several roles. They might tell the story from the mother's point of view or even one of the individual kittens. Is one kitten more forgetful than others or loses things more frequently than its siblings? How does each kitten feel about losing their mittens and not being allowed to eat the pie initially?

Goal: "Children will engage competently in group activities." You can help children work successfully in groups by ensuring the task is clear. For very young children, the task for "group" work may be to share materials and engage in friendly talk as they work. Or it may be in engaging in a choral reading of certain words or phrases as a whole or in small groups of children.

Aesthetic and Creative Development

Goal: "Children will use, experiment with, and gain control over a variety of art media." *Three Little Kittens* is illustrated using Pinkney's trademark pencil-and-watercolor illustrations. Watercolors are excellent to use with young children because they are inexpensive, easy to clean up, and don't damage classroom surfaces or children's clothing (of course, children can always wear an old shirt as a smock). Pinkney uses warm colors with plenty of white space in the background of his illustrations. Point out to children the expressions on the kittens' faces, from initial delight to despair, to satisfaction. Children can either paint directly on a piece of paper or draw their illustration and then paint in the colors.

Goal: "Children will respond favorably to diverse styles of art and music." Children could be asked what they notice about the illustrations and encouraged to give a variety of responses. Bring in other versions of the *Three Little Kittens*, such as Paul Galdone's reissued version published in 2011 or one illustrated by Lorianne Siomades (2000) or the comic-book style by Barbara McClintock (2020) with an original twist at the end. They might tell how the illustrations in the three books differ, describing the different styles of art and media used. One preschool teacher shared that a small group of two- and three-year-olds spread the books on the table, studied them, and pointed out different things they saw. The children also made up stories to go with the illustrations. In addition to comparing illustrations, children can also sing the *Three Little Kittens* nursery rhyme. Pinkney's version contains the words and music for the rhyme, which can easily be found on the hard casing under the book jacket. Finally, as you read aloud the rhyme, have children dramatize the actions of each little kitten as well as their mother.

A Book for Primary Grades

Just as there are many possibilities for toddlers and preschool children to enjoy and respond to *Three Little Kittens*, so are there opportunities for primary-grade students to enjoy and respond to Jacqueline Woodson's *The Day You Begin* (2018). "There will be times when you walk into a room and no one there is quite like you" begins this lyrical story about feeling different, overcoming fears, and having a sense of belonging. The characters' emotions swell because of the way they talk, the food they eat, or even their inability to engage in the same activities as other children.

Language Development

Goal: "Children will hear the flow of language through the rhythm and rhyme of the text." As you read *The Day You Begin* aloud, children will hear the cadence of the lyrical language written by Woodson. For example, "And all that stands beside you is your own brave self—steady as steel and ready . . ."

There is also the repetitive phrasing that begins with, "There will be times . . ." Discuss with children how Woodson uses descriptive words and phrases to create images in their minds. Ask children why Woodson starts several sentences with, "There will be times." Create a chart with words and phrases that Woodson writes that "tickle" their ears and ones they want to remember. When revisiting *The Day You Begin*, view the video of Jacqueline Woodson reading it aloud (https://www.youtube.com/watch?v=KDs5d_qFbEs) and discuss how she emphasizes certain words and phrases.

Goal: "Children will communicate effectively, both orally and in writing." Brainstorm expressive words about feelings and emotions. Then, have children tell or write about a time when they felt different. Or have them respond to Woodson's question at the video's conclusion, "What makes you so fabulously different from everyone else you meet?"

Intellectual Development

Goal: "Children will engage in problem-solving." Read aloud Jacqueline Woodson's *The Year We Learned to Fly* (2022), illustrated by Rafael López. In this companion story to *The Day You Begin*, a brother and sister are stuck inside on a rainy day. Their grandmother urges them to, "Lift your arms, close your eyes, take a deep breath, and believe in a thing." This repetitive phrase occurs when the children say they are bored, are angry at each other, or when they move, and no one wants to play with them. Discuss with children how the brother and sister solved their problems through imagination and their ability to "learn to fly." Create a list of problem-solving strategies that they could use to change something negative into a positive action or behavior.

Goal: "Children will develop skills in a variety of thinking processes." Conduct a picture walk through *The Day You Begin* and *The Year We Learned to Fly*. After each book, write down what children observed in the illustrations. Or you might want them to observe the action in each story and the reactions of the characters. Compare the two books. What is the same and what is different in the story and the illustrations? Children could draw a picture of one thing that happened in either *The Day You Begin* or *The Year We Learned to Fly*. Then have them form groups based on which book they chose. Next, children can share their pictures and then sequence them in the order they occurred in the story. This strategy uses various thinking processes as children draw, describe, and organize the picture according to the story sequence.

Personality Development

Goal: "Children will develop positive and realistic self-concepts." *The Day You Begin* focuses on developing positive self-esteem and self-concept. This occurs when children recognize their uniqueness and begin to share their stories.

Create a "This is me" book by having children first draw a self-portrait. Next, provide sentence stems such as "My favorite food is . . ." or "My favorite place is . . ." or "What I can do well is . . ." or "I am fabulous because . . ." to create pages for their books with sentences and drawings.

Goal: "Children will explore how emotions are portrayed through text and visual images." Using sticky notes, walk through *The Day You Begin* and *The Year We Learned to Fly*, and ask children about the emotion being expressed by the characters. Write down the emotion and place the sticky note next to that character. There are both primary and secondary characters in both books that can be used for this activity.

Social and Moral Development

Goal: "Children will view a situation from more than one perspective, seeing the viewpoint of another person." If you could interview one of the characters in *The Day You Begin*, what would you ask that person? Have children write down a list of questions and then share these in small groups. They could record these questions as well as new understandings based on their interpretation of what is stated in the text and shown in the illustration for that character.

Goal: "Children will empathize with a book character." As children learn to "read" another's feelings, they also become more sensitive to those feelings. Have children think about how they would feel if something similar happened to them, such as being laughed at, eating foods others are not familiar with, or not having a turn to play on a team.

Aesthetic and Creative Development

Goal: "Children will recognize how the use of color and space are used to express emotions." As you conduct a picture walk through *The Day You Begin*, have children talk about the colors that Rafael López used to create the illustrations. Point out the differences in the background color surrounding some of the characters, especially when they are feeling different. Examine the front and concluding end pages in *The Day You Begin* and *The Year We Learned to Fly*. What do they notice about the use of color and differences in the illustrations from front to back? Several times in both books, a character is separated from others, as shown by the use of space. How does this help to understand how the character is feeling?

Goal: "Children will identify how visual images and symbols are used as metaphors in *The Day You Begin* and *The Year We Learned to Fly*." In the final minute of the video, https://www.youtube.com/watch?v=KDs5d_qFbEs&t=316s, Jacqueline Woodson shares how illustrator Rafael López uses rulers throughout *The Day You Begin* as a metaphor for measuring ourselves with others. Have children revisit those pages and discuss why they think he used a ruler this way. In viewing *The Year We Learned to Fly*, a bird appears in various illustrations. Ask children why López might have included a bird on these pages and what it means.

Selecting Response Activities

Many, although not all, of these goals and activities are compatible with one another for the books discussed. Given these possibilities, far more than you would actually do with any one group of children, your task becomes deciding which to pursue. Here are three general suggestions for determining the merit of specific response activities for extending and enhancing books.

First, the activity should enhance the literature, not detract from it. Toddlers or preschoolers dramatizing *Three Little Kittens* actively participate in the story, help build the suspense, and work together to develop their understanding of it. They enjoy the predictability of the language and the plot. They are more likely to want to hear the book again, dramatize it in various ways, and think positively about literature. If, however, you require children to practice individually with flashcards until they have learned the words each animal says or to memorize the rhyme, many children will likely view literature as a source of frustration. They will not be eager to have you read more books, let alone repeat *Three Little Kittens*. A deeper understanding or appreciation for the literature will not have been gained.

Second, the activity should emerge naturally from the book. The Day You Begin is an engaging story using lyrical language and expressive illustrations. It is also a story that many children can relate to. Generally, children have all felt different at some time and may struggle with self-esteem. The notion that everyone has a story and all children are fabulous in their own way is an important message from the book. How an author tells a story through language and imagery lends itself to children responding in a like manner. Identifying descriptive words and brainstorming with others will provide additional vocabulary for written responses to the story. Illustrations depicting diverse characters offer the opportunity to discuss race, gender, and ability. The characters' expressions also assist in conveying emotion and meaning. *The Day You Begin* may be seen as a book to begin the school year. However, it is vital to think about what it's really about rather than assume it's about the first day of school. Throughout the year, children seek acknowledgment from others and are encouraged to "find the places inside your laughter and your lunches, your books, your travel and your stories." Envision the possibilities for literature rather than limiting a book's potential.

Third, the activities should match both the needs and abilities of the children. Making watercolor illustrations allows toddlers and preschoolers to explore the artistic technique using materials they can manipulate successfully. Having primary-grade students generate questions to ask a character in *The Day You Begin* gives children the experience of planning an interview, using oral language and listening skills, and reporting accurately, in writing, what another has said. The response activities for both books relate to early childhood education goals explored throughout *Literature and Literacy for Young Children: Envisioning Possibilities in Early Childhood Education for Ages 0–8*. Deciding which are most appropriate means knowing your group of children well, being able to assess and rank their needs, and knowing which needs will be met in other ways. It also means recognizing that any group of children will have a range of needs and abilities and that you will be planning activities for small groups or individuals much of the time. Some toddlers and preschoolers are able to cut out intricate shapes; others still need practice controlling scissors and benefit from cutting large, less-detailed shapes. Some of the children may need help learning to work cooperatively with others. Some may need to work alone before they are ready to contribute to a group project. Determining which activities should be suggested to which children is a professional skill of teaching and child-care work.

Recognizing the Larger Context

The sharing of a single book fits within the context of all the literature the children experience, and the literature fits within the context of their lives both at home and at school. Your planning will be more effective if you consider the larger picture as you make decisions about literature and literature-based activities.

Literature-Rich Curriculum

As you select individual books and plan your curriculum, group some of the books into units or use graphic organizers as described in previous chapters. Ideas for grouping may emerge as you look at the literature, a particular author or illustrator's work, or several books expressing a similar topic or theme. Sometimes you may need to search the internet to assist in identifying books that fit the topics you intend to develop. With *Three Little*

Kittens, you might want to introduce other Mother Goose nursery rhymes illustrated as a single rhyme, such as Keith Baker's *Hickory Dickory Dock* (2007), or that appear within a collection like *The Arnold Lobel Book of Mother Goose* (2022).

With *The Day You Begin*, you might look at other books illustrated by Rafael López, such as *Just Ask! Be Different, Be Brave, Be You* (Sotomayor, 2019) or *Maybe Something Beautiful: How Art Transformed a Neighborhood* (Campoy, 2016), because he effectively expresses emotions through his art. You also might select books about characters that portray emotions in several stories, such as David Shannon's *No, David!* (1998) and *David Gets in Trouble* (2002). There are also Mo Willems's "Pigeon" books or Ian Falconer's "Olivia" stories.

You can sequence some units throughout the school year, and the placement of these units may help determine their success. Keep other units and books in mind but be flexible in planning when they will be presented. For instance, the units mentioned might come at any convenient time, whereas holiday books obviously need to be scheduled to coincide with the event. Check your general plan to guarantee that you develop a balanced literature curriculum with fiction and nonfiction, fantasy and realism, poetry, and classic and contemporary stories.

Engaging Children with Literature

Plans for bringing children and books together must always revolve around the specific children you are working with. Children must be able to create meaning from the books you share because they are touched by them—through the topic, language, emotion expressed, and intellectual stimulation they provide. You should have books that depict a diverse set of characters so that children see themselves and the people they know in books and come to know and appreciate others who are different from them. You will want children to experience literature in various formats depending upon the age of the child—board books, hardcover and paperback, audiobooks, and those shared through digital means—so that they have the opportunity to appreciate the strengths of each. You will begin to think not just of the world children find themselves in at the moment but the world in which they will live in the future. Most of all, you want children to find literature as a source of joy and knowledge, which will guide not only your selection of books but also how you share them with children.

Reading and Writing Activities from Internet Sources

For this final chapter, activities from various internet sources supporting reading and writing with young children have been compiled. Early childhood educators generously share ideas, templates to use with children, and book suggestions.

Reading Activities

- Toss the balloon or beach ball activity can be used with sight words, as explained on this website. A variation is to write who, what, where, when, why, or how on the beach ball or balloon. Whatever word is shown once the child catches it is the one they must answer about the story. https://masandpas.com/magic-letters-first-letters/
- Explore this website for numerous ideas for teaching reading and writing. The ideas, as well as corresponding websites, are included. https://www.teachingexpertise.com/classroom-ideas/preschool-activities-literacy/
- Combine reading and relaxing during story time with this terrific idea for creating Discovery Bottles that feature items related to a story that can be passed around during read-aloud to calm restless toddlers or preschoolers. https://teachpreschool.org/2015/04/27/childrens-book-in-a-bottle/
- Hands-on activities for toddlers and preschoolers focused on picture books can be found at https://teaching2and3yearolds.com/picture-book-activities/
- Coordinating art projects with picture books is featured at https://www.deepspacesparkle.com/art-and-literature-2-2/
- Activities for emergent readers and beginning readers are plentiful on the Reading Rockets website. https://www.readingrockets.org/article/25-activities-reading-and-writing-fun. This site also has information about children's book authors and illustrators
- Creative ideas for primary-grade students to enhance their comprehension and engage in retelling are shared on this useful website. https://www.weareteachers.com/first-grade-reading-comprehension/

Writing Activities

- Use Playdough with toddlers to increase strength in finger and hand muscles for holding a pencil or pen. This website contains a recipe for making your own Playdough. https://mumslittleexplorers.com/best-playdough-recipe-homemade/

- Ideas for learning centers for emergent writers and also suggested books written in various formats. https://www.naeyc.org/resources/pubs/yc/nov2017/emergent-writing
- Writing and art are combined in this activity where an adult writes letters or a child's name with white crayon or wax, and then the child paints over it to reveal what is written. https://masandpas.com/magic-letters-first-letters/
- Simple and easy writing ideas for preschoolers. https://www.teachingexpertise.com/classroom-ideas/pre-writing-activities-for-preschoolers/
- Explains a variety of different formats for young children to use for writing. https://www.readingrockets.org/reading-101-guide-parents/first-grade/writing-activities-your-first-grader

Book Suggestions and Extension Activities

- Picture books to teach children about kindness. https://www.weareteachers.com/kindness-books-for-kids/
- Excellent site for locating books by topic, age, series, and for reading aloud. https://imaginationsoup.net/
- Publisher-sponsored websites that offer booklists by age and topic, as well as teacher guides. www.readbrightly.com; https://www.abramsbooks.com/academic-resources/teaching-guides/; https://www.leeandlow.com/educators/teacher-s-guides; https://www.chroniclebooks.com/pages/ed-resources (be sure to click on "details" after arriving at the selected book site)
- Australian website with response ideas for picture books. https://www.teachingwithpicturebooks.com.au/picture-books/
- Resources for parents, teachers, and librarians in locating diverse books and strategies for locating and sharing them with children. https://diversebooks.org/resources/

Professional References Cited

Johnson, N. J. & Giorgis, C. (2007). *The wonder of it all: When literature and literacy intersect.* Heinemann.

Children's Literature Cited

Baker, Keith. (2007). *Hickory dickory dock*. Harcourt.

Campoy, Isabel F. (2016). *Maybe something beautiful: How art transformed a neighborhood*. Ill. Rafael López. Clarion Books.

Galdone, Paul. (2011). *Three little kittens*. Houghton Mifflin Harcourt.

Lobel, Arnold. (2022). *The Arnold Lobel book of Mother Goose*. Simon & Schuster.

McClintock, Barbara. (2020). *Three little kittens*. Scholastic.

Pinkney, Jerry. (2009). *The lion & the mouse*. Little, Brown and Company.

Pinkney, Jerry. (2010). *Three little kittens*. Dial.

Shannon, David. (1998). *No, David!* Scholastic.

Shannon, David. (2002). *David gets in trouble*. Scholastic.

Siomades, Lorianne. (2000). *Three little kittens*. Boyds Mills.

Sotomayor, Sonia. (2019). *Just ask! Be different, be brave, be you*. Ill. Rafael López. Philomel Books.

Woodson, Jacqueline. (2018). *The day you begin*. Ill. Rafael López. Nancy Paulsen Books.

Woodson, Jacqueline. (2022). *The year we learned to fly*. Ill. Rafael López. Nancy Paulsen Books.

Index

Note: *Italic* page numbers refer to figures.

Made in United States
Cleveland, OH
19 August 2025

19567898R00162